C000146225

Digital Literacies in Education

RETHINKING EDUCATION
VOLUME 8

Series Editors:

Dr Marie Martin

Dr Gerry Gaden

Dr Judith Harford

PETER LANG

Oxford · Bern · Berlin · Bruxelles · Frankfurt am Main · New York · Wien

Yvonne Crotty and Margaret Farren (eds)

Digital Literacies in Education

Creative, Multimodal and Innovative Practices

PETER LANG

Oxford · Bern · Berlin · Bruxelles · Frankfurt am Main · New York · Wien

Bibliographic information published by Die Deutsche Nationalbibliothek.
Die Deutsche Nationalbibliothek lists this publication in the Deutsche
Nationalbibliografie; detailed bibliographic data is available on the Internet
at http://dnb.d-nb.de.

A catalogue record for this book is available from the British Library.

Library of Congress Control Number: 2013934513

Cover image by Yvonne Crotty.

ISSN 1662-9949
ISBN 978-3-0343-0928-8

© Peter Lang AG, International Academic Publishers, Bern 2013
Hochfeldstrasse 32, CH-3012 Bern, Switzerland
info@peterlang.com, www.peterlang.com, www.peterlang.net

All rights reserved.
All parts of this publication are protected by copyright.
Any utilisation outside the strict limits of the copyright law, without
the permission of the publisher, is forbidden and liable to prosecution.
This applies in particular to reproductions, translations, microfilming,
and storage and processing in electronic retrieval systems.

Printed in Germany

Contents

Foreword

New technologies offer a rich variety of ways in which learners can interact, communicate and collaborate; however, both learners and teachers need to develop a complex set of digital literacies in order to harness the potential of these media. This edited collection is an output from a DIVERSE conference held at Dublin City University in 2011. It is an authoritative work outlining different strands of digital literacy research and is timely given the increasing impact that technologies are having on education. It covers both theoretical discourses on the topic, along with practical empirical studies of the use of different technologies, such as podcasts, mobile devices and virtual worlds.

Yvonne Crotty sets the scene for the book in Chapter 1, describing the origins and focus of the DIVERSE 2011 conference, which included keynotes from two eminent speakers, Michael Wesch and Roy Pea.

In Chapter 2, Michael Wesch provides a philosophical account of the impact of new media and the means by which social and participatory media enable us to actively engage, interact, communicate and collaborate; as he states, 'We were celebrating empowerment, new forms of connection and community, and new and unimaginable possibilities.' He states that this is not just a technology revolution but also a social one. Despite this potential, his research and the research of others shows that students are not extensively engaging with new media and lack the critical literacy skills to make informed judgments about the relevance of resources they find for their own studies.

Roy Pea and colleagues focus on a study about fostering collaborative learning through the use of digital video technologies for collaborative knowledge construction in a classroom. The study provides evidence of how to improve guidance for student teams solving a complex authentic task in history.

In Chapter 4, Vance Martin describes the use of wikis to foster democratic teaching. He uses an action research approach and draws in particular on the work of Vygotsky, Lave and Wenger and the concepts of social production and the open source movements. He concludes that '[Technologies] can offer all students the chance to find their voice, and become creators in their own education.'

In Chapter 5, Theo Kuechel plots the evolution of audiovisual technology over the last sixty years and, in particular, explores the potential shift of the use of these media from one-way presentation to the promotion of different pedagogical approaches. He describes a pedagogical model developed as part of a JISC-funded project, which consisted of the following elements: watch/observe, analyse/predict, empathise, create, share/publish and collaborate.

Stephen J. McNeill and Joshua N. Azriel also argue that we are witnesses to a global communication revolution, in Chapter 6. They describe a study using cell phones for journalism with a group of communication students. They used the phones to gather data on a new item and to produce a newspaper-style article.

In Chapter 7, Glen Williams focuses on visual educational resources. He argues that 'Visual content can be harnessed to enliven our classes, provide illustrative examples, and enhance learning.' He summarises the work of Hariman, Lucaites and Finnegan on the power of visualization, and concludes by arguing that we need to help students develop visual literacies in order to participate in today's media-rich environment.

Yvonne Crotty and Margaret Farren, the editors of the book, describe the development of information and communication technologies at Dublin City University, in Chapter 8. The chapter begins by describing the Irish government's policies on ICT in education over the last twenty years or so. It goes on to describe the establishment of the Centre for Teaching Computing at DCU, along with a Masters in Computer Applications for Education that has now developed into the Masters in Education and Training Management (eLearning).

In Chapter 9, Jack Whitehead focuses on Self-Study of Teacher Education Practices (S-STEP), drawing on Schön's research. He concludes by stating that 'the generation and legitimation of living educational theories takes place in contexts that have been influenced by different historical traditions and sociocultural influences and that these contexts are in a constant process of transformation'.

Virtual worlds are the focus of Chapter 10, by Sabrina Fitzsimons. Her interest is in understanding immersion in virtual worlds and the stages one moves through: from separation, through transition and finally transformation. She describes her own experience, using an ethnographic approach, and argues that it is a challenging and experiential learning process.

In Chapter 11, Fawei Geng and colleagues describe the development of podcasts at Oxford University; the initiative built on Oxford's initial developments from 2008 onwards. In particular, there were a number of shortcomings identified with the then approach to developing podcasts, namely: remoteness of contributors, scattered hosting and split collection interfaces. The JISC-funded OpenSpires project aimed to address these and to establish a rich Open Educational Resource repository. Evaluation of the resource indicated a number of benefits: motivating distance learners, supporting existing students, helping teachers in their professional development, and reuse in the classroom.

Rüdiger Rolf and colleagues describe, in Chapter 12, a lecture capture system developed at the University of Osnabrück and, in particular, a project funded by the Mellon Foundation, Matterhorn, which involved thirteen partners.

In Chapter 13, Meghan Dougherty and Adrienne Massanari outline best practices for bloggers. They begin with an overview of the type and purposes of different blogs, ranging from personal diaries through to information portals. The chapter provides a useful set of tips and hints for creating and maintaining blogs.

In a postscript to the book, Mathy Vanbuel and Sally Reynolds describe the establishment of the MEDEA awards scheme in 2007, which aimed to recognise and reward excellence in media to support learning.

What I particularly admire about this book is the rich set of empirically based examples of the use of different technologies to promote different pedagogical approaches. Together, they give an excellent picture of the potential of new technologies for education, but also demonstrate that both teachers and learners need to develop a complex set of digital literacies in order to harness this potential. Providing practical examples (as in this book), along with more structured guidance for the design of learning interventions, is the way to achieve this. As Michael Wesch states in Chapter 2, we are poised for a revolution in education. Technologies truly have the potential to transform; the question is, are we as teachers ready to embrace this potential?

Gráinne Conole

Introduction

This book offers the opportunity for new ways of thinking about teaching, learning and research. It shares inspiration and guidance and suggests what digital technologies have to offer for education, research and project management.

The research papers in this book have been selected from a range of international professionals working in different educational contexts, e.g. academics, researchers, practitioner-researchers, multimedia specialists, computer and audiovisual services personnel and software developers. What the authors all have in common is a shared interest in what digital media has to offer to the educational project. We believe that these contributions will promote discussion and greater knowledge and understanding about teaching, learning and research, as linked to digital technologies. These papers offer you, the reader, a range of interests; themes range from the impact that podcasting and use of mobile devices have, to guidelines for blogging and exploring virtual worlds. Different methodological approaches are used e.g. empirical research, action research, researching your own practice and ethnography. The papers offer stimulating reading about e-Learning, social media and web-based technology, and provide cutting edge examples for education practitioners who are interested in research in this growing academic field.

Technologies and pedagogies examined in the book go beyond those that are text-based to incorporate visual forms of literacy. The authors promote students getting involved in producing and sharing digital media artefacts, having a voice in their own learning, developing media literacy skills that are linked to social awareness and new ways of participating and working in the world. New digital technologies have enabled us to collaborate, communicate, work together and learn from each other in ways that were not possible in the past. We aim to equip students for the media rich world in which they live and work, in so doing, we have to create conditions that support their development of key competencies so that students become creators of knowledge though the use of technology and not mere consumers of others' artefacts.

Background

In June 2011 Dublin City University hosted the 11th Annual DIVERSE Conference with the local organising team inviting a range of keynote speakers, including Professor Michael Wesch and Professor Roy Pea, to present their practice and research linked to the Conference theme of 'Creativity: Enhancing our Vision for the Future'. International speakers from a wide range of disciplines – education, anthropology, applied psychology, cultural anthropology, art and design, communications, research and software development – presented their papers at the Conference. This book publication emerged from the DIVERSE 2011 Conference.

Organisation of Book

Chapter 1

Yvonne Crotty, a lecturer at Dublin City University, outlines the backdrop to the International DIVERSE Conference. She describes the planning and production that was involved in capturing the DIVERSE 2011 Conference theme 'Creativity: Enhancing our Vision for the Future.' The Conference provided the opportunity for Dublin City University (DCU) students to develop video production skills as part of the 'DIVERSE Live' project. This paper highlights the connections made between the various groups: post-primary students, principals, ICT teachers, industry personnel and the Conference keynote speakers and presenters, during a truly unique event.

Chapter 2

Michael Wesch is a cultural anthropologist and media ecologist at Kansas State University. In his paper 'New Media Literacy: What's at Stake' he points to how the 'information revolution' has brought about new ways of relating to and interacting and collaborating with one other. He believes that we must practise seeing the world both *big* and *small* – simultaneously exploring the larger structural, global connections and patterns while also seeing the minute details of the everyday that ultimately co-create these larger structures.

Chapter 3

Roy Pea, Director of H-STAR Institute, Stanford University, Carmen Zahn of the University of Applied Sciences, Northwestern Switzerland, Karsten Krauskopf of the Knowledge Media Research Centre, Tuebingen, Germany, and Friedrich W. Hesse, Executive Director of the Knowledge Media Research Centre, Tuebingen, Germany, present evidence for the use of web-based video tools to support students' collaborative learning. An experimental study with sixteen-year-old learners (who were working on a History topic), compares two types of guidance for student collaboration: dyads-task-related guidance and social interaction-related guidance.

Chapter 4

Vance Martin, a post-doctoral research fellow at the University of Illinois at Urbana-Champaign, discusses how action research helped him to research a concern he had in his practice regarding the use of a traditional course textbook for History teaching. He demonstrates how a wiki supported students to learn History through the process of writing their own textbook. The emergence of more democratic practices was evident through this research study.

Chapter 5

Theo Kuechel, an independent consultant and researcher in educational technology, explores the evolution over the past sixty years of the use of moving images for learning in schools. Drawing on past and current evidence, the paper predicts how emerging trends in web enabled video will increase the potential for learning. Editing tools are becoming prominent on mobile and handheld devices and in the cloud, whilst the publishing and sharing of video is now instantaneous through real time streaming services.

Chapter 6

Stephen J. McNeill and Joshua N. Azriel of the Department of Communications, Kennesaw State University, Georgia, propose that social media has brought to life a new digital literacy. They believe that this change in communication reflects the rise of Citizen Media. In their own words, this means 'the average individual communicating and contributing to the marketplace of ideas'. In a pilot study with Communication students the authors discuss how interviewing, photography and writing were produced on a cell phone and posted on WordPress's web site using its mobile application.

Chapter 7

Glen Williams, Chairperson of Communication Studies, Southeast Missouri State University, argues that students need to develop information literacy skills, including visual literacy. He believes that this is paramount if we are to equip students for the media rich world in which we live and to help them develop their abilities as effective producers and consumers of both images and words.

Chapter 8

Margaret Farren and Yvonne Crotty of the School of Education Studies at Dublin City University trace the evolution of Government policy in Ireland with regard to ICT in Education since 1992. They report on a particular approach to professional development at Masters degree level at DCU offered by the Masters in Education and Training Management (eLearning) programme. The programme attracts a cohort of high calibre professionals from a range of work contexts i.e. education, industry, banking, nursing, government departments, and the arts.

Chapter 9

Jack Whitehead of Liverpool Hope University and the University of Bath distinguishes the practical principles used by educators to explain educational influence from the propositional theories of the disciplines of education. Whitehead suggests that visual representations can express the energy-flowing and values-laden explanatory principles in explanations of educational influence in learning.

Chapter 10

Sabrina Fitzsimons from the Mater Dei Institute of Education, Dublin, gives an account of her own journey into a second life (SL) environment before she brought students into the environment. The research methodology employed in her study was ethnography. In her study, she gathered a range of data in the SL environment including in-world photography.

Chapter 11

Carl Marshall, Fawei Geng and Rowan Wilson of Oxford University Computing Services share the impact of iTunes U at Oxford University and describe how it enabled podcasting to flourish across the University. The authors explain the 'Listening for Impact' project that examined data and sought new information to provide an insight into the uses and value of Oxford University's podcasts.

Chapter 12

Rüdiger Rolf, Nils Birnbaum and Markus Ketterl describe the organisation of lecture recordings at the University of Osnabrück in Germany, developed in-house. In 2008 they joined an Opencast community comprising developers of open-source lecture recording systems from across the globe. The paper describes how they worked collaboratively to create the vision for the next generation lecture recording system.

Chapter 13

Meghan Dougherty and Adrienne Massanari from Chicago's School of Communication at Loyola University offer a guide to best practice in blogging and provide questions for bloggers to think about as they create and maintain their blog. The authors advise bloggers to reflect on the consequences of what they write – especially about other public or private citizens.

Postscript

Mathy Vanbuel and Sally Reynolds, ATiT, Belgium, provide the background and information about the MEDEA Awards, established in 2007 to recognise and reward excellence in media use in education and training. The MEDEA Awards have extended through the European Commission supported project called MEDEA: EU, which means the Awards operate in German and French as well as English.

YVONNE CROTTY

1   On A World Stage: DIVERSE Conference 2011

> Vision without action is a dream. Action without vision is simply passing
> the time. Action with vision is making a positive difference.
> — JOEL BARKER

'DIVERSE 2011 Highlights' (Crotty, 2011) <http://www.youtube.com/
watch?v=9KmdjQLXg8k&feature=player_embedded>

Introduction to DIVERSE

The acronym DIVERSE stands for *Developing Innovative Visual Educational
Resources for Students Everywhere*. The first DIVERSE Conference took
place in Derby, UK in 2001 and focused on all aspects of video production
and videoconferencing in education, research and project management.
The Conferences expanded to include the convergence of these visual
technologies with other online technologies and the idea of 'presence
production' (Knudsen, 2002), for learning along with interactive television, virtual reality, computer games techniques and handheld access to
moving images. In 2011 the DIVERSE Conference took place at Dublin
City University, Ireland. The DIVERSE Conference is an annual event.
Previous DIVERSE Conferences have taken place in the Netherlands, the
USA, Canada, Norway, as well as locations around the UK.

The DIVERSE Conference offers a platform to share creative ideas with an international group of like-minded people interested in cultivating the imagination and expanding the horizons for learners across the globe. The contributors to this book provide a window into some of the presentations at DIVERSE 2011, ranging from the affordances of digital video technologies, use of mobile devices, impact of podcasting and guidelines for blogging. This was the first time the Conference took place in Ireland and it also provided the opportunity to disseminate the creative and visual practice-based research work that I am supporting on the Masters in Education and Training Management (eLearning) – MEME – <http://yvonnecrotty.com/>.

The DIVERSE Committee consists of a core international group of academic and technical experts, chaired by Pieter Van Parreeren from InHolland University. The Committee usually decides on the location for the Annual Conference approximately eighteen months in advance. There are certain traditions in place for the Conference but the local organisers are given the freedom to add their individual stamp to the event.

As a musician, singer and teacher of Music at second level education for fifteen years, performance has always played a key part in my life. This was one of the reasons I accepted the invitation to organise the International DIVERSE Conference at Dublin City University (DCU) in June 2011. In organising such an event I was able to link the various communities together that were interested in developing and using visual media in teaching, research and creative enquiry: academics, teachers, researchers, learning technologists, software developers and project managers to name but a few.

I attended the DIVERSE Conference for the first time in 2008, when it was organised by Tom Visscher and Pieter Van Parreeren at InHolland University, Haarlem. Many of the Conferences that I had attended previously lacked a dynamic between the various delegates and presentations that talked *about* the use of technology, due to a lack of internet connection at the venues. Text-heavy slides seemed to dominate the presentations and there was little use of visuals to enhance the Conference venue or the presentations. In contrast DIVERSE 2008 at InHolland University had a live television studio running in parallel with the presentations, under the guidance of Professor Aase Knudsen from Lillehammer University in Norway and Dr Mike O'Donoghue from Manchester University, UK. This initiative provided postgraduate media students with an opportunity to learn the practicalities of television production. Overall I experienced a warm inclusive atmosphere where the various communities had something to contribute.

Another initiative at DIVERSE 2008 was the 'Creative Concept Coffee' (CCC), a coffee break forum that enabled delegates to network with each other and brainstorm ideas with the possibility of starting a collaborative project. This initiative was the brainchild of Dr Lori Schnieders of the University of Southern Maine, USA and a member of the international DIVERSE Committee. The idea of CCC was that the winning team from the Conference would present their collaborative project at the Conference the following year. In addition, a video conferencing Master Class took place between a music teacher at InHolland University, and a student studying the cello, who was based in the USA. This Master Class demonstrated the potential of the visual element of technology for enhancing teaching and learning and showed a Conference Committee that was willing to take a risk by demonstrating the benefits of cutting edge technology to education.

After my successful bid to host the 2011 Conference, the committee provided me with an opportunity to lead a team and co-create an open space that would combine academic excellence and creativity. From the outset I wanted the Conference delegates to have a holistic and enjoyable experience by awakening their senses using a multi-modal approach and in this way they would be ready to learn from the cognitive experience. At times there seemed to be a disconnect between the head and the heart; the academic world of rigour and validity did not equate with the ever-changing emotional lives that delegates experienced outside of the academic presentations. I had experienced a tension between these two worlds that was contrary to my belief that a variety of experiences can enrich the world of academia.

DIVERSE Ireland 2011 was held over a three day period from 26 to 28 June. It hosted 121 international delegates as well as presenters. There were eight keynote speakers and a cohort of 220 principals and Information and Communication Technology (ICT) coordinators from the second-level sector in Ireland who also were given an opportunity to attend the keynote presentations. A visionary workshop on inquiry based Science Education took place during the Conference as part of the European Seventh Framework project 'Pathway to Inquiry Based Science Education' and was attended by thirty Science teachers from across Ireland. The local Conference team included seven representatives from the University and six volunteers from the local second level school who worked under the guidance of John Harney, an undergraduate from DCU. A thirty-seven strong television crew, called 'DIVERSE Live' were responsible for filming the event and editing highlights. The Helix venue provided two technical staff for each of the four parallel sessions that ran over the two days and also included their own event management and catering staff.

DIVERSE Ireland 2011 – planning and production

Creating the vision to engage your audience

'DIVERSE 2011 website' <http://diverse2011.dcu.ie/>

In organising a scholarly Conference that captured the Conference theme of DIVERSE 2011, 'Creativity: Enhancing our Vision for the Future', there needed to be structures put in place to scaffold the event. Producing a Conference event is like a live stage production; the vision has to be understood by all involved so that everyone is inspired to work together towards a successful outcome. My task was to translate the agreed vision into practice.

To extend an Irish welcome – céad míle fáilte – to our international guests was a key focus. The introduction of different forms of representation in the venue aimed to create an atmospheric learning environment that catered for more than the cognitive dimension. I believed that the Conference would transform people's understanding of the learning processes.

With the agreed plan in place, seven key elements formed the structure of DIVERSE 2011:

1. Web presence

I felt that an engaging, informative and interactive user-friendly web presence would generate interest from the outset. I wanted to create an atmosphere on the website before people arrived at the Conference. Prior to the 2010 Conference in Maine, USA, I had worked on some key areas to ensure that I had website content that included the following elements:

(i)   Theme of the Conference and titles of the various Conference strands;
(ii) Branding material – the design of the DIVERSE Ireland logo and posters;
(iii) Engaging keynote speakers with research in areas that linked practice and theory.

Continually adding content to the website encouraged people to visit the site regularly and check for updates and notices. It offered a sense of what was to come and embodied all things cultural, scholarly, social, visual and engaging while respecting the traditions established by the DIVERSE community. Twitter added impetus to the event and was monitored by Leone Gately, a graduate student of MEME in DCU and also a member of the local DIVERSE team.

2. A venue

It was crucial that the venue was aesthetically pleasing and fit for purpose. Research says that it is not the room but the actual venue that is important (Whitfield, 2009). In relation to organising conferences, Gosling states: 'There has been a drive to produce something different, something exciting and original to add value to an event ... to ensure their company, brand or corporate message stands out from the crowd' (2002, p. 23).

As a delegate at previous Conferences I would have preferred an unusual setting over a hotel or academic venue (Whiteling, 2007). The availability of the Helix Theatre on our DCU campus, all rooms equipped with the latest technology and their proximity to each other, was the perfect solution and such a venue would motivate and give an incentive for people to attend (Roythorne, 2007). Good quality accommodation on campus provided an extra opportunity for people to socialise, share research ideas and collaborate at the end of each day.

The potential success of the event would not derive from the venue but from its overall management; the success of the event involved attention to detail with logistics being a major component (Allen, 2000).

'Helix Site Visit Slideshow' (Heaney, 2011) <http://vimeo.com/27249734>

3. Visual experience

- Logo

I designed the logo in the shape of a woman to depict the mythical symbol and emblem of Ireland, Kathleen Ni Houlihan <http://diverse2011.dcu.ie/welcome.html>. The use of key landmarks in Dublin aimed to join the old with the new. Patrick Kavanagh, the Irish poet, is sitting on the landmark seat by Dublin's Grand Canal Bank Walk; the newly built Spire on O'Connell Street, Daniel O'Connell's statue and the Halfpenny Bridge gave a sense of place and culture. The choice of greens and white – colours associated with Ireland – was intended to give a fresh look and clarity to the website. These images were placed within the website header.

- Balloons

My wish to include balloons at the Conference venue came when I observed the artistic work of Raquel Reynolds, who had transformed many venues into colourful and fun places with life-sized balloons <http://www.funky-balloons.ie>. The strategic placement of the figures to greet delegates at the door of each plenary session provided a talking point and dispelled the myth that all academic Conferences have to be totally serious. The eight-foot balloon of Kathleen Ni Houlihan was situated at the entrance

Figure 1 Kathleen
Ní Houlihan logo
(mythical symbol of
Ireland)

to the Helix and immediately added a sense of fun to the Conference. All
balloons also matched Conference colours.

• Animation

At previous Concerts I had organised or at which I performed, I included
some form of multi-media resource. For the DIVERSE Conference, I
worked in collaboration with John O'Riordain and Seamus Brett, technical experts in animation and music respectively who helped transform my
ideas into reality drawing on the designs and concepts that I used on the
website and combined these with Irish dance tunes to add a cultural and
professional dimension in between the scholarly presentation sessions. This

animation was also integrated into the live broadcasts that took place at the end of each day.

'Live Opening' (Crotty, 2011) <http://www.youtube.com/watch?v=BJ BOLID_bwA&feature=relmfu>

- Photo competition

The initial idea for a photo competition came at a Workshop on Visual Literacy and in the preparation of an e-Portfolio workshop that I teach each year to a group of undergraduate students taking an extra curricular module. Requests for volunteers after this session resulted in Alan Lyons, an amateur photographer, expressing an interest in being involved in organising the photo competition. Alan distributed the call for photographs through the National Photographers' Association and secured reputable judges for the competition. However, the idea for the competition proved too ambitious and a lack of entries meant that we could not run with the planned photo exhibition. Nevertheless, I still wanted to include a photographic exhibition as part of the Conference and Alan put me in contact with Peter Byrne, a local photographer, who agreed to exhibit black and white photographs with an Irish theme. These added to the cultural aspect of the Conference.

- Video competition

I produced a video to launch this competition. This created links with other communities such as Video in Teaching and Learning (VITAL), <http://vital-sig.ning.com> and to collaborate with them on the generation of content in order to raise an awareness of the Conference. The video competition, similarly with the photo competition, received few entries. By June 2011 however, the video call had over 600 hits that cultivated an interest in the DIVERSE Conference itself.

Video 'Final Competition' (Crotty, 2011) <http://www.youtube.com/ watch?v=on7g-2GBZvo&feature=relmfu>

- Clothing: tee-shirts

In order to set a professional tone and ensure there was a sense of care for the delegates, black tee-shirts for the Conference film crew, white tee-shirts for the local volunteers and navy-blue tee-shirts for the DCU local team were purchased. This helped to make key staff easily identifiable so that the delegates knew who to contact if they needed help. Generating a sense of unity among the different members of the crew was also important to ensure cooperation and the successful workflow across the different elements of the Conference. A good support network is important and so all groups met at the same time each day for a briefing and met at the end of the Conference day to evaluate the day's events (Allen, 2000).

4. A cultural encounter

Providing an Irish experience to our international guests between the presentation sessions through the musical interludes/animation and an evening concert event was intended to link the Conference to Ireland's cultural heritage. Our cultural capital is deeply embedded in our ontology. The inclusion of a four-part harmony male vocal group performing Irish songs at the opening of the Conference and during break times further reinforced the cultural dimension. A walking photography workshop of Dublin also sought to combine the educational, social and cultural dimensions of the Conference.

At the DIVERSE 2012 Conference in Leuven, Belgium, I met with Ingrid Bruynse, a South African delegate, who had attended the DIVERSE Conference in Dublin. She recalled her experience of DIVERSE 2011 and emphasised how the inclusion of music, visuals with the academic themes had made the 2011 Conference a 'fabulous whole experience'. She also described the strange feeling that she had experienced upon hearing Irish music and this motivated her to go in search of her own genealogy only to discover that she was of Irish extraction. The following video captures the immense joy and value Ingrid experienced and demonstrates that it is important never to underestimate our cultural and musical expression.

'Never underestimate your Cultural and Musical Expression' (Crotty, 2012) <http://vimeo.com/45691283>

5. Linking to the wider community

I have always seen the organising of events as an opportunity to link to the wider community, to be more inclusive and also contribute to it being a more significant occasion. In addition to organising the main DIVERSE community, I linked other groups in Ireland that I felt would benefit from the experience: post-primary students, Principals, Information and Communication Technology representatives and industry representatives in general.

(i) Linking with post-primary students:

Arcodia and Reid (2008) talk about volunteers playing a significant role in the organisation of conferences. From my own experience as a secondary school teacher, when I worked with students during the production of musicals and various projects, I had seen how volunteers greatly enhanced the running of any event. Events like the DIVERSE Conference provide an authentic learning experience for students that can help them with career choices when they leave school. Some of the postgraduate students from MEME at DCU are teachers in the local post-primary Girls school and I was delighted to be able to link in with their Transition Year (TY) students.

Before the Conference, I worked with these TY students preparing them for their roles at the Conference. I covered topics such as the logistics of event management, sponsorship, branding, catering, hospitality and sound production. I wanted the students to have a general knowledge of all aspects of organising an event before they experienced working along-side professionals. I also highlighted the importance of planning an event properly, the strategy I was implementing and the operational aspects in which they would be involved.

From my experience of planning an event there needs to be both a strategic perspective and an operational schedule. I rotated the schedule so that each of the students would get a chance to work on different areas.

This could have hampered the efficiency of the operations but because they communicated so well as a team, using the group facility that I had set up on Facebook, all aspects of their brief were adhered to throughout the Conference. The improvement in their social skills, communication skills, confidence and self-esteem was heartening to see and the event was also an excellent capacity-building opportunity for these students. Their presence during Conference preparations provided fun and enjoyment and generated a real sense of goodwill for everyone involved. Each student was assigned a group of delegates and a keynote speaker and this worked very well.

It was important that the students learned from the event and that they knew they were instrumental in making the event a success. Central to my philosophy was the idea that it had to be a reciprocal relationship, so that they would feel appreciated for the work they did at the event. I asked each student to write a reflection of their experience after the Conference so that they could consolidate their learning. The following comment from Ciara, a Transition Year student, demonstrates the change in her thinking and what she had learned:

> Over the Conference, I had the opportunity to work with many professionals. From the delegates with excellent teaching experience to the staff in the Helix with catering and event managing experience, everyone around us had something which we could learn from. DIVERSE gave me and the volunteers as a team the opportunity to do many things we never had before. I learnt how to communicate with people in all professional situations, how to work as a team within our volunteer team alongside the overall DIVERSE organisation team. I experienced waitressing which I had never attempted before, I developed skills with office equipment such as laminators and guillotines, sound equipment and most of all I discovered how much work goes into event management and how to make sure an event runs to according to plan. (Ciara Dawson, Dominican Convent, Dublin, July 2011)

John Harney graduated in 2011 with a BSc in Financial and Actuarial Maths and was involved in the day-to-day running of this post-primary volunteer group. His reflections demonstrate that there was a great sense of individual well-being to be achieved while working as part of a bigger team. It also shows the transformative effect this event had on him.

Managing a team as I did was wonderful experience for me and helped me to become more confident in my own communication and organisational skills. I found that I was able to connect with people and build up a relationship with them quickly. I also found that people trusted me which was very flattering. On a personal level, as I was just finished my degree, it really helped me recapture a sense that passion for your chosen path in life is the key to fulfillment. While I was very content with the path I was on at the time, I had a niggling feeling that there was something else I should do. I have since taken steps to pursue what I feel I am called to do in the world, and I feel that my experience at the conference played a part in this. (John Harney, Personal Communication, 15 June 2012)

(ii) Linking with post-primary Principals and Information and Communication Technology teachers:

Continuing Professional Development (CPD) for teachers is a significant part of our work in DCU's School of Education Studies. A grant of up to €90,000 was allocated by the Department of Education and Science (DES) of Ireland in 2010 for the purchase of hardware in post-primary schools in Ireland and I received a number of enquiries from ICT coordinators and Principals before the DIVERSE Conference asking me to advise them on how they could best spend the funding. This prompted me to find a way to link the needs of these Principals to the DIVERSE Conference presentations so they could learn from the good practice in place in post-primary schools in Ireland. The post-primary teachers who had successfully completed the Masters programme were already integrating technology in their subject areas and I knew that this would inspire others to learn from their experience of integrating ICT into the curriculum. I know that Principals are very busy people and it is difficult for them to keep up-to-date with technological innovation. The National Centre for Technology in Education (NCTE) personnel, who are located on the DCU campus, and more specifically Tom Lonergan, a student on MEME collaborated with me on a CPD day as an adjunct to the main Conference.

I wanted to extend an invitation to representatives from each school (Principals or ICT coordinators). It is my belief that Principals do not need to be technologists but can act as advocates for the creative use of technology and stay connected to the future needs of their students. I invited a maximum of three people from each post-primary school. This

invitation included attendance at the keynote presentation from Dr Michael
Wesch, a Professor of Cultural Anthropology at Kansas State University
and internationally known for his video work with students. This added a
sense of excitement to the professional development day with the sharing
of educational practice by an international expert. Past and current students from MEME presented their applied research work and how they
were making effective use of technology to transform their own teaching
and learning and the learning of students and teachers in their schools.

Mary O'Toole, a Chemistry teacher, who was in Year One of the
Masters programme, attended the event with her principal:

> My Principal was much more positive about the possibilities available to school
> having attended the 'Stay ConnectED' day. We got a whole new computer room of
> 30 Apple Mac computers. It might have taken much longer for her to understand how
> effective this move was had she not had a chance to see examples of other teachers
> research work. (Mary O'Toole, Personal Communication, 4 June 2012)

(iii) Linking to industry:

Industry personnel with a business interest in ICT in education and training
were invited to partner with us for this event; this helped generate funds
to ensure a successful CPD day. The downturn in the economy and the
exponential rise in companies going into liquidation meant that Irish companies had to show a return on investment and had to be very discerning
about which events they supported. Over the years I have become aware
that teachers are often wary of dealing with the business world. However,
I am also cognisant that many educational innovations would not have
come to fruition without the input and support from industry and the business world. There is a requirement on us to explain what we, as educators,
can share with industry and industry in turn can share new technological
developments e.g. custom-made accessible, usable technology that links
with the curriculum.

DIVERSE is an international Conference and I understood that local
business sponsors would not see international delegates as prospective
clients. But the addition of the ICT teachers and Principals for the CPD
seminar day entitled 'Stay ConnectED' gave vendors real links with schools

and made it financially viable for them to support the Conference. It was essential that all parties would benefit as I did not want to involve industry until I had a firm commitment from Principals and teachers that they would attend the Conference. Confirmation of 220 delegates representing Principals and ICT coordinators allowed me to proceed with the CPD venture and secure my commitment to industry. This provided an opportunity for educators to explore their technologies and to partner with industry-school initiatives.

6. Video LinkED – Video linking to education with 'DIVERSE Live' TV workshop

At the beginning of this chapter I expressed my satisfaction at finding a Conference that appealed to me when at DIVERSE 2008 in InHolland University. The presence of a broadcasting event in the form of a TV studio was an exciting innovation first introduced by Professor Aase Knudsen and Dr Mike O'Donoghue in Lillehammer, Norway during 2007. As an observer and newcomer to the DIVERSE community in Haarlem, the hidden nature of the studio detracted somewhat from the possibilities that an opportunity such as the TV studio could afford others to learn about the live streaming process. This was a driving force behind my wanting to include a live studio at the hub of activity for the DIVERSE Conference 2011.

As a performer I envisaged great possibilities for having such a workshop located in the centre of activity. I am not a technical expert in live television production but when I mooted the idea at the Maine Conference in 2010 to Aase Knudsen, an expert in this field, and subsequently to Mike O Donoghue, both were enthusiastic about the possibility of trying this idea out. We envisaged this as being central to the proceedings in order to:

(i)   Create an energy;
(ii) Give students a hands-on experience of how to work multiple cameras;
(iii) Allow delegates to see the workings behind the television studio.

I wanted to professionally document the event as I felt that it would be easier for subsequent Conference organisers to get sponsorship and encourage prospective delegates to attend busy quality footage showing people attending an enjoyable, professionally organised multi-modal event. A good set of photographers and videographers might have been sufficient and less expensive if documenting the Conference was my sole aim; however, it was not.

7. Opportunity to learn

Another important aspect to 'DIVERSE Live' was that it would give the students a real opportunity to develop their own video production skills. There were two cohorts of students I particularly wanted to involve: the students on the Multimedia degree in the School of Communication who had studied the technicalities of audio and video production as part of their undergraduate multimedia studies, and the Masters in Education and Training Management (eLearning) – MEME – students, who had developed educational video resources as part of their postgraduate studies. The first cohort also included two international groups of students from Manchester University, UK and the University of Lillehammer in Norway. They were under the guidance of Mike O'Donoghue and Aase Knudsen respectively and of Alberto Ramerez, another member of the International DIVERSE Committee.

Both student groups viewed the 'DIVERSE Live' project from different perspectives. The MEME group were concerned with the educational message of the video transmissions (VTs) and focused on the content. The undergraduate students from the School of Communications were concerned with the actual brief of being a producer or cameraman, with less concern for content from an educational viewpoint; they appeared more concerned with deadlines and logistics. The MEME students had initially embarked on the project with less confidence in their technical ability assuming that they were not as knowledgeable despite having previously been told that their vision and managerial skills would traverse specific skills. I had also emphasised that their creative side and visual literacy skills, fostered during their studies, would prepare them as well as their peers for this project, provided they believed in their abilities. The following is a reflection from one the MEME students Gemma Clarke:

> DIVERSE was a one of those unique rare opportunities that life sometimes presents to you. It was a mad crazy roller coaster of a week. We were literally thrown in at the deep and had to produce one hour live broadcast for three days in a row. While we had some training in video production, the learning curve was enormous. Not only did we acquire a lot of additional technical skills but most importantly we came away with a deep appreciation of how well we (the Masters elearning group) had learned to work together so well on our course. This was particularly apparent especially at the more stressful points throughout the week. Where other groups were becoming more dysfunctional, we remained steadfast, supporting and encouraging each other to do the best we could. Not only we were a true collaborative learning unit, we also got this rare opportunity to appreciate and understand what we had become as individuals and the confidence we had gained throughout our Masters programme. For me that was the best part of it all. (Gemma Clarke, Personal Correspondence, 18 September 2011)

The maturity of the postgraduate students enhanced the overall project and ensured the stability needed to achieve the successful outcome. The postgraduate students were beyond having a particular title for the sake of it and were more concerned with the task in hand. Mike O Donoghue had prepared and collated a comprehensive handbook for the event which incorporated the roles of a TV production crew defining the various job specifications. The marriage of the experienced technical team from the Norwegian group, in Aase Knudsen, Kathrine Mørkved, Pål Finnkroken and Ina Madsen Rogne along with Damien Hickey and Eoin Campbell from DCU, sharpened the focus for the technical running and success of this part of the project.

After DIVERSE Ireland and post evaluation

Although the project achieved its goals and was very successful, there are some changes I would make if organising a similar event. I believe that dividing the large group into smaller teams so that they could work on content, one month before the Conference, would assist greatly in achieving more effective and smoother running of the event. Collaboration via Skype or through Facebook groups in order to carry out research, storyboard and work on possible topics in advance would avert unnecessary panic. Such a process would have given students a better chance to enjoy building relationships and working together. There could have been a better opportunity for students to get to know each other and take pride in each other's work, rather than having to focus on trouble-shooting near the deadlines. My observation from student feedback was that their inclusion before DIVERSE started was a little too rushed and that they would have benefited from more training as a group. This appeared to put unnecessary stress on inexperienced groups instead of being a more enjoyable educational experience for all involved. The following extract is from Niall Murphy, an undergraduate student on the Multimedia Degree in the School of Communications:

> As a student studying multimedia, DIVERSE live was the perfect opportunity for me to gain some out-of-class experience in the area of live production. For me, DIVERSE taught me things that I couldn't learn from sitting in the classroom and gave me an insight into the real workings of the media industry. Although it only took place over a few days, the whole experience was invaluable to me and is something that has opened doors to new and similar experiences for me.
>
> I thought the whole project was very well organised but if there was one thing I could change it would be adding a couple of days of detailed training for everyone before the Conference began as I felt some of the production team were unsure of a few things.
>
> Overall, it is something I would do again and I would have no hesitation in advising people to getting involved next time. (Niall Murphy, personal reflection feedback, 23 June 2012)

'DIVERSE Live' was a resounding success and the feedback I have included highlights the huge learning curve the participants were on and how glad they were that they had partaken in the event.

Team building – things don't just happen

Organising and managing events is a task I have always enjoyed. Choosing a dynamic local team to help with the organisation of the Conference was vital. I have always found leading a small core group to be more productive than working with a larger and more dispersed committee. It was important to me that this event involved the DCU community and that this was reflected by inviting a cohort of people to contribute to DIVERSE from across the various Faculties on campus. Having a diverse group involved in the event would give them a sense of social pride (Derrett, 2003). At a time of job cuts within the university sector this event would play an important part in creating trust and cohesiveness among the DCU community and indeed the DIVERSE community members themselves (Gursoy, Kyungmi, & Uysal, 2004). Although different Faculties were involved, there was a sense that we were all together in one higher education establishment and our overall goal was about educating people. It was also an opportunity that all Faculties would benefit from learning how to develop and incorporate visual media into teaching, learning and research, so individuals from across the University were included – Humanities and Social Science, Engineering and Computing, Science and Health, the Business School, as well as representation from the Learning Innovation Unit and Oscail. This meant that a spread of people from across the University was represented and a good group dynamic created.

Creating a sense of well-being amongst the group was a main priority. The Conference also needed a clear vision and direction. As mentioned in the section on volunteers, planning was a crucial starting point; I knew it would optimise the team and the resource structures and encourage all stakeholders to understand their roles and work cooperatively (Bramwell,

1997). I worked with Dr Margaret Farren, to identify possible members for the local team. It was vital to know exactly what was needed from each person and that good, clear management and leadership was provided in order to provide the best experience possible for my volunteers in utilising their skills for a successful Conference. In recruiting volunteers I wanted to contribute to community spirit and have a social impact that would contribute to diversity and include a wide range of backgrounds (Van der Wagen, 2006).

Once structures were in place and briefs assigned, team members could use their creative initiative to complete their tasks. Emma O'Brien of the Biomedical Diagnostic Unit in DCU took charge of organising a new, very successful strand in e-Health. Dr Margaret Farren and Morag Munro ensured quality presentations by reviewing the papers and making the final call. Peter Tiernan, Ger Cannon and Eamon Coughlan took charge of the technical requirements and Leone Gately looked after the social media and dissemination of news. Weekly meetings from mid-March to June helped to keep our spirits high. For each meeting, I always tried to have another new visual dimension ready to add another layer of understanding to what was about to happen.

Looking back

There have been articles written about the Conference and feedback has been very positive. Dr Mark Childs, who was the DIVERSE Chair from 2005–2008, documented his reflections in the Association for Learning Technology (ALT) newsletter which was published in Autumn 2011. Like the many musical productions and other projects I have been involved in, it was difficult to get a true perspective on the impact of the Conference at the time. Reflection needs to occur some time later to evaluate the event properly and give a true reflection of what has taken place. Acknowledging the merits and the areas that need to be improved is easier with perspective. Some time on, I am now happy with the energy that was generated at DIVERSE 2011, and I enjoy hearing accounts that highlight the joy experienced and the impact the Conference had on individuals and on the wider social formations.

By documenting the events, I have tried to be mindful of all the good-will DIVERSE generated and of its impact in sharing knowledge. My objective in demonstrating the potential of visual media in teaching, research and learning was achieved, so I succeeded in marrying the head and the heart and sense and soul (Wiber, 1998).

The video footage from the Creative Coffee Concept winners captures some of the ongoing impact of DIVERSE 2011. DIVERSE 2011 in Dublin can be improved and built upon so that others within the DIVERSE community, and future DIVERSE local Conference organisers can benefit.

'Looking back – DIVERSE 2011' (Crotty, 2012) <http://vimeo.com/ 45483779>

References

Allen, J., *Event Planning, The Ultimate Guide to Successful Meetings, Corporate Events, Fundraising Galas, Conferences, Conventions, Incentives and other Special Events* (Ontario: Wiley, 2000).

Arcodia, C. & Reid, S., 'Professional Standards: The Current State of Event Management Associations.' *Journal of Convention & Event Tourism* 9/1 (2008), 60–80.

Ball, A. & Tyson C., 'Non Satis Scire: To Know is Not Enough.' *American Educational Research Association 2012 Annual Meeting Call for Submissions, Vancouver, British Columbia, Canada.* Retrieved 10 October 2011 from <http://www.aera.net/ AnnualMeetingThemeHighlights/tabid/12577/Default.aspx>

Bramwell, B., 'Strategic planning before and after a mega-event.' *Tourism Management* 18/3 (1997), 167–176.

Childs, M., DIVERSE 2011 [Issue 24]. Message posted to <http://newsletter.alt. ac.uk/2011/08/DIVERSE-2011/>

Crotty, Y., 'How Am I Bringing an Entrepreneurial Spirit into Higher Level Education' (2012).

Derrett, R., 'Making sense of how festivals demonstrate a community's sense of place.' *Event Management* 8/1 (2003), 49–58.

Gosling, J., 'Unusual venues: An event less ordinary.' *Conference and Incentive Travel* (2002, November/December), 23–28.

Gursoy, D., Kyungmi, K., & Uysal, M., 'Perceived impacts of festivals and special events by organizers: An extension and validation.' *Tourism Management* 25/2 (2004), 171–181.

Roythorne, P., 'Venues: Standing out from the crowd.' Retrieved 22 September 2007 from <http://meetingsreview.com/news/view?id=929&print=1>

Van der Wagen, L., *Human Resource Management for Events* (Oxford: Elsevier Ltd, 2007).

Whitehead, J., 'To Know Is Not Enough, Or Is It?' Paper presented at the 2012 Conference of the American Educational Research Association in Vancouver on 14 April 2012. Retrieved 12 May 2011 from <http://www.actionresearch.net/writings/jack/jwaera12noffke200212.pdf>

Whiteling, I., 'Unusual venues found to be big draw for delegates.' Retrieved 24 September 2008 from <http://meetingsreview.com/news/view?id=856&print=1>

Whitfield, J.E., 'Why and How UK Visitor Attractions Diversify Their Product to Offer Conference and Event Facilities.' *Journal of Convention & Event Tourism* 10/1 (2009), 72–88.

MICHAEL WESCH

2   New Media Literacy: What's at Stake?

Over twenty-five years ago, Neil Postman described American culture of the late twentieth century as being marked by a discourse of *irrelevance*, *incoherence*, and *impotence*, placing the blame on the one-way electronic mass media onslaught of context-free information. He challenged us to imagine ourselves sitting in front of a television watching the most serious and *important* newscast available and to ask ourselves, 'What steps do you plan to take to reduce the conflict in the Middle East? Or the rates of inflation, crime and unemployment? ... What do you plan to do about NATO, OPEC, or the CIA?' He then '[took] the liberty of answering for [us]: You plan to do nothing.' It was 1985. Affordable hand-held video cameras, the Web, and the social media platforms that could potentially transform us into active media participants and create a user-generated media alternative were unavailable.

Those of us who care about media participation, expression, and citizen engagement have all at one time or another been excited by the possibilities and promises of new media. Most of us can point to a particular moment when we thought that this era of irrelevance, incoherence and impotence might be coming to an end as the dawn of new media displayed its first glimmers on the horizon. My moment came while surveying the *Numa Numa* viral video craze. Just before the launch of YouTube, Gary Brolsma orchestrated a dance to a Moldovan pop song that commentator Douglas Wolk would say 'single-handedly justifies the existence of webcams'. He uploaded the video in December 2004 and soon attracted millions of viewers. When YouTube launched later that year people, who before this time had no means of sharing a video with the world, recorded themselves dancing the *Numa Numa* and shared it with the world. Soon, tens of thousands of webcam dancers joined 'the Internet's version of the Macarena', a giant virtual Conga Line stretching around the world across space and time. While in themselves the videos may seem to be of little significance I could not help but think that those of us who had joined the dance were celebrating something more profound than *Numa Numa* itself. We were celebrating empowerment, new forms of connection and community and new and unimaginable possibilities. It may sound like hype and there was plenty of hype in those early days of YouTube but consider what we were dancing in front of: about one billion little boxes scattered all over the world with little glass dots that could take in and transmit our image to any one of those other one billion little boxes. As an anthropologist concerned with the long view of human history, I'm not sure if it is possible to overstate the significance of such an event.

But here we are six years since the launch of YouTube, along with the whole fleet of other potentially revolutionary social media platforms, and a more sobering reality is starting to become apparent. Quick surveys of my own students at Kansas State suggest that fewer than 4 per cent of students have ever edited and published a video for the public before entering my class, yet they consume four times as much video as they do text. Nearly all students report that they frequently use Wikipedia, but fewer than 10 per cent know what a wiki is, or how a wiki works. Fewer than 5 per cent have ever edited a wiki. A similarly small percentage know what an RSS feed is, or how to use a social bookmarking service (both of which are powerful methods for online research, information gathering, and information sharing.) While all of them frequently use Google and other search engines to find online information, studies from Diana Oblinger and others have consistently demonstrated that university students are not good at finding or identifying high quality materials (e.g. <21cif.com>). In short, the so-called *digital natives* are very good at entertaining themselves online, but are not so good at educating themselves online. They live in a world that gives them tremendous potential, but they lack the most basic skills to harness and leverage this potential.

There is a great deal at stake. At the base of what many have called the *information revolution* are really new ways of relating to one another, new forms of discourse, new ways of interacting, new kinds of groups, and new ways of sharing, trading and collaborating. This is a social revolution, not just a technological one, and its most revolutionary aspect may be the virtually unlimited potential for digital technology to do and be almost anything, mediating human relations in an almost limitless variety of ways. Media, as Postman reminds us, are not just about sending and receiving information. They are the means by how we relate to one another, affecting much more than just how we communicate. It took tens of thousands of years for the first substantially new medium (writing) to emerge after humans spoke their first words. It took thousands more before the printing press and a few hundred again before the telegraph. Today a new medium emerges every time somebody creates a new application. A Flickr here, a Twitter there, and a new way of relating to others emerges.

Commonplace distinctions between *new* and *old* media fail to capture the real changes now taking shape. It is not just about the fact that most old media is going digital, thereby being absorbed into the webs of participation I have been describing here. That is just a small part of the story. The changes we are now participating in are too pervasive to be captured by standard definitions of media that are predicated on notions of one-way commercial media giants. Old media is something you watch or read. It exists apart from you, as something to talk about and criticise. You can turn it on and off or put it away. It is only from an old media perspective that we would be concerned about amateurs taking over the production of media (e.g. Keen, 2007), or that we might be awash in too much information. Such concerns miss the bigger picture by focusing on the transmission and reception of information, and draw attention away from more realistic and serious issues that we must face as we recognise how pervasive digital media now are in our everyday lives.

Giving our students basic skills is not enough. Even higher order ideals that we have rallied around for several decades, such as critical thinking and information literacy, fail to inspire the kinds of learning, values, and dispositions we need. In the words of Henry Jenkins, we need to move beyond information literacy to participatory literacy, and embrace more holistic goals that recognise the more far-reaching effects of this new media environment (2006). Gardner Campbell calls it digital citizenship, and it is much more than a simple skill set as implied by the 21st Century Skills movement (2010). We must help create a way of being-in-the-world in which people recognise and actively examine, question, and even re-create the (increasingly digital) structures that shape our world.

This means going beyond the traditional rallying cries of critical thinking in education. The educational goal of critical thinking blossomed in the media environment dominated by television. Many educators quite rightly embraced it (and continue to embrace it) as a means of limiting the damage done by television. Critical thinking takes on a particular relevance when we recognise that television is not just a conduit for the delivery and consumption of trivial information, but is also the primary cultural production machine providing the pieces to be used by our students in their search for identity and recognition.

'Onslaught', a Dove cosmetics product commercial, demonstrates the point, showing a young girl bombarded by a flurry of media messages driving her toward a future of low self-esteem, false body-image, and an unending desire to *fix* herself. The lyrics underscore the point, 'Here it comes, the breeze that'll blow you away, all your reason and your sane, same with your minds.' The commercial demonstrates the real need for critical thinking to save our minds from the relentless breeze of commercial media that threatens to blow us away.

But the remixes of the video demonstrate that we can no longer be content with simply protecting ourselves from this breeze. We can blow back. One remix called 'A message from Unilever' (2007) simply notes that Unilever is the parent company for both Dove (the creator of this wonderful programme rallying against the sins of the beauty industry) and Axe (the creator of many of the more objectifying and distasteful ads that are creating the problem in the first place). Using imagery from Axe as 'the breeze that'll blow you away,' bombarding the young girl with objectifying imagery from Unilever's own ad campaign, thereby reveals their hypocrisy.

Another remix, created by Greenpeace (2008), shows a young girl in Indonesia taking in a flurry of images of the trees in the environment around her being destroyed to clear the way for palm plantations providing palm oil for Dove products. The song is the same, but with parodying lyrics, 'There they go, your trees are gone today, all that beauty hacked away. So use your minds'. The video ends with the young Indonesian girl walking away from a recently cut down forest, and a subtitle that reads '98% of

Indonesia's lowland forest will be gone by the time Azizah is 25. Most is destroyed to make palm oil, which is used in Dove products.'

The video raced to over 1 million views on YouTube. Two weeks later Greenpeace activists were invited to the table with senior executives at Unilever who then signed an immediate moratorium on deforestation for palm oil in Southeast Asia (Greenpeace, 2009). Greenpeace noted that it was the single most effective tactic they had ever used.

Recall Postman's challenge in 1985. 'What are you going to do about [major world issues you hear about on TV] ...?' He can no longer take the liberty of answering for us. We are no longer constrained to doing nothing. We can talk back. We can create. Critical thinking remains essential and important. But it is no longer enough.

There is no more room for complaining about one-way media commercial giants anymore. The new media environment of today is nothing more nor less than what we collectively make of it. Educators now take on a double responsibility, not only to create students who are media literate in the old school sense of being able to think critically about media they consume, but also to create students who can effectively create, share and collaborate.

The need for new media literacy extends beyond video literacy. As I write this the web is moving increasingly off the desktop and laptop screen and into our everyday lives. Global Positioning System coordinates and billions of two-dimensional barcodes and RFID tags embedded in products are increasingly used as hyperlinks in the real world. Many mobile devices now double as augmented reality devices overlaying information about the items in your environment as you aim your mobile devices camera around your surroundings. The type of information we will see is ultimately up to us. The battle for a better media environment becomes a battle for the view, a battle for what will be seen and unseen, known and unknown.

Digital code will increasingly set the most important laws of our societies. Code will set the forms and structures through which we interact. Spider bots, spambots, spybots, and other invisible applications will increasingly feed from and feed off a growing database of our most mundane movements and actions. The issues surrounding code as law will become ever more pervasive and salient. The digital citizens we hope to create must be media ecologists themselves, recognising how the codes shape and structure our interactions with one another, how they encourage or discourage different types of intentional and unintentional information sharing and how they shape the overall discourse of our culture.

To bring these issues to familiar territory, consider that the largest public spaces in the world at this particular moment are Facebook and YouTube. Hundreds of millions of people gather virtually at these sites every day to connect with one another. Of course, these connections are highly mediated, and Facebook and YouTube, like all media, have certain structures and forms that encourage and enable some forms of communication while discouraging and sometimes even disabling other kinds of communication. The code itself sets the rules. 'Code is law' as Larry Lessig so succinctly noted (1999).

Already, there are signs of an imbalanced and unfair code at work in the background of YouTube. The automatic content identification system can be set by copyright holders to automatically take down a video with copyrighted material, regardless of whether or not that material was used legally (for criticism under the laws of Fair Use or Fair Dealing, for example). The user may contest the take-down, but if the copyright holder denies the claim of Fair Use, the user must obtain a lawyer and file a counter claim, something that is much too risky and expensive for the average user to do. As a result, tens of thousands of videos have been removed, some of which may have been of some great significance.

Contrary to the hype, new media alone do not create a more just, open, transparent, and participatory world that can move us beyond the irrelevant and incoherent banter Postman found on television. Consider the 2008 US political campaign when CNN teamed up with YouTube for what they called 'history in the making,' a 'groundbreaking format' that allowed viewers to submit the questions. Unfortunately, the only thing new about the debate was that the questions tended to be highly entertaining, a little laugh to punctuate the flurry of talking points delivered by the candidates. Disagreements were mentioned but not debated. It was old media remediating the new, absorbing it into its forms. We were still, in Postman's words, 'amusing ourselves to death'.

So how can we use new media, or create new media, to conquer the narcissistic disengagement that we see today in a culture that is still ruled by trivialities? I have noted that basic skills, even complicated skills like coding, are not enough. And as Maxine Greene has written, 'superior technical competencies, like basic skills themselves, are insufficient in the face of holocausts, famines, budget deficits in the trillions, unimaginable wealth controlled by corporate interests' and on the list of problems runs. If we really want our students to engage this world and help recreate it, 'what kinds of intelligences are required?' she asks (1995).

Of particular importance to digital citizenship is what Maxine Greene called the *social imagination* which she describes as 'the ability the capacity to invent visions of what should be and what might be in our deficient society.' The social imagination begins with the ability to see things as if they could be otherwise, to see givens as contingencies. And, following Greene a bit further, we must practise seeing the world both *big* and *small* – simultaneously exploring the large structural global connections and patterns while also seeing the minute details of the everyday, and of individuals, that ultimately co-create these larger structures. And therein lies the key to it all. Digital citizenship requires an ongoing exploration of the world and how it is co-created, how our understandings of the world are also co-created, and how we can move toward new creations and a new world if needed.

If one needs an indication that what we are doing in our traditional schools might not be working, consider that the most potent machine ever invented for creativity, sharing, learning, and collaboration (the Web) finds its primary use in university classrooms as a distraction device. We live in a world that is quickly racing toward ubiquitous computing, communication, and information at unlimited speed about everything everywhere, accessed and uploaded from anywhere on all kinds of devices, all of which makes it easier than ever to connect, organise, share, collect, collaborate, and publish with almost anybody and to almost anybody in the world. How did we end up in a situation in which the institutions we have designed for learning see this as a distraction rather than an asset?

Media is what we make of it, from the information we find, share and create, to the actual media forms through which this information flows and through which we connect with one another. Our responsibilities are

as profound as the opportunities are rich, and the stakes are high. For the
structures and forms of media we create, create *how* we can create, and perhaps more importantly, how we will relate with one another. Each time we
create a new medium we are not only remaking the media environment,
we are remaking ourselves. We need to create creators more than ever –
not just so they can create the future. Where code is law we need to create
creators to ensure we have a future in which creators can create and freely
share their creations.

References

Arendt, H., *The Human Condition* (Chicago: University of Chicago Press, 1958).

Campbell, G., 'Media Fluency?' Retrieved 2010 from <http://gardnercampbell.net/
    blog1/?m=201005>

Dewey, J., *Experience and Education* (New York: Macmillan Publishing, 1938).

De Zengotita, T., *Mediated: how the media shapes your world and the way you live in
    it* (New York: Bloomsbury Publishing, 2005).

Greene, M., *Releasing the Imagination* (San Francisco: Jossey-Bass Publishers, 1995).

Greenpeace, 'Dove Onslaught(er)'. Retrieved 2008 from <http://www.youtube.com/
    watch?v=odI7pQFyjso>

Greenpeace, 'Public Pressure for Indonesia's forests works, Ask Unilever'. Retrieved
    2009 from <http://www.greenpeace.org/international/campaigns/forests/
    asia-pacific/dove-palmoil-action/>

Jenkins, H., *Confronting the challenges of participatory culture: Media education for the
    21st Century* (MacArthur Foundation, 2006).

Keen, A., *The Cult of the Amateur: How Today's Internet is Killing Our Culture* (New
    York: Broadway Business, 2007).

Lessig, L., *Code and other laws of cyberspace* (New York: Basic Books, 1999).

Postman, N., *Amusing Ourselves to Death.* (New York: Penguin Books, 1985).

Ryeclifton, 'A message from Unilever.' Retrieved 2007 from <http://www.youtube.
    com/watch?v=SwDEF-w4rJk>

Taylor, C., *The Ethics of Authenticity* (Cambridge: Harvard University Press, 1991).

Wesch, M., 'From Knowledgeable to Knowledge-able.' *Academic Commons* (January
    2009).

CARMEN ZAHN, KARSTEN KRAUSKOPF, FRIEDRICH W. HESSE
AND ROY PEA

3   Digital Media in the Classroom: A Study on How to Improve Guidance for Successful Collaboration and Learning in Student Teams

Computational technology and digital media can greatly enhance the possibilities for creative knowledge construction in social learning situations. However, there are open questions related to the guidance of group interactions in desirable directions, especially when novice learners face complex authentic learning tasks. For example, a major concern expressed from the instructional perspective is how instructive guidance should be designed in accordance with human cognitive functioning (e.g. Kirschner & Sweller, 2006). In addition, Computer Supported Collaborative Learning (CSCL) research has emphasised the necessity of considering the complex relations between tasks, tools, interaction processes and learning outcomes (e.g. Van Drie, Van Boxtel, Erkens, & Kanselaar, 2003). Here we tap into these issues, examining the example of digital video technologies used for collaborative knowledge construction in a classroom setting. Specifically, we investigate in an experiment *how* instructive guidance can be balanced for middle-school students in order to support skill-intensive socio-cognitive processes during a short collaborative design task for History learning with different digital video tools.

The potential of digital video technologies reaches far beyond the dynamic presentation and illustration of visual information. With digital video tools, learners may zoom into and out of digital video sequences, insert hyperlinks into videos in order to relate visual information to other instructional materials and arrange video sequences for discussion and reflection.

Such functions are expected to afford, for example, detailed observations (e.g. Smith & Reiser, 2005), multiple perspectives (e.g. Goldman, 2004) or the understanding of complex concepts in ill-structured domains (Spiro, Collins, & Ramchandran, 2007). The affordances of digital video technologies can be restructured for youthful learners in classrooms, so that students can either create their own representations (e.g. multimedia documents) or arrange video contents in order to understand and explain complex subject matter (Zahn, Pea et al., 2005). This usage, in the sense of *learning through design* (e.g. Kafai & Resnick, 1996), goes far beyond teacher-centred approaches where videos on curriculum topics are only watched by individual learners or in whole-class models.

Over the last several years, we have investigated collaborative design with video tools. Evidence from our experimental studies has indicated that specific affordances of video tools (e.g. of WebDIVERTM, Pea et al. 2004), when employed in design tasks for History learning, can support learners' social interactions to become more productive than those performed with simple technological solutions, resulting in improved learning outcomes (e.g. Zahn, Pea, Hesse, & Rosen, 2010). Yet, initial field studies with sixteen-year-old students (Zahn, Krauskopf, Hesse, & Pea, 2010) showed that the positive effects of video tools were sometimes limited to an *action level*, and students would have needed more guidance to optimise their collaborative design process. This finding is consistent with findings from Barron (2003) showing that student groups can have problems engaging in productive knowledge-building conversations during video-based mathematics problem solving. It is also consistent with related evidence showing that collaborating students need help in organising, planning and conducting scientific inquiries (Edelson, Gordin, & Pea, 1999), in scientific argumentation (Kollar & Fischer, 2004) and in accomplishing scientific design projects (Kolodner et al., 2003).

Two sources of problems can hinder productive socio-cognitive processes when students perform design tasks with digital video tools: the complexity of collaboration with *video tools* and the complexity of collaborative *design*. We have demonstrated in prior research how specific video tools can influence collaborative learning (e.g. Zahn, Pea, Hesse & Rosen, 2010). In the present study, we take into account their *differential* complexity (Zahn, Pea et al., 2005) when they are used as design tools for learning. *Design* tasks generally consist of creating and structuring content for an anticipated audience according to the aesthetic standards of the media at hand. They include the setting of design goals and complex processes of knowledge transformation, as was proposed earlier by related cognitive research (e.g. Bereiter & Scardamalia, 1987; Goel & Pirolli, 1992; Hayes, 1996). According to Détienne (2006) *collaborative* design includes the management of task interdependencies and of multiple perspectives. Correspondingly, design activities relate to the levels of the design problem/design solution and group cooperation. Moreover, when designers use complex and sometimes unfamiliar *digital tools* (video tools in our case), they coordinate their collaboration by establishing a social problem space that is distributed over the cognitive systems of at least two people *and* a digital artifact, creating new coordination problems familiar in distributed cognitive systems (Streek et al., 2011). Based on this shared context, they negotiate their choices of design goals and their understanding of content, task schemas, genre knowledge, and task relevant strategies (as in *collaborative writing*, e.g. Lowry, Curtis, & Lowry, 2004). The importance of the shared (multimodal) context for design was repeatedly emphasised (Détienne, 2006).

Consequently, although designing video or other artifacts with digital tools is highly desirable for students because it is cognitively engaging, students may sometimes be cognitively overwhelmed by the complexity of having to find a design solution, manage the group and use an unfamiliar digital tool. They actually may need guidance throughout the process so that learning through design can take place. Based on previous research on the nature of design (e.g. Détienne, 2006), we might provide such guidance, tackling either *cognitive design task*-related issues or *social interaction*-related issues (similar to Fischer et al. (2002), the distinction of *content-specific* and *content-unspecific* instructional support or Weinberger et al. (2005) *epistemic* vs. *social scripts*). It is still open whether guiding students' design activities or their social interactions would lend important support for successful task completion – or whether students might feel restricted by too much guidance and be impeded in their creativity and learning. Also, the mediating role of the digital video tools for collaboration under such conditions is quite unclear. Hence, in our study, we compared the two forms of guidance using two types of video tools, and we explored whether interactions would occur.

Experimental study

Method

Participants: 148 students (81 male, 65 female, 2 no answer) from four different German high schools located in Southwestern Germany participated in the study. Their mean age was $M = 16.2$ years ($SD = 1.0$). Prior to the study we obtained written consent from the students' parents and the school administration. The sample size varies minimally due to problems with data availability from stored design products and videotaped interactions.

Study design: The study was conducted in a computer classroom set up at our institute. Classes accompanied by their respective teachers came to the Institute on regular school days and as part of their regular History Curriculum. Upon arrival they were randomly grouped into dyads and assigned to one of the four experimental conditions of a 2×2 study plan. The first factor, *Guidance* (cognitive design-related vs. social interaction-related), determined which type of instructive guidance was provided to support the collaborative accomplishment of a visual design task: guidance either emphasising the cognitive aspects of the design task (e.g. setting a design goal, planning a design concept, tailoring information *for an audience*), or guidance focusing on smooth collaboration (e.g. developing *common* ground about design goals and design decisions, determining *communication* rules for discourse practice). The second factor, *Video Tool*, determined whether students worked with WebDIVERTM (Pea et al., 2004) or Asterpix as their design tool: the tools differed on a generic level in

either supporting collaborative analysis (WebDIVER tool for guided notic-
ing) or collaborative linking of information (Hypervideo tool Asterpix).
With WebDIVER, learners' cognitive/collaborative analysis is heightened
by their ability to zoom into and out of digital video sequences, and arrange
digital video sequences for discussion and reflection. With the Hypervideo
tool, Asterpix, the collaborative ability to insert new knowledge artifacts
into an existing digital video is heightened by hyperlinks relating visual
information to other materials. All other circumstances were kept constant
across conditions.

Task: A visual design task based on a historical newsreel was employed.
This task had been carefully developed for the purpose of studying computer supported History learning with digital video tools in a realistic
classroom (e.g. Zahn, Krauskopf, Hesse, & Pea, 2010). It follows central
educational goals in the domain of History in German middle school education (Krammer, 2006). Furthermore, it is theoretically founded in cognitive and collaborative frameworks of advanced learning and knowledge
building approaches (e.g. Scardamalia, 2002). During this task, students
work on a newsreel about the Berlin blockade in 1948, so that it can be
published, e.g. on a website of a virtual History museum. They are asked
to analyse and comment on the newsreel so that future visitors of the virtual museum can develop a good understanding of both the content and
the style of the newsreel as a propaganda instrument. To accomplish the
task, the students can use a collaborative video tool (see Tools section).
The constructive activity of designing content for a web page of a virtual History museum provides learners with a framework for comparison
and re-organisation of knowledge, as they produce their own ideas and
work creatively with them. During the collaborative design process, it is
assumed that learners appropriate the video content to their own thinking
purposes and develop advanced thinking skills. The learning goal and a
special challenge for the students is to understand that the newsreel is not
only *showing* the History topic (Berlin 1948) but that the newsreel itself
is a History topic (i.e., a newsreel as an historical means for propaganda).
In other words, historical content knowledge is closely intertwined with

developing advanced thinking skills (Scardamalia, 2002), such as being able to analyse and critically reflect on video messages.

Materials and Tools: The video used in the visual design task is a digitised version of an historical newsreel originally produced by the Allied forces (USA/Great Britain) and shown to the German public during the Berlin blockade in 1948. It covers news information about the airlift established in 1948 by the Allied forces when Russia tried to cut off Berlin from traffic of goods. It consists of ninety-five single pictures and lasts five minutes. The video used in the transfer task is a modern sixty-five-second TV-Clip by the German Green Party (Buendnis 90/Die Gruenen) from the 2006 nationwide election in Germany. The texts used in the experiment contain 350–1,500 words each. The content of the texts provides detailed information on three sub-topics: accounts of the historical context of Berlin in post-war Germany, information on media History and newsreels in post-World War II Germany, and a short introduction on film theory. Guidance was implemented in text-based form within the computer environment used for general task instruction. The texts differed between conditions in their descriptions of how one should best proceed to solve a visual design problem. The video tool used for computer-supported learning in the visual design task was either WebDIVER or Asterpix. WebDIVER is one of the software programs developed in the DIVER Project (<http://diver.stanford.edu>) at Stanford University. It is based on the metaphor of enabling a user to *dive* into videos for expressing points of view regarding precise spatio-temporal video areas of one or more source videos. Asterpix is a commercially available hypervideo tool. It is based on the idea of enabling users to select areas of interest and place graphical hyperlinks into a source video.

With the functions offered by WebDIVER, users can select either a temporal segment or a spatio-temporal sub-region of a video by mouse-controlling a rectangular selection frame (acting like a camera viewfinder) to *pan* and/or *zoom* into view only that subpart of a video that they wish to feature, and then interpretively annotating their selection via a web interface. Each dive movie clip and its associated annotations is represented in a panel in the dive, and a remix of the video clips and annotations can be played to experience the dive. Asterpix was a Web 2.0 tool (<http://

www.asterpix.com/>, no longer available) with functions based on the hypervideo idea: users could isolate dynamic, sensitive regions within video materials, provide text commentaries to these regions and add links to other web resources. The links could further be discussed by means of an integrated e-communication tool. Thus, users could include their own annotations and knowledge in a video and share them with others in a group or community (cf. Zahn et al., 2005).

Procedure: A week before the students came to our lab, they filled in questionnaires that assessed their prior knowledge and other control variables. The *experimental* sessions consisted of the following steps: In Step 1 (preparation phase), the students individually read the overall instructions, including the different types of guidance (either guidance for effective design or guidance for effective social interactions during design). Then they read the History/media texts and watched the video showing the historical Berlin-Blockade newsreel from 1948. They briefly practised the use of the video tools to establish familiarity. In Steps 2, 3 and 4 (collaborative design and learning phase) the participants worked collaboratively in dyads at a computer. In Step 2 (planning), those students in dyads in the *social interaction*-related guidance condition were asked to write down the content they would like to cover in their design products and how they would like to coordinate their design work. Those students in dyads in the *cognitive design*-related guidance condition were asked which design goals they would aim for. In Step 3, the dyads were asked to design their product according to their initial ideas using either WebDIVER or Asterpix. In Step 4 (evaluation) the dyads were asked to evaluate the quality of their own products and teamwork. When students were done, they continued with Steps 5 and 6 (test phase), where self-assessment questionnaires and knowledge tests were completed individually. In Step 7, the participants individually accomplished a transfer task (TV ad, see Materials section). They were then thanked and released and returned to their schools with their teachers. During the whole procedure, the teachers were present and tutors were also available for any questions or technology problems.

Measures: To assess prior background knowledge in the domain of History, computer expertise or expertise in film and media production, a pre-questionnaire (self-assessment) and a multiple choice knowledge test were administered. To assess the effectiveness of our text-based instruction as implementation of guidance (manipulation check), we asked the subjects to select a maximum of three alternatives from six statements about the task's characteristics (three social characteristics, e.g. 'one of the most important aspects of the learning unit was good communication' and three design characteristics, e.g. 'one of the most important aspects of the learning unit was to design for a target audience'). To assess collaborative design performance, the design products created by the dyads with WebDIVER or Asterpix were analysed. From these products, the following categories of data were obtained: *video selections/sensitive areas with comments, style features commented,* and *interpretations* in the comments. Additionally, dyadic interactions were captured with a webcam and a screen recorder (Camtasia Studio by TechSmith). The proportions of talking time in the categories *design planning, design action, design evaluation, technical issues, problems,* and *off task* (related to total amount of talking time) were extracted from the video data using video analysis software (Videograph©).

To assess treatment effects on learning outcomes, a post-test was administered, consisting of a multiple choice test measuring historical topic knowledge and a transfer task tapping advanced visual analytic skills. The multiple choice post-test consisted of eight items. A sample item of this test is:

> At the beginning of 1946 Germany is ...
> a) ... a unified nation,
> b) ... divided into four sectors,
> c) ... divided into an Eastern and a Western part,
> d) ... divided into 16 Länder.

The theoretical maximum for this test was 13 points, and it had a satisfactory internal consistency, Cronbach's $\alpha = .71$.

The transfer task part of the post-test was assigned to reveal skills of critical analysis and reflection in response to a video message. It consisted of two questions relating to a political TV ad from the 2006 nationwide German government elections.

> Please analyse the following video sequence by answering the questions
> 1) Which film techniques were used?
> 2) What might have been the intention of using them?

The questions were open ended.

Results

We will first present results substantiating the comparability of our conditions, and then results obtained from quantitative analyses of the design products and post-tests. Due to assumed interdependence of students working in one dyad, we determined dyads as the unit of analysis and used data aggregated within dyads (cf. Kenny, Kashy, & Cook, 2006). The level of significance for all analyses was set to .05.

Comparability of the conditions: 2 × 2 between subjects ANOVAs with the factors Guidance and Video Tool revealed no significant differences between the conditions concerning participants' age, prior experience with computers in general and video software in particular, their History grade, or their dispositional interest in History (all $p > .10$). The dyads also did not differ significantly between conditions concerning within-group composition related to age, gender, prior knowledge, History grade, or historical interest (all $p > .10$). In addition, student dyads did not differ in their appraisal of the task, the appraisal of their teamwork or the amount of invested mental effort during task work (all $p > .10$), indicating that the participants' overall positive attitudes towards task and performance were similarly high in the four conditions. In sum, the conditions can be considered comparable. However, historical knowledge showed a marginally significant interaction, $F(1, 68) = 3.86, p = .05$, partial $\eta^2 = .05$, showing that for students working with WebDIVER, those participating in the cognitive design-related guidance condition scored higher on the pre-test ($M = 10.23, SD = 2.55$) than students in the social interaction-related condition ($M = 8.22, SD = 2.20$), $t(34) = 2.53, p = .02$. For students working with Asterpix, there were no significant differences. All ANOVAs reported here were also run as ANCOVAs controlling for interest in History and prior knowledge, and they are reported when they show different results.

Manipulation check: An ANOVA revealed no significant difference between conditions concerning their scores in *design task* characteristics, Fs < 1, *ns*, but a significant difference for the *social task* characteristics for the factor Guidance, $F(1, 68) = 15.51, p < .001$, partial $\eta^2 = .19$. More social task items were chosen by students who had received social interaction-related guidance than by students who had received cognitive task-related design guidance. Our text-based implementation of guidance by task instructions can thus be considered effective for eliciting the students' awareness of the design problem in all conditions and the students' increased awareness of the *social* demands of the collaborative design task in the social interaction-related conditions.

Design performance: Interrater reliability for style features and interpretations were satisfactory, Cohen's $\kappa \geq .94$. ANOVAs revealed a significant main effect for the factor Guidance: The mean scores in all the mentioned indicators were significantly higher for the products of dyads in the condition with social interaction-related guidance, than for those from dyads in the condition with cognitive design-related guidance, in terms of *number of comments*, $F(1, 67) = 6.46, p = .01$, partial $\eta^2 = .09$, *number of style features*, $F(1, 67) = 4.78, p = .03$, partial $\eta^2 = .07$, and *number of interpretations*, $F(1, 67) = 4.63, p = .04$, partial $\eta^2 = .07$. Hence, design performance in the visual design task was higher in the social interaction-related guidance conditions than in the other conditions. No further main or interaction effects were found. Thus, the two forms of video tools were not used in different ways – at least in relation to the quantitative indicators of design performance we applied here.

Historical topic knowledge: Analyses of the scores from the multiple choice post-test on knowledge about the History topic revealed a total mean score $M = 7.54$ ($SD = 2.46$) out of 13 possible points. We conducted a mixed $2 \times 2 \times 2$ ANCOVA with the two between-subjects factors Guidance and Video Tool and the within-subjects factor Pre-Post-Test to test for differences in the gain in individual factual knowledge. After controlling for the differences in pre-test scores, the results still showed a significant increase in factual knowledge over time, $F(1, 67) = 34.80, p < .001$, partial $\eta^2 = .34$. However, there were no significant differences between the conditions, $Fs < 1, ns$, and no significant interaction, $F(1, 67) = 1.93, p = .17$, indicating that the students in both conditions had developed an understanding of the historical content.

Critical analysis and reflection

The students' written answers to the transfer task questions were coded independently by two raters. For the coding procedure, coders considered a pre-defined default solution created by an expert in visual media production (first author of this paper). The solution comprised exemplary stylistic features used in the TV ad (e.g. camera, music, montage), as well as examples for correct interpretations of such elements (e.g. close-up of a person's face aims at creating emotional involvement). Based on this example, raters counted the number of named style features and interpretations. Also, the elaborateness of the answers was rated on a 3-point Likert scale (1 = simple, 3 = elaborate). Interrater reliability was satisfactory for the number of style features, Cohen's $\kappa = .91$, and the elaborateness rating, Cronbach's $\alpha = .80$. However, rater agreement for the number of interpretations of these style features was very low, Cohen's $\kappa = .10$. Closer analyses revealed that the raters differed greatly with regard to how strictly they applied the coding scheme. For further analyses we decided to only use the coding of the more conservative rater. The analysis of the transfer test results revealed a total average of $M = 1.97$ ($SD = 0.74$) for 'number of style features', $M = 0.37$ ($SD = 0.23$) for 'number of interpretations' and $M = 1.19$ ($SD = 0.47$), and for 'elaborateness of the answer'. ANOVAs revealed that the means of all these indicators were significantly higher in the answers of students in the conditions with social interaction-related guidance, than in the conditions with cognitive design-related guidance: *number of style features*, $F(1, 68) = 7.96$, $p = .01$, partial $\eta^2 = .11$, *number of interpretations*, $F(1, 68) = 4.36$, $p = .04$, partial $\eta^2 = 06$, *elaborateness of the answer*, $F(1, 68) = 4.11$, $p = .047$, partial $\eta^2 = .06$. Overall, effect sizes were of medium to large size. There were no effects of the video tool factor, $Fs < 1.1$, *ns*, or any significant interactions, $Fs < 1$, *ns*. Thus, although all students developed a comparable understanding of the topic, the learning outcomes in terms of advanced thinking skills (critical analysis and reflection) were higher when social interaction was supported in the student dyads.

Dyadic interactions: For analyses of dyadic interactions, we coded the proportions of time that students engaged in activities belonging to one of the categories 'design planning', 'design action', 'design evaluation', 'technological issues', 'problems' and 'off task' (related to total amount of talking time, $M = 21.52$ minutes, $SD = 4.46$). 20% of the videos were coded by a second rater and agreement was on average satisfactory, median of Cohen's $\kappa = .64$. However, 2 × 2 ANOVAs with the two between-factors, Guidance and Video Tool, yielded no significant differences between the conditions.

Discussion

Our results provide evidence from an experimental study that helps to answer the question of how to improve guidance for student teams solving a complex authentic design task for History learning with the support of web-based video tools. Results indicate that while using either of the advanced video tools we offered was generally effective, differences in the types of guidance we implemented (*cognitive task*-related vs. *social interaction*-related guidance) resulted in different learning outcomes. Firstly, the immediate design products of the dyads' task work were of better quality. Secondly, individual students scored significantly higher in a transfer test evaluating critical analysis and reflection skills. Concerning factual knowledge about the topic ('Berlin blockade'), no differences and no trade-off effects in performance in a multiple-choice post-test emerged. Moreover, during the students' dyadic interactions, similar amounts of time were devoted to the subtasks 'design planning', 'design action', 'design evaluation', 'technical issues', 'problems' and 'off task' behaviour in all conditions. Thus, the differences in the transfer test were neither at costs of other learning outcome measures, nor could they be explained by a first (superficial) analysis of specific students' interaction time spent on task. This finding was not confined to a specific tool used in our study.

Results show that given the conceptual differences of the video technologies (WebDIVER and Asterpix) described above, the benefits of supporting the social problem space persist. We thus conclude that the dyads with social interaction-related guidance learned *more* than the dyads with cognitive task-related guidance, and we conjecture that even given different affordances for the two video tools, social interaction-related guidance improved the quality of dyadic interactions on a deeper content level. And this leads us to the question of *how exactly* that quality was improved.

In a next cycle of analyses we will investigate differences in the content of dyadic interactions. These findings will add further answers to the question of *how* instructive guidance can be balanced for middle-school students in order to support skill-intensive socio-cognitive processes.

When interpreting the results reported here to draw conclusions for school practice, we need to consider the following issues: In this study we created a highly controlled, computer-supported experimental setting, thereby enabling us to draw causal conclusions. We exposed students to a short-time visual design task for a regular History lesson, which is different from large design projects performed over several weeks. So the results cannot be generalised to such projects. However, we compared our results from this experiment with the results from an earlier field study in a real, 'noisy' classroom situation with a comparable sample of students and with the same short task and test items (Zahn, Krauskopf et al., 2010). Results revealed general gains in factual knowledge (pre- to post-tests) similar to those obtained in the field. No indications of influences of the artificial experimental situation (positive or negative) were found. From the analyses, we may thus conclude that students of the age group investigated here seem to have sufficient working patterns for completing short design tasks (establishing a design problem space), but not necessarily for social interaction (establishing a social problem space). This might be the case because design tasks are often used in school-based education and students are familiar enough with them to perform the necessary activities. However, they seem to be less able to activate effective ways of team interaction from their everyday school experiences. In other words: guidance repeatedly emphasising the aspects of design problem solving, thereby focusing on the design product, may *not* improve the learning addressed here, but guidance improving collaborative activity (coordinating teamwork and communication) can. For design-based interventions such as this, the result may be somewhat unsurprising, but certainly worth highlighting. The strength of the social interaction-related guidance described here is such that it calls for further analysis across a broad range of collaborative learning environments. For teachers this issue would be important in practice if, indeed, their guidance of students' collaborative task work in real lessons were focused on social interaction processes. This perspective is consonant with related views across different domains and digital media (e.g. Barron, 2003) – and hopefully stimulates further Computer Supported Collaborative Learning research.

References

Barron, B., 'When smart groups fail.' *The Journal of the Learning Sciences 12*/3 (2003), 7–359.
Bereiter, C. & Scardamalia, M., *The Psychology of Written Composition* (Hillsdale, NJ: Lawrence Erlbaum Associates, 1987).

Détienne, F., 'Collaborative design: Managing task interdependencies and multiple perspectives'. *Interacting with Computers* 18/1 (2006), 1–20.

Edelson, D.C., Gordin, D.N., & Pea, R.D., 'Addressing the Challenges of Inquiry-Based Learning Through Technology and Curriculum Design.' *The Journal of the Learning Sciences* 833, 834 (1999), 391–450.

Fischer, F., Bruhn, J., Gräsel, C., & Mandl, H., 'Fostering Collaborative Knowledge Construction with Visualization Tools.' *Learning and Instruction* 12 (2002), 213–232.

Goel, V. & Pirolli, P., 'The structure of design problem spaces.' *Cognitive Science* 16 (1992), 395–429.

Goldman, R., 'Video perspectivity meets wild and crazy teens: Design ethnography.' *Cambridge Journal of Education*, 2/4 (2004), 147–169.

Hayes, J.R., 'A new model of cognition and affect in writing' in M. Levy & S. Ransdell, eds, *The Science of Writing* (Hillsdale, NJ: Erlbaum, 1996) 1–27.

Kafai, Y.B. & Resnick, M., eds, *Constructionism in Practice: Designing, Thinking, and Learning in a Digital World* XII (Mahwah, NJ: Lawrence Erlbaum Associates, 1996).

Kirschner, P.A. & Sweller, J., 'Why Minimal Guidance During Instruction Does Not Work: An Analysis of the Failure of Constructivist Discovery, Problem-Based, Experiential, and Inquiry-based Teaching.' *Educational Psychologist* 4/2 (2006), 75–86.

Kollar, I., Fischer, F. et al., 'Internal and external scripts in computer-supported collaborative inquiry learning.' *Learning & Instruction* 17/6 (2007), 708–721.

Kolodner, J.L. et al., 'Problem-Based Learning Meets Case-Based Reasoning in the Middle-School Science Classroom: Putting Learning by DesignTM Into Practice.' *Journal of the Learning Sciences* 12 (2003), 495–547.

Lowry, P.B., Curtis, A., & Lowry, M.R., 'Building a Taxonomy and Nomenclature of Collaborative Writing to Improve Interdisciplinary Research and Practice.' *Journal of Business Communication* 41 (2004), 66–99.

Pea, R. et al., 'The DIVER™ Project: Interactive Digital Video Repurposing.' *IEEE Multimedia* 11/1 (2004, January–March), 54–61.

Pea, R.D., 'Video-as-data and digital video manipulation techniques for transforming learning sciences research, education and other cultural practices' in J. Weiss, J. Nolan, J. Hunsinger, & P. Trifonas, eds, *International handbook of virtual learning environments* (Dordrecht, The Netherlands: Kluwer Academic, 2006), 1321–1393.

Scardamalia, M., 'Collective Cognitive Responsibility for the Advancement of Knowledge' in B. Smith, ed., *Liberal Education in a Knowledge Society* (Chicago: Open Court, 2002), 67–98.

Smith, B., & Reiser, B.J., 'Explaining behavior through observational investigation and theory articulation.' *Journal of the Learning Sciences* 14 (2005), 315–360.

Spiro, R.J. et al., 'Reflections on a post-Gutenberg epistemology for video use in ill-structured domains: Fostering complex learning and cognitive flexibility' in R. Goldman, R.D. Pea, B. Barron & Derry, S., eds, *Video research in the learning sciences* (Mahwah, NJ: Erlbaum, 2007), 93–100.

Streek, J., Goodwin, C., & LeBaron, C., eds, *Embodied interaction: Language and body in the material world* (Cambridge: Cambridge University Press, 2011).

Weinberger, A. et al., 'Epistemic and social scripts in computer-supported collaborative learning.' *Instructional Science* 33/1 (2005), 1–30.

Zahn, C. et al., 'Advanced Digital Video Technologies to Support Collaborative Learning in School Education and Beyond' in T. Koschmann, D. Suthers, & T.-W. Chan, eds, *Computer Supported Collaborative Learning 2005: The Next 10 Years* (Mahwah, NJ: Lawrence Erlbaum, 2005), 737–742.

Zahn, C. et al., 'Comparing Simple and Advanced Video Tools as Supports for Complex Collaborative Design Processes.' *The Journal of the Learning Sciences* 19/3 (2010), 403–440.

Zahn, C. et al., 'Digital Video Tools in the Classroom: How to Support Meaningful Collaboration and Critical Thinking of Students?' in M.S. Khine & I.M. Saleh, *New Science of Learning: Computers and Collaboration in Education* (New York: Springer, 2010).

VANCE MARTIN

4 Using Wikis to Democratise Teaching

History courses can reify the status quo or highlight the need for societal change. History teachers need to consider this, their views and the students' future. This paper explores one way that change in practice can be encouraged through the use of educational wikis. The most famous wiki may be Wikipedia, but wikis in general are openly editable, online writing software. In an educational context they can allow multiple users to interact and create knowledge. It is through the introduction of wikis in my own instruction that my class has become more democratic. I am defining democratic learning as critiquing democracy while pursuing its intended goals, including issues of race, gender, national identity, and subjectivity (Giroux, 2000; Noffke, 2000).

I began the use of wikis in my History classes in the fall of 2008. This began due to frustration with required texts, and a belief that students needed to learn skills for a digital future. At that point in my teaching, I was integrating my own ideas with current literature on technology usage. However, my assessment of what worked was limited to end of semester feedback from students and my own end of semester reflection. This changed in the spring of 2009. As I was nearing the end of my graduate coursework, I attended my first class on action research. Action research brought a process of change to my instruction, and would be the framework for much of my future work. My beliefs about exposing students to various points of view, mixed with ideas about integrating technology into the classroom, would change my classes drastically. This study is the evolution of my practice over three semester-long action research cycles. Integration of technology with purposeful planning, acting, observing, and reflecting has made my courses more democratic.

Background

Before discussing the evolution of practice, it will be useful to think about some of the literature which was influential in bringing about change. Several constructivist learning theories were fundamental for this study. The first was the constructivism of Vygotsky (1978). Vygotsky developed the concept of a zone of proximal development. Simply put, a learner has a level of understanding that s/he may reach independently and a possible level of understanding that s/he may reach with external help. Through social interaction with an expert other, the learner can be pushed into a zone of proximal development toward that next level. In the digital world, almost anyone can help a learner to the next zone or stage as the roles of expert and novice are constantly in flux. An example of this could occur in a wiki, or openly editable html platform. Within a wiki students can add material, and be helped by others who may comment on their writing style or question where they found the information. This can also create a situation related to the ideas of Lave and Wenger (1991). These students are exchanging ideas, learning from others, and while not in true *apprenticeship* situations, are certainly learning as peripheral participants and experts.

Another theory which was valuable was Bruckman's (Zagal & Bruckman, 2008) revision of Papert's (Papert & Harel, 1991) constructionism. Bruckman applied constructionism to wikis, noting that those who put their work in the public arena care more about its production, which could be valuable for students posting publicly. She also believes that knowledge is acquired through give and take, through offering little pieces and adding more to it. This allows the learner to create and thereby build greater knowledge which is also a potential afforded by wikis.

A second area of literature which was useful related to the potential of the open source movement. Benkler (2007) discusses the potential of the learning, creation, and economy of social production. He gives examples of groups of people taking on many small jobs to complete a greater project which would otherwise not be completed. This can be seen with NASA crowdsourcing the mapping of the moon or college students tagging archival pictures as part of a perceived game. For this study, the idea was applied to a group of college students taking a History course in which they were responsible for adding and editing content to an ongoing course text. This also relates to ideas discussed by Lessig (2004). He discusses how modern students have taken Music or Art and remade it, or remixed it, making it relevant for a new era. In the process these students are learning skills for a digital future, but also creating media for the current and future societies.

Method

The research method employed for this study is action research (Caro-Bruce, Flessner, Klehr, & Zeichner, 2007). Action research is a cycle: plan, act, observe, and evaluate (Anderson, Herr, & Nihlen, 2007). For my study it was used initially to assess wiki implementation in my classroom over three semesters. As the instructor and researcher I was careful to keep in mind the two roles: to observe my own practice, and to help the students learn.

This study was conducted in a Midwestern United States Community College of 10,000 students. The students in the study took US History I: 1492–1877. They ranged in age from eighteen to fifty, with an average class size of twenty. Most students were white, with a few African-Americans and Latinos. Just over half the students were male. Many of the students who take this class do so because it is required for teacher education students. The data included instructor reflections, observations of the class, the wiki, artifacts from the class and interviews. The data was used in each action research cycle to evaluate each semester while planning for subsequent semesters. The information was coded based on findings over time as well as themes which arose through research on the topic.

Discussion

I started using wikis in the fall of 2008 in my course on the History of the United States, 1492–1877. I began the project for two reasons. The first was dissatisfaction with a chosen course textbook. By having students write a course text, they could integrate points of view which were not reflected in the publisher's text. The second related reason was that having the students write a textbook in a wiki would be a record of what they found to be important which could resonate with future students. The setup of the project was that students were responsible for a certain time period and a chosen chapter. They would be required to add the most material to this chapter, but also read what other students added and make edits accordingly. This would require them to gain in depth knowledge on one period, but also read what others were writing and get an overall picture on related periods. In this first semester we used the wiki that came with the college's course management system. I found it to be cumbersome, not allowing anyone to edit anything unless the current editor logged out. This made many students simply say, 'I wasn't able to edit,' or, 'It didn't work'. So in the second semester I changed to pbwiki, later called pbworks.

In the spring of 2009 I began my first action research cycle using pbwiki. Pbwiki is a freely available, public wiki site. With suitable amounts of storage available for educators, they offer upgrades for paying customers. This platform was chosen because it allowed students to know if someone was editing a page and it offered greater flexibility in layout. Based on student feedback from the previous semester I outlined how many edits they needed to make. I decided thirty total edits was appropriate, suggesting two edits per week over fifteen weeks. Again students signed up for a chapter and were supposed to make edits to other people's chapters. They had access to the old wiki but were basically starting from scratch. It was during the first semester I began actively observing as part of an action research cycle. I taught the class as I had taught previous classes. I stood in front of the class, sometimes walking from side to side, and used PowerPoints to show the students what topic we were on. I felt that the students would add information which they found interesting in the text from my lecture or from classroom discussions. From there they would do their own research and make additions to the wiki. The wiki would really be a reflection of what the students thought was interesting.

The semester began in mid-January. It was mid-February before anyone added anything to the wiki. I initially thought some of the problem was that students had to sign up for a username and login with pbwiki, and that this extra process caused a problem. No one seemed to want to be the first person to add anything to a blank wiki in case it was *wrong*. The students wanted some sort of leadership and outline on how to add material. However, I wanted this to be their wiki, so I had given them little in an attempt not to lead them in a particular direction. By early March a small number of students began adding to the wiki. Someone would add several paragraphs of information, and someone else would go through and edit it. Some of these edits were changing 'Indians' to 'Native Americans', or fixing punctuation, or moving material around to fit chronologically. Some people included pictures to illustrate ideas. This began to increase over March and April.

As the semester neared its end in late April, the students began to present their final papers to the class. In the last week we discussed their papers, what they learned, and what they thought about the class and wiki for the future. Some students felt that a group project would be valuable. This was presumably based on the idea that at several points during the semester, before tests, I would break students up into groups and give them the essay questions for the tests. They would then discuss these and report back to the rest of the class. Apparently this caused a lot of group connections outside of scheduled classes that the students found valuable. As I looked back on my reflections and thought about what the students had said, I made some changes for the next semester. I decided to add a group project. I also decided that I would not teach the class standing in front of them but sitting with them. This stemmed from literature I was reading as well as my own reflections. I noted that before each class I sat and discussed things with the students. We all seemed comfortable and they were able to ask lots of questions. When class began this feeling changed, becoming more formal and one-sided. So I planned to sit for the fall semester.

As I was planning for a second action research cycle in fall 2009, I decided that I would incorporate a group assignment where the students would think about something that concerned them in the modern world, and I put them in several groups of similar interests. During the first week, each student came up with two problems they were worried about. At the end of the week they narrowed a list of forty concerns down to five. I divided the students into groups to focus on these five areas. They then shared their contact information so they could begin working on the project outside of class. Because I added this extra group component, I decided to deemphasise tests with essays and multiple-choice instead, using quizzes with multiple choice options.

Class started in mid-August. In the first and second weeks there were questions about the wiki and group projects. I taught the class sitting with the class in a circle, integrating my observations from the Spring. I covered the material that I normally would about European, African, and Native-American history pre-1492. The first students had signed up for the third chapter beginning with Jamestown in 1609. In the syllabus I had said students would be responsible for the material when it is covered in class. Some of the students in the first weeks had asked what this meant and I told them they would have to present to the class. So at the beginning of the third week of class the students began to present what they had researched to the class.

The first students did a great job and set the tone for the whole course. As we continued to sit in a circle classmates presented what they had researched to each other. The students had become the teachers. My role began to be less instructor and more fellow learner. I would fill in for students who were absent and if something was factually incorrect I would question the student about where they got the information. Sometimes this would allow modelling of research, as the student or I could use the computer at the front of the room to search for more information. This allowed the class to see how information was found and to question the validity of each site that was chosen, leading to more questions. Students who presented added the material that they taught to the wiki. In this semester it seemed to be easier for the students since there was some outline from the previous semester but still lots of room to add material. While in the previous semester the material had mainly been textual with a few pictures, this semester there were videos, music, pictures, text, and one case, a machinima project. Machinima is the use of 3D computer graphics, typically from a videogame to create a movie. The creator records hours of footage and edits it into a short film, which may or may not be related to the original game. Students began to see how History was constructed as they questioned what their classmates added to the wiki but not necessarily what they taught in class.

In the spring of 2010, I only made one change to the setup of the course. This was my third action research cycle of this project. While the students in the previous semester had been part of a group, they had trouble fitting their material into the class discussion and sometimes even into the wiki. So this semester I had students make sure they added the material to the wiki and presented their group project as a mini-lecture to the class, when appropriate. With two semesters of material in the pbworks wiki, a change began to occur. Discussions focused on the validity of the material but not in the wiki. While students did question somewhat what was online, they were less concerned with openly questioning what was there, and more concerned with questioning how their classmates knew what they presented.

Additions to the wiki in this semester became more fractured. Two semesters worth of material had been added. Some students did not know how they should integrate more material into what was already there. So new material was added, but at the end of the wiki. Or new sections were added that were not present in the wiki so that there wasn't a need to integrate the material. However, as students presented their material to the class, discussions and arguments arose. How did the student know what they were saying? Was it an opinion or fact? An example of this is one of the students, Jean, an African-American, traditional college-aged female. She presented on the same day about the Nat Turner rebellion and the battle at the Alamo. As she discussed Nat Turner, she told the class that she thought he was a serial killer. This launched a discussion of what made someone a serial killer, who made the decision, and the importance of extenuating circumstances and points of view. As she discussed the Alamo, she gave a very pro-Texan point of view on the battle. This also launched a discussion about the Mexican side of the story, and where she had found her information. Classmates were now questioning her to get at an underlying understanding of History.

What had occurred in the first two semesters online was now occurring in the classroom. One of my students, Roberto, felt the change could be attributed to his generation:

> You're always going to find that people want to talk to people, and see their emotions, and the way they feel about it firsthand, not necessarily over a computer. You would be surprised by how people dislike Facebook 'cause they don't like Facebook disagreements. It's a very looked down upon thing in the Y generation.
>
> It happens a lot, but it's a very tacky thing and you'd be surprised, some of the most tacky people will tell you that's a tacky thing. (Interview, 16 June 2010, transcript)

Significance

There have been changes in both my practice and understanding of teaching through this process. When I began teaching, my style was more traditional. However, as I began my graduate work and began to actively observe my own practice, changes began to occur. Some of these changes reflect what was working within the classroom, while some of them related to educational literature which I was reading. I initially began this use of technology because of problems with traditional texts. I also felt that the students could learn through the actual physical process of writing about History. This related to the constructivist literature of Vygotsky, and Lave and Wenger. I hoped that students would be able to push each other towards a greater level of learning through use of the wiki. Within the first few iterations of the wiki, I believe this occurred online. As one person added material, their classmates negotiated the work, changed words and phrases, and moved around some of the information. Later editors would fill in where there were holes that needed more information. Within the last iteration of the class, this occurred less online and more within the classroom, as students learned classroom behaviours from one another and built on what was presented or discussed previously, and learned to question each other about the material.

Building on Bruckman's use of Papert, I also felt that if students researched what they were interested in and knew the material was public, they would put more effort into the projects. I believe this happened somewhat in the spring and fall of 2009 on the wiki. In the spring of 2010 I think it made a transition to the actual classroom. My initial belief is that as the students perceived less room to add new material to the wiki, they began to question more what was presented within the class. However, this could also be a change as the project progressed, or related to different students over time, or perhaps even a different emerging generation of students.

What initially began as frustration with textbooks and a belief that students could learn History through the process of writing changed even more through reflecting on the ideas of social production and open source movements. My practice evolved through reflection in the action research cycle. Initially I integrated multiple formats and viewpoints into my own instruction. However this pedagogical method still relied on the instructor as expert. This evolution was from the traditional expert in front of the classroom to a co-participant in a learning experience. The goals of the wiki were to reduce biases based on race, gender, religion, and socioeconomic condition, or at least raise awareness of these biases. That position is inconsistent with an instructor as expert. By reflecting upon the students' experiences, the class, and the goals I changed my own practice to embody these goals.

While observing the Spring 2010 class, I was initially surprised by how the students conducted themselves democratically. On further reflection and analysis, it is consistent with the goals of the project, just not in the way I expected. Using a wiki allows endless amounts of text, pictures, video, and permutations of these. They can be edited by an entire class at any point in the day. By its very nature this takes the control away from the instructor and places it with the class. I believe this change is a dramatic and important change toward democratic education, and democratising pedagogy. As we go further into a digital age, democratic education will become more important (Giroux, 2000; Noffke, 2000). Within a United States context there are racial, religious, gender, and economic divides, without adding divides based on digital skills or globalisation. It is becoming more important to allow students to have a voice and train them for critical thinking to navigate the traditional and emerging worlds.

An important issue related to democratic education and action research is that of trust. There needs to be a relationship of trust between the students and the instructor as researcher. This trust operates on several levels. The first is that neither side will allow harm or ridicule. The second is that an open environment is created to allow for exchanges of knowledge and understanding. It is difficult for an instructor to trust the students to present material but by extending the opportunity, I believe most students will live up to the expectations set.

A final theme which arose in this study was related to ideas of democratic education and the work of Freire (2009). In essays and interviews, I asked the students how they felt about teaching the class and writing in the wiki. Some students enjoyed the process, some did not. Upon reflection it seemed that there was a pattern to this but it did not necessarily correlate to performance in the class. Upon further examination it correlated to students who might be classified as a minority. Those students who were part of the majority were able to do the assignments but they did not feel that the work was relevant to them. Students who were from a minority, whether based on race, religion, gender, or economics, felt empowered with these assignments. They were able to add a voice to History which had never been there. This made it valuable and important to them. A course which they'd been able to simply pass in the past now became important because they could research what they wanted and add what they researched.

Conclusion

We often assume education must occur in the same manner as it has for the past 150 years. However, for the majority of human history it has not occurred this way. More often it occurred in a manner similar to that described by Lave and Wenger (1991). With digital technologies we are at a point where we have the potential for changing education and society. Digital technologies can illuminate inequalities and discrimination, today and in the past. They can offer all students the chance to find their voice, and become creators in their own education. This can occur through active reflection on literature and practice.

References

Anderson, G.L., Herr, K., & Nihlen, A.S., *Studying your own school: An educator's guide to practitioner action research* (Thousand Oaks, CA: Corwin Press 2007).

Benkler, Y., *The wealth of networks: How social production transforms markets and freedom* (New Haven, CT: Yale University Press 2007).

Caro-Bruce, C., Flessner, R., Klehr, M., & Zeichner, K.M., *Creating equitable classrooms through action research* (Thousand Oaks, CA: Corwin Press 2007).

Freire, P., *Pedagogy of the oppressed* (New York, NY: Continuum, 2009).

Giroux, H.A., 'Democratic education and popular culture' in D.W. Hursh & E.W. Ross, eds, *Democratic social education: Social studies for social change* (New York, NY: Falmer Press, 2000), 85–96.

Lave, J. & Wenger, E., *Situated learning: Legitimate peripheral participation (learning in doing): Social, cognitive and computational perspectives* (Cambridge, UK: Cambridge University Press, 1991).

Lessig, L., *Free culture: The nature and future of creativity* (New York, NY: Penguin Books, 2004).

Noffke, S.E., 'Identity, community, and democracy in the New social order' in D.W. Hursh & E.W. Ross, eds, *Democratic social education: Social studies for social change* (New York, NY: Falmer Press, 2000).

Papert, S. & Harel, I., 'Situating constructionism' in S. Papert & I. Harel, eds, *Constructionism.* (New York, NY: Ablex Publishing Corporation, 1991).

Vygotsky, L.S., 'Interaction between learning and development' in M. Cole, V. John-Steiner, S. Scribner, & E. Souberman, eds, *Mind in society: The development of higher psychological processes* (Cambridge, MA: Harvard University Press, 1978), 79–91.

Zagal, J.P. & Bruckman, A., 'Novices, gamers, and scholars: Exploring the challenges of teaching about games.' *Game Studies*, 8/2 (2008).

THEO KUECHEL

5 Video for Learning: Past, Present and Future

Educators have long been aware of the potential of audiovisual learning through moving images. Moving images have been regularly available to teachers and schools through TV broadcasts since the 1950s, and before that as film screenings. These formats dictated *how* and *when* teachers were able to let children watch educational broadcasts or films.

Historically, as an educational practice, watching moving images (film, TV and video) in school has been a whole class activity. Despite major developments in both the delivery platforms and video technology, most educational use of video is still predicated on a paradigm of whole class viewing, where the primary purpose of the video content is to illustrate or exemplify a subject, concept or idea.

Over the past sixty years there have been a number of milestones which have explicitly changed or extended the possibilities of how moving images (in today's context, video), can be used for learning. Parallel and convergent developments in ICT and moving image technology have offered teachers greater control of the media and new opportunities to use video for learning in innovative ways. Although some teachers have taken advantage of these opportunities, such use is not widespread and video is still not fully incorporated within everyday classroom practice. Video is still seen as *a window on the world* or *an expert, a substitute teacher that presents one-way knowledge to students* rather than offering a constructivist tool for learning.

This chapter looks at the evolution of using moving images for learning, primarily in the schools sector over the past sixty years (although Further Education and Higher Education are also included). This chapter argues that teachers can now achieve significant benefits for learning with video, benefits that go far beyond simply using video to illustrate content. It suggests that if educators implement pedagogical frameworks that consider different approaches to using video for learning, and thereby exploit the potential of emergent web based video technologies, teachers can equip themselves with a very powerful knowledge building toolset.

Past

Moving images have been available on a regular basis to teachers and schools for well over sixty years. Educators have long been aware of the value of the moving image in developing understanding and have taken advantage of this to engage, inspire and motivate learners (Cruse, 2008).

Although historically, a variety of audio/visual media, including film strips, slides and movie screenings, had been used previously, for most schools the first meaningful engagement with moving images for learning have been through Schools TV broadcasts that originated in the 1950s. In the UK, the BBC began school TV broadcasts in 1957 and by 1974, 80 per cent of schools were viewing the BBC broadcasts. In the USA the 1950s saw many licences granted to Universities and public bodies to create educational TV resources; and by the end of the 1960s 'tens of millions of students were receiving televised instructions on a daily basis' (Molenda, 2008).

Most early educational TV broadcasts followed a formalised model of learning, and the broadcast schedules dictated how educational TV could be fitted into the curriculum. In order to include the broadcasts in their lessons, schools would need to arrange their timetables around these schedules. Usually schools would only have one television, often in a central hall or focal area, and whole classes would view the program together, often moving to that specific room or school space in order to do so.

From today's perspective, the style of many of the early educational TV broadcasts might appear dry or stilted. However, they did cover most genres still found in today's educational video. These included filmed lectures, talking heads, visualisations, and dramatic reconstructions. They were produced with tight scripts and timings in a style developed for the time (Kuomi, 2006). Such content and production values evolved over a long standing tradition of public service broadcasting from a number of countries including the UK and the USA, and are still in use today.

Nevertheless, there were exceptions to predictable subject based offerings. Even in the late 1950s and early 1960s, some school television programmes did tackle controversial or sensitive issues such as race. From the 1960s onwards there was a move from purely expository content to a more cognitive approach (Molenda, 2008). This trend was amplified by innovative approaches such as *Sesame Street* from the USA, which tried, and succeeded, in making learning more engaging and child centred, using content implicitly mapped to curricular criteria. *Sesame Street* is still influential on current 'educational' TV formats.

TV and video content for schools was and still is often supplemented with lesson plans, curriculum notes or study guides in order to add extra value for learning. Initially these were usually created by the content producer. In recent years there has been a greater emphasis on these materials being augmented with resources developed by teachers.

Video recording

A significant milestone in the use of moving images for learning was the development and mass market adoption of the Video Cassette Recorder (VCR) during the late 1970s. Schools rapidly bought into this technology because it gave teachers the opportunity to *time-shift* the recordings and play them at a convenient time. VCRs gave teachers control over *when* the video could be shown, enabling teachers to make a better use of the school day.

The successful take-up of the VCR in schools incentivised educational content producers to offer content on pre-recorded video tapes. This resulted in teachers having a real alternative to live broadcasts. Correspondingly, teachers also began to use the technology to bring 'home taped' material in to school, even though such content was not designed with a school audience or education as the primary audience. This practice soon raised the issue of copyright in schools. VCR technology was not welcomed by the content industry. Jack Valenti, then Head of the MPAA (Motion Picture Association of America), decried the 'savagery and the ravages of this machine' (*Wikipedia*), foreshadowing the future copyright controversies which were later to become commonplace as content moved to digital platforms.

Nevertheless, using videocassettes was very much a linear process and videos would normally be played and watched from beginning to end. Although it was possible to start and stop a video during playback, VCRs use analogue technology and this was not an accurate procedure, often fraught with difficulty for the unwary or inexperienced.

All this changed forever with advent of the microcomputer. By the late 1980s the display capability and processing power of computers had become sufficiently advanced to allow video to be displayed and viewed effectively on a computer monitor. Although compared with today's stand-ards videos were small and of a much lower quality, this was a significant breakthrough. Initially, video was mainly accessed or played directly from a range of optical media including CD's, Interactive Videodiscs, Video CD's, and from the early 2000s onwards, DVDs. These formats allowed users to stop, start and replay sequences of video in order to analyse parts of the video, or to illustrate topics selectively by choosing the sections of relevant content. Video content on a DVD could be divided into chap-ters that could be selected and played non-sequentially and accessed from menus or lists of contents.

A project whose significance should not be underestimated in the his-tory of audiovisual learning was the BBC Domesday Project. Undertaken in 1984 and published in 1986, its mission was to capture a snapshot of life in the UK by combining geographical and cultural media and data. In some ways this was a forerunner of our crowd sourced interactive media. A collaborative venture between the BBC schools and the public produced two laser vision data discs containing over 80,000 images, OS Maps and professional video footage. Unfortunately the combination of the high cost of hardware and its technical complexity meant it was never able to fulfil its true educational potential. Many of those concepts were to re-emerge later, facilitated by internet based platforms.

Computer based Digital Video (DV) extended the understanding and interpretation of a topic by enabling non linear (non sequential) viewing of video content. Teachers could use this either for navigational purposes – in order to fast forward, pause, rewind to specific parts of the video – or to analyse the video content itself – stopping, speeding up and slowing down the movement. This allowed a new level of visual analysis previously only available to professional filmmakers, enabling teachers to analyse movement and phenomena.

Along with the development of DV came the concept of the *clip*, as a short self-explanatory sequence of video, ideal for illustrating a concept or a process. An international survey of 472 educators (Burden & Kuechel, 2010) found that the preference of a majority of educators (77 per cent) was for short clips of between three and ten minutes. This suggests that most teachers who use video agree it is much easier to convey ideas and processes, using clips rather than programmes. Clips also allow teachers to make better use of lesson time, a fact also noted by other researchers.

> Shorter clips afford educators the ability to use highly focused learning objects across disciplines and in a variety of learning settings. Shorter clips also address the issue of educators' time constraints, both in preparation and in the classroom. (Mardis, 2009)

Internet hosted video emerged during the late 1990s, enabling computers to access video content on the web in streaming or downloadable formats. In reality early experiences were not always positive in schools – bandwidth restrictions, and the functionality of the hardware meant regular classroom use was impractical. For example, RealPlayer, one of the earliest streaming media players, had security issues and installed unwanted components on to users' computers.

PC and Apple (Mac) users rightly or wrongly identified compatibility issues between the different download formats for Windows (.wmv) and Mac OS (.mov) files as a barrier to making full use of video in schools. Some content providers became aware of this and made their video content available in both formats. Overall, it may be said that for many teachers, the technology was not seen as sufficiently mature in order to support learning on a meaningful scale.

This perception began to change with the arrival of Flash enabled video format (.flv) in 2002. Video could now be viewed on a browser thus diminishing the importance of the cross-platform issue. Many video providers including the BBC shifted their video content to Flash video and by 2003 it was becoming increasingly common on the Web.

The launch of YouTube in 2005 together with faster broadband connections in school signalled a recognition of the growing importance of online video, and advisory bodies such as Naace[1] and Becta (British Educational Communications and Technology Agency) referenced video sites and content in their reports and communications. By 2006 the quantity of online videos, on YouTube and elsewhere had grown exponentially. In the UK, school network managers reported to Becta that one in twenty web requests were for YouTube videos.[2]

Converging with internet video, desktop video editing tools arrived on the market during late 1999. At the forefront of this consumer focused approach to video editing was Apple's iMovie software which came pre-installed on the iMac DV, offering a one stop, out of the box solution which required no set up and was intuitively easy to use. iMovie was followed in 2001 by Windows Moviemaker, included as part of the Windows XP operating system.

Easy to use software tools meant it was now possible to edit video directly on the desktop, using simple copy and paste / drag and drop techniques. The combination of desktop software and relatively low cost camcorders moved videography from the professional arena to the amateur, a paradigm shift that would later be echoed on the internet with the emergence of Web 2.0 and social media.

Although initially only a small number of pathfinder schools were involved in making videos, the practice soon gained momentum with

1   An advisory body for ICT in schools.
2   The data does not distinguish between teacher and student use.

websites and communities such *DVinED* and *Apple Learning Interchange*,[3] providing support and exemplars of practice. At first mainly incorporated into 'media'-centric studies, the use of DV did start to extend out to the wider curriculum. This was kick-started in the UK by two innovative projects initiated by Becta: the Digital Video Pilot Project in 2002, and the Teaching and Learning with Digital Video Assets Project in 2003. Whilst the DV Pilot Project focused on the practical and aesthetic aspect of making video, the Teaching and Learning with Video Assets Project was more ambitious. It sought to combine educational video content with production processes. Ahead of its time, the DV Assets Project introduced the idea of *remixing*[4] students' own video footage with existing video clips from a number of video libraries including *Pathé News*. This project was successful in that it demonstrated the potential for combining students' and teachers' creativity in using digital media with subject knowledge.

The project found that engaging with video helped teachers and students develop a greater understanding of the potential of film and video, not just for subject exposition but for critical thinking and deep learning.

> There is a clear link between the analytical skills necessary in English and those involved in deconstructing a piece of film, both in terms of technical film language and the messages and values contained within the piece, especially the implicit ideological elements. (Teacher DV Assets Project, Kuechel & Burden)

This theme was to re-emerge strongly with the advent of YouTube and other Web 2.0 tools after 2005. Indeed, if YouTube and Web 2.0 had been available at the time, one might speculate that the outcomes of these projects would have been disseminated much more widely. This is because learning processes are much more easily facilitated through internet enabled video and user generated content, both dominant elements in educational video today. The facility to embed YouTube content within web pages and wikis means video content can be easily shared, enabling creation and

3   ALI site closed 2010.
4   Although common in the music world, the term *remixing* was not in general usage at the time of the project.

development of new resources. It was later acknowledged by Becta that the technologies would lead to:

> a convergence between the characteristics that have redefined online community and those that have characterised online content creation. (Facer et al., Becta, 2007)

Present

Video technology and practice has moved from occupying a specialist niche within specific school departments into the mainstream classroom. This has been made possible by smart-phones and inexpensive cameras such as *flip cams* that enable easy one-touch recording. When such tools are combined with easy to use video editing software, on desktop, mobile or hand held devices there can be a democratisation of the video process allowing a critical mass of actors, both educators and students, to participate in pedagogical video activities.

Desktop and mobile editing tools are now being supplemented by video editing tools hosted in the cloud. YouTube currently offers video editing which in addition to the usual transitions, filters and adjustments includes image stabilisation and captioning.

Most schools now have an adequate, or better, broadband connection to the internet and watching online video, whether downloaded and/ or streaming, is now commonplace in many schools. A good number of schools also purchase or subscribe to internet-enabled video clip libraries. These are often supported with well-designed curriculum focused resources. Teachers regularly access online video services including YouTube, and if prevented from doing so by schools filtering and blocking access, they will readily access those services out of school. Whilst the evidence suggests that viewing video is increasing, it is still predicated on a traditional didactic pedagogy:

> It would appear that users in all sectors conceptualise the use of video essentially as a whole class teaching and learning resource, Although there was an opportunity for users to illustrate other more personalised patterns of use (e.g. on individual devices or screens) very few did so, leading us to conclude that video is still perceived, by the majority of users, as a for whole class pedagogy. (Kuechel & Burden, 2010)

Denning is aware of the potential for learner interaction with video and argues that in order to move from a passive use of video to an interactive model teachers must be instrumental in using video *in combination with other instructional strategies* because:

> Videos can allow learners to make their own input into learning experiences and to realize the personal importance of learning itself. It is up to the teacher to develop processes and circumstances to get the most 'interactive learning' value from video and to help bring the video experience into the real world of the student as learner. (Denning, no date)

In studies with colleague Kevin Burden also identified a number of common practical factors that affect the wider take up of video in schools:

• Filtering and blocking of YouTube (and other online video services)
• Technical issues and access to resources
• Time management for previewing and selecting video
• Permissions and copyright
• Finding suitable video

It seems unlikely that until these issues are addressed and become sustainable at an institutional level, rather than a classroom or individual level, and until there is a critical mass of institutions using video regularly, strategically and in depth, the full pedagogical benefits of video will not be realised. Currently it seems there are no examinations (other than those where video is part of the expected outcomes) that allow video or video-enhanced texts as part of a student's submission. This is an area that is ripe for further research and investigation.

The persistence of YouTube

Any child entering a school in the developed world during 2011 will have
grown up alongside YouTube. For many it will be as familiar a part of their
world as television, and although there are other services available, YouTube
has become synonymous with watching video on a computer.

Children and young adults are likely to use YouTube on a daily basis
to check out the latest 'essential' viewing, often in one or more of the following categories: funny, music, sport, or supporting a social conversation
centred on these, with their peers (Davies & Merchant, 2009). Davies and
Merchant also reach the following conclusion:

> This kind of activity is one that could be easily cloned, with teachers embedding
> YouTube clips into new online spaces such as class blogs, wikis.

Whilst the authors acknowledge that it is unlikely that a teacher's choice
of video would be the same as that of their pupils, they intimate that the
potential for using the viral capacity of video to enhance learning is an area
ripe for further research.

YouTube is at the forefront of many innovations in online video, regularly introducing new feature sets and tools. A simple but effective example
is the Playlist Bar, which makes managing, sharing and tagging of video
sources really easy. These tools all serve as a model for how other educational platforms might facilitate educational content. The latest addition
is the YouTube Video Manager which allows users to build a playlist, check
subscriptions and review their viewing history.

YouTube in school

Teachers are increasingly turning to YouTube; for many teachers and educators it is the first place they will look to find video resources (Burden &
Kuechel, 2010). It is also increasingly used as a search tool by both teachers

and students (Merchant and Davies, 2009). YouTube is the benchmark to which other video platforms, including educational video platforms, are compared.

As teachers increasingly recognise the educational value of YouTube platform and content, and despite the routine blocking of the service by educational organisations, local authorities and schools, many will access the service out of school in order to download the video file and convert it to a desktop format for use in class (Burden & Kuechel, 2010). However such strategies – which, incidentally, break YouTube's Terms of Service – are unsustainable because they rely on individual expertise and commitment, or may not have been sanctioned by the school leadership, who in some cases may not even be aware of the practice.

It can be argued that in order to leverage the educational value of YouTube, teachers should engage with, and promote, the educational affordances of the service, for example YouTube's *channel* structure. Channels, featuring content created both by 'users' and established providers, such as the BBC, National Geographic or major universities often host unique content relevant to subject specialisms and areas of study, offering teachers a quick and easy way to find and curate content from *trusted* sources. Such strategies may help convince other stakeholders, including other teachers, school leaders and parents of the value of YouTube. Some schools are engaging at this level and have set up their own school channels.

Several education specific video platforms such as *TeacherTube* and *SchoolTube* have replicated, or adapted, the style and functionality of YouTube. These services aim to offer a safe moderated alternative to YouTube. However, they do not have the traction or the range and amount of content available on YouTube.

The educational potential of YouTube is also implicitly acknowledged by third party services that are designed to filter or manage YouTube content. Many educators' criticisms of YouTube are not directed at the video content itself, but at the standard and suitability of the user comments attached to the videos. Comment Snob has been developed to filter comments on YouTube. Other services, for example, VueSafe and SafeWatch, allow teachers to present YouTube videos in an independent space respectively.

Another proactive service which could also be used for moderation is TubeChop, which can be use to *trim* and *select* required parts of a video, in a way that can be compared to using a desktop video editing programme. This is a more constructivist approach with the potential for knowledge building.

Pedagogically focused video platforms

Some video platforms have been developed to offer more than an online library of videos, by using different pedagogical approaches to delivering video content.

A good example of this is WatchKnow.org, a non-profit video crowd-sourced platform developed by Wikipedia co-founder Larry Sanger to provide free educational videos delivered over the internet. Viewed any time, from anywhere, WatchKnow aggregates and curates educational content from a number of video libraries, including YouTube, TeacherTube and Google Video. The videos are organised by curriculum area and subjects and can be filtered for age suitability.

WatchKnow is a peer moderated community for managing video content, and it functions like a wiki. Prospective contributors can join the WatchKnow community to add videos plus metadata, as well as being able to edit and rearrange the video categories. There may be a great deal of value for teachers in becoming involved in the work of this community. Working with video at this level is likely to facilitate a deep consideration of the learning potential of the individual videos they are managing.

Taking a different approach is Edutube Plus, an EU (eContent Plus) funded initiative designed to combine video and learning in an everyday classroom environment, in schools across Europe. Developed by a consortium of seventeen EU partners, Edutube Plus offers a framework to combine curriculum and subject metadata with teachers' learning objectives and lesson planning. The platform is designed to combine the benefits of a multilingual video library with pedagogical tools and to test its potential in an international marketplace. Its stated aims are to:

> create a European hybrid, multilingual video-based service for schools ... [which will] integrate thousands of multi-lingual curriculum-related video-clips by major European educational TV & video providers, with tools ... to enrich the library with user-generated clips. The [service] ... will enable users to develop, translate and share video-based learning scenarios and lessons, to search resources using terms related to their national curriculum and to use video in a pedagogically relevant manner in-class.

Although there were some initial technical issues with the pilot version of the platform, data from teacher feedback and evaluation during and after the project pilot confirmed that teachers across Europe were keen to use the platform for video based curriculum activities and international collaboration.

The attribute of the Edutube Plus platform that was highly valued by teachers and which differentiated it from other educational video libraries was the integration of several innovative pedagogical tools within the platform. These tools enabled teachers to create 'Learning Scenarios' to scaffold video clips in an educational context, and to upload their own videos. They were able to benefit from translated metadata (including curriculum ontologies), and video descriptions into their language of choice. The Edtube Plus pilot also enabled schools to establish a number of successful international partnerships to facilitate international projects and collaboration on learning with video.

Edutube Plus hosts video clips, extracted from professionally created content. These were selected using pedagogical video selection criteria developed by the University of Hull, based on work by ATiT in Belgium, the VideoAktiv project and Jack Kuomi. These were integrated with a platform provided by LeSite (France) after following the pedagogical aims and structure specified by the Greek Ministry of Education and RACTI in Athens. The platform also allows registered users to upload user generated content to its library and this is seen as a part of the platform that is growing in importance.

Developing pedagogical frameworks for video

Currently most educational video libraries and portals are organised on a subject or content basis. Whilst there is a great deal of value in this for helping teachers locate quality of video content for their subject, the downside of such systems is that teachers may not look outside their subject specialisms, and consequently overlook video resources that could offer new cognitive experiences for their students. Denning (no date) states:

> The viewing context for the message and the instructional strategies found within the presentation are critical factors in how learning is fostered by a particular instructional presentation.

In order to offer an alternative to the orthodox model of using video in school, recent work by Atkinson, Burden and Kuechel for JISC (2009) developed a pedagogical framework for learning with video in HE:

> The use of digital video has reached a crossroads where educators are beginning to perceive the added value which video can contribute to carefully designed and appropriate learning contexts. (Burden & Kuechel, 2010)

Initially developed to support teaching and learning with the JISC Newsfilm Online video archive, its purpose was to separate the content of the video from a presumed curriculum subject focus, and consider how it might be used in different contexts. The framework was similar to Denning's model except that it also included elements 4 to 6 in the list below:

1. Watch/Observe
2. Analyse/Predict
3. Empathise
4. Create
5. Share/Publish
6. Collaborate

By cross referencing the above ways of using video with both traditional and emergent learning spaces, as represented in the matrix, we have a framework illustrated below (Table 5.1) focusing on the learning space. This space is completely flexible and educators can use it to extrapolate the potential for individual video clips.

Table 5.1 Pedagogical Framework for Learning with Video

Assembly					
Lecture					
Class					
Workshop					
Group					
Individual					
Virtual					
Mobile					
	Watch/ Observer	Analyse/ Predict	Empathise	Create	Share/Publish

For example, whilst the content of a (familiar) video clip such as the Tacoma Narrows could be used as an illustration in Physics, it could also be used to allow students to empathise with the motorists and pedestrians trying to cross the bridge, or it could be stopped at a critical point before its conclusion in order to pose the question: what do you think will happen next – and why?

Future

It may be fairly safe to extrapolate that the technical quality and delivery of video, both professionally produced and user generated, will continue to improve and offer high quality, engaging and interactive visual experiences. There is a consensus that video will become even more ubiquitous (Good, 2010), and that the future of learning will rely heavily on video content that is internet enabled, especially cloud based services. Editing tools are already becoming prominent on mobile and handheld devices and in the Cloud, whilst the publishing and sharing of video is now instantaneous through real time streaming services.

Personalised and self-directed learning with video is likely to be a dominant factor, as evidenced by models already being developed and adopted. In his Ted Talk, Chris Anderson (2010) presents a video of the six-year-old *lil demon* breakdancing, stating: 'He's doing dance tricks ... that probably no other six-year-old in history has done before.' Anderson then asks rhetorically, 'And how did he learn this? ... what drove him to spend the hundreds of hours this must have taken?' The answer, of course, is the internet and, by default, YouTube. Anderson then describes the evolution of communities, in this case dancers, who use web based video to improve their skills and demonstrate their capability. It seems logical to extrapolate that this personalised learning in a community context, with shared goals, should be transferable to 'education' per se.

Currently the most significant implementation of using video for personalised learning is *Khan Academy*. This initiative by Salman Khan has a mission to *deliver a world-class education to anyone anywhere*, using over 2,100 YouTube videos on Maths together with some videos on Science, Astronomy and History. Khan's video content is delivered in a mini-lecture format that offers bite size chunks of knowledge.

Although there are many examples of recorded lectures and mini-lecture videos on the Web, Khan Academy differs because it includes tests and exercises that can help students gauge and determine their knowledge, understanding and performance. These metrics offer some excellent formative assessment, guiding the student and providing multilevel feedback, incentives, and branching recommendations for the next stage of study.

The blending of assessment metrics and video to support learning, measure and incentivise progress is also evidenced by another service, English Central, which incorporates speech recognition technology to help English learners improve their speaking and pronunciation skills.

Learners choose from a selection of online videos, including user recommended clips, available on the English Central platform, and then listen to a section of the video and record their own voice speaking that section. As well as being able to hear and compare their recording with the original, the English Central software 'scores' their recorded submission and highlights the words that need attention. Learners can work with individual words, phrases or sentences and the platform also includes linked dictionary tools which will help the learners with interpretation and meaning.

Combining text and video – captions and subtitles

The practice of overlaying moving images with text in the form of subtitles or captions has been around for a long time. Initially used to provide a text translation of a film or video, or to help those who are deaf or suffer from loss of hearing interpret audio, subtitles and captions are coming under renewed scrutiny by educators and educational researchers because of the ways they can extend learning.

Whilst the immediate benefits of subtitles for translation and accessibility are obvious, there are other ways in which subtitles and captions can enhance learning. Recent research by Brij Kothari in India suggests that Same Language Subtitling (SLS) led to:

> an incremental but measurable contribution to decoding skills, across the group that generally saw the subtitled TV program [as compared to those who did not]. (Kothari, 2004)

Kothari found that by adding *karaoke* style subtitles to television and film song broadcasts it increased reading and engagement by a neo-literate audience, developing their literacy skills as they joined in with the songs.

Historically, subtitling has been a specialist skill, not within the reach of most educators because it required dedicated technicians and professional level hardware. This changed over the past few years with the emergence of a number of Web 2.0 tools and services designed to allow users to create and add subtitles to online video.

Whilst YouTube allows you to add captions to video that you upload yourself, there are a growing number of cloud based services including Universal Subtitles and DotSub that enable users to create and add subtitles to any online video. Such tools are relatively easy to use and can provide excellent cognitive tasks, for example matching the text to the video time codes. Encouraging students to subtitle and caption video can provide benefits including deeper engagement with subjects and development of higher order thinking skills.

Offering students real practice in subtitling and captioning will stimulate learning on a number of levels. This can include: understanding and learning of languages, problem solving, reading and even coding and timeline based work. Subtitles offer language teachers translating and language teaching tools by reaching global audiences and being accessible to the deaf and hard-of-hearing.

Semantic video

Future implementations of video for learning are likely to be based on semantic video, meaning video that is aware of the content within it, enabling deep linking, and that is searchable by properties including audio, colour, shape or movement. Several projects are presently underway researching and experimenting with such systems.

The *Mozilla Drumbeat* project (2011) blends HTML 5.0 and Popcorn. js technology to create interactive video. As the video playhead moves along the video timeline, it triggers related data to appear in the surrounding information panels at contextual points in the video.

The HTML 5.0 enabled video also provides any user generated notes, licensing information and any available captions. The captions can be automatically translated into other languages. This is the twenty-first-century destination of the path on which the BBC Domesday project set out. It is now possible because it is web based and not reliant on specific hardware technologies.

Although the video is still the focal point, this video tool provides an excellent model of a learning framework. It transcends the confines of the lesson plan, or learning template. It is a complete knowledge building system. Teachers may consider it in terms of: how could I use this? The design is modular but it goes far beyond the limited potential of SCORM based learning objects.

This video tool offers a knowledge building framework that can be adapted to many pedagogical instances. For example, if we use a clip that is universally familiar, such as the aforementioned Tacoma Narrows footage, students would not only be able to watch the video of the actual event but also have/include access to maps, references and eyewitness accounts. With the video as a starting point, it can access and call upon global conversations and knowledge sharing tools.

Content search

Another application of semantic video is searching for audio or visual content within a video sequence. Research by Dr Marcel Worring from MediaMill, University of the Netherlands, has been directed at looking at how content such as colour, shape, form, movement and audio can be located within a video search.

The processes employed by the MediaMill semantic video search engine are an amalgamation of various branches of computer science including 'image and video processing, computer vision, language technology, machine learning and information visualization' (MediaMill 2010).

Conclusion

We are now entering the age of *smart video* where:

> Eventually, all videos will be searchable with speech recognition and audio indexing software. Even the vast and eclectic YouTube database will be searchable for any spoken word or phrase. (Lindstrom, 2011)

When video is enhanced with these smart, semantic capabilities, educators must extrapolate how best these emergent tools, platforms and video communities can support and extend opportunities for learning.

Emerging evidence and research as outlined in this paper suggests that video will become a keystone for educational texts, and also a hub for educational communities. The potential for educators to use video will only be limited by their imaginations and willingness to engage with, experiment and participate in this exciting and challenging space.

References

Anderson, C., 'How web video powers global innovation'. Retrieved 8 January 2011 from <http://www.ted.com/talks/chris_anderson_how_web_video_powers_global_innovation.html>

Atkinson, S., Burden, K., Kuechel, T., 'JISC Newsfilm Online; Teaching and Learning with Digitised Resources'. Available at <http://misc.jisc.ac.uk/JISC/>

Bell, L. & Bull, G., 'Digital Video and Teaching'. *CITE* 10/1 (2010).

Bijens, M., Vanbuel, M., Verstegens, S., & Young, C., *Handbook on Digital Video and Audio in Education.* (Socrates-Minerva EC: VideoAktiv Project, 2006). Available at <http://www.videoaktiv.org/>

Burden, K. & Kuechel, T., 'Evaluation Report Becta Teaching and Learning with DV assets' (2004). Available at <http://www.bee-it.co.uk/Guidance%20Docs/Becta%20Files/Reports%20and%20publications/104%20Teaching%20and%20learning%20with%20digital%20video%20assets%202003-2004.pdf>

Burn, A., Reid, M., & Parker, D., 'Evaluation Report of the Becta Digital Video Pilot Project, BFI' (2004) Available at <http://homepages.shu.ac.uk/~edsjlc/ict/becta/research_papers/what_the_research_says/dvreport_241002.pdf>

Clement, C., Silver, J. et al., 'A New Public Media – A Plan for Action' (2010). Available at <http://www.freepress.net/sites/default/files/fp-legacy/New_Public_Media.doc.pdf>

Cox, M. et al., 'An investigation of the research evidence relating to ICT pedagogy' (2004). Available at <http://dera.ioe.ac.uk/1601/1/becta_2003_attainment-pedagogy_queensprinter.pdf>

Cruse, E., 'Using Educational Video in the Classroom: Theory, Research and Practice' (2008). Available at <http://www.libraryvideo.com/articles/article26.asp>

Davies, J. & Merchant, G., *Web 2.0 for Schools* (Oxford: Peter Lang, 2009).

Denning, D., 'Video in Theory and Practice: Issues for Classroom Use and Teacher Video' (No Date). Available at <http://www.edbqhs.org/Teachers/pdf/VidPM.pdf>

Facer, K. et al. in *Emerging Technologies*, 2 (2008). Available at <http://www.mmiweb.org.uk/publications/ict/emerging_tech03.pdf>

Good, R., retrieved 25 January 2010 at <MasterNewmedia.org>

Khan, S., 'Lets Use Video To Reinvent Education'. Retrieved 12 May 2011 at <http://www.ted.com/talks/salman_khan_let_s_use_video_to_reinvent_education.html>

Kothari, B. & Pandey, A., 'Reading Out of the Idiot Box: Same-Language Subtitling on Television in India' (2005). Available at <http://www.dcmp.org/caai/NADH255.pdf>

Koumi, J., *Designing Video and Multimedia for Open and Flexible Learning* (Oxford: Routledge, 2006).

Literacy 2.0, 'DOE Debuts Audio-indexed Video Database'. Retrieved 28 February 2011 from <http://www.literacy20.com/2011/02/doe-launches-audio-indexed-video-database/>

MediaMill Semantic Search Engine (University of Amsterdam) (2010). Available at <http://www.science.uva.nl/research/mediamill/>

Megalou, E. Retrieved 16 April 2011 at <http://www.edutubeplus.info/news/the-edutubeplus-closing-conference-was-successfully-held-in-athens>

Molenda, M. & Spector, P., *Handbook of Research on Educational Communications and Technology* (Oxford: Taylor Francis Group LLC, 2008) (Third Ed.).

Tyner, K., *Arts Education Policy Review* Vol. 96, No. 1. (September/October 1994). Retrieved 2 June 2011 from <http://www.laplaza.org/about_lap/archives/mlit/media_10.html>

Websites and organisations

ATiT <http://www.atit.be/>

British Pathé News <http://www.britishpathe.com/>

Domesday Project <http://www.domesday.org.uk/>

DotSub <http://dotsub.com>

DVinED <http://www.dvined.org.uk/>

Edutube Plus <http://www.edutubeplus.info/ EnglishCentral http://www.english-central.com>

HYTML 5 Video demo <http://webmademovies.etherworks.ca/popcorndemo/>

LeSite <http://www.lesite.tv/>

Khan Academy <http://www.khanacademy.org/>

Naace <http://www.naace.co.uk/>

Mozilla Drumbeat <https://www.drumbeat.org/en-US/projects/>

RACTI <http://www.cti.gr/>

REELSEO Semantic Video Indexing <http://www.reelseo.com/semantic-video-indexing/>

SchoolTube <http://www.schooltube.com>

Stevens, L., La Vaca Lola clip <http://www.universalsubtitles.org/en/videos/rj3mvm X1gUGL/es/>

Teacher Tube <http://www1.teachertube.com/>

TubeChop

Universal Subtitles <http://universalsubtitles.org/en/>

Voicethread <http://voicethread.com/>

VuSafe <http://www.m86vusafe.com/>

WatchKnow.org <http://www.watchknow.org/>

YouTube <http://youtube.com>

YouTube Edu <http://www.youtube.com/education?b=400>

STEPHEN J. MCNEILL AND JOSHUA N. AZRIEL

6 News Reporting from Mobile Devices: A Pilot Study

The beginning of the twenty-first century is witnessing remarkable technological changes. Access to communication is unparalleled at this time compared with other moments in history. Even in regions of the world with disadvantaged communities in Africa, Central America and Asia, the numbers of individuals using social media continues to grow at enormous rates. When governments block their public's access to online content, people still turn to the internet to download and upload information. While countries such as China and Iran censor the internet, citizens in both countries find ways to communicate with their cell phones using social media such as Twitter and Facebook. These actions reflect the truth that mobile communication devices such as cell phones and netbooks are becoming the standard sources for global communication. With the 2010 US Presidential Campaign, the world saw firsthand the seeming overhaul of 'politics as usual' as then-candidate Barack Obama went overseas to campaign for President. People from around the world were watching, even if they weren't directly involved. The same could be said for the Arab Spring as well.

Facebook Beacon, a controversial targeted advertising tool, sent user information from other websites directly to Facebook to target potential advertising and marketing for Facebook users. After only two years, Beacon was discontinued due to ethical concerns of privacy and numerous lawsuits, most notably from moveon.org. However, search engines such as Google use trending and other analytics to both provide targeted advertising to users and to develop *cookie pools* (as demographic information) to offer to potential advertisers.

As the printing press sparked a literacy movement, social media has ignited a new digital literacy that is making a great impact on our lives. Governments can try to stand in the way, but in the long run they will inevitably fail. We are witnessing a global communications revolution that is more powerful than any one government's ability to control it. Global communication has several *backbones* or layers. Censor one avenue of digital communication and another is available. Thirteen years ago, in 1999, Lawrence Lessig boldly and correctly wrote in *Code and Other Laws of Cyberspace* that the internet inherently brings freedom of speech to the world because of its technological infrastructure. With mobile communication devices, his prediction is correct.

All this change in communications reflects the rise of *Citizen Media*. Simply stated, citizen media is the average individual communicating and contributing to the marketplace of ideas. Individuals now have the power to shape local, national, and global conversations and debates. People using their cell phones to photograph a news event and uploading it to a website, blog, or social media website is no longer revolutionary. *Citizen Journalists* are often the first to report a news story and send images to a newsroom. Videos of protests are just as likely to be uploaded to Facebook, Twitter, and YouTube as they are to be seen on television. Foursquare was also designed for mobile phone users but acts as a location based social networking site, similar to the properties displayed on Facebook Places. Places, which was a reaction to Foursquare, will diversify itself by providing coupons and other miscellany based on the user's location. We live in an age when people in almost any corner of the world contribute to a global marketplace of ideas. What was previously the communications venue for the few and privileged has opened up to the public. We are as likely to communicate with co-workers, friends, and relatives who live thousands of miles away as we are with our neighbors. The ongoing development of user-friendly software and technologies increases citizen media outreach.

In United States history, Thomas Paine and Benjamin Franklin were the citizen media activists of their time because they owned or had access to a printing press. They influenced the early politics and culture of the USA. Today, new media has given birth to millions of Benjamin Franklins who distribute their opinions online on any topic to an unlimited global audience and influence their own communities, while the film or the video game continues to structure our world view.

As technology advances, journalists are called upon to use equipment such as cell phones to assist them in their reporting duties. Cell phones that have access to the internet and contain built-in features for recording audio and video can help journalists report the news without the need to carry heavy recording equipment such as video cameras, microphones, and audio recorders. The iPhone is an example of a mobile device that can accomplish all these tasks. Other cell phone operating systems, such as an Android or Blackberry, also contain similar features. These common, everyday devices can be used to assist reporters in interviewing, recording photos and videos, and writing news copy for their stories. While not a substitute for broadcast quality video cameras or a state of the art digital camera, in a breaking news scenario cell phones can be a valuable journalism tool.

The task

A pilot study in June 2010 at Kennesaw State University's Department of Communication studied the effectiveness of using these cell phones for news gathering. A group of thirteen communication students who were enrolled in COM 3310 Concepts in New Media completed an assignment that required them to use their cell phones with data plans for accessing the internet to produce a newspaper style story. The results from this pilot study show which types of cell phones worked best in aiding the students in producing a newspaper style story.

The students were given the assignment of covering a news story only using a cell phone. They had to write an eight to ten paragraph newspaper style story that included a headline and byline. Students were instructed to present a local city or university oriented news story to the professor for approval.

Approximately half the students owned a cell phone and paid for a monthly data plan that provided internet access. These students were paired with another individual in the class who did not own a cell phone with a paid data plan. Working in pairs, they used the cell phone to interview, photograph, and write the story. With a total of thirteen students, one individual – who owned a cell phone with a paid data plan – worked alone on the assignment. The finished story could be posted either on the Blogger (www.blogger.com) or WordPress (www.wordpress.com) web sites. These two sites have templates that the students could use to write their stories, which in turn could be presented as a newspaper style story. Blackberrys, iPhones, Androids, and Windows-operated phones as well as a Sanyo Sprint data-based phone were used. Each group turned in written notes detailing their successes and/or failures using the smartphone for the assignment. In fact, the Pew Foundation predicted as early as 2008 that by the year 2020 most people across the world will be using their smartphone as the primary means of connecting to the internet. In developing nations, the smartphone could leapfrog over the laptop, just as cell phones leaped over landlines in many developing nations in the 1990s.

Citizen journalism (CJ movement and aesthetic)

Citizen reporters, or civic journalists, are on the rise. Often called bloggers, these reporters are more than just simple texters. Using Flickr, Facebook, YouTube, or any other social networking site, regular people are covering stories in a multimedia atmosphere. Video, audio, print stories, and photos from the location all come together. While traditional media such as AP are regularly accomplishing this task, what is remarkable is the equal playing field citizen journalists seem to have. Citizen journalists, or CJs, are also actively collaborating with traditional media, such as CNN's iReport. We have also seen some of the most compelling journalism coming from Tehran in Iran, during turbulent times within the city and nation. Almost all the footage that we see can be found on YouTube, all shot by regular people, trying to show us the atrocities of their current situation. This also leads to discussion on the *Citizen Media Aesthetic*, or user-generated aesthetic content. This content provides perspective and important instrumental and warning surveillance, but at the stake of professional quality of the storytelling, from a production and reporting perspective. Storytelling now is un-authoritarian, non-linear, not left-to-right (professional sports broadcast production routinely reacts to video game design in their broadcasts). In many cases, gatekeeping becomes a serious problem as well, as CJs may not be objective or knowledgeable in the areas they are reporting in. However, one can never mistake the service to journalism citizen media accomplishes, especially from a utilitarian point of view.

In reality, modern technology has always been the line between creator and audience. Web 2.0 has already erased the concept of gatekeeping in our media message delivery. The ease of the technology has made us all automatons: the media as a global warming all its own. Ronald Bettig (1996) wrote that these developments are situated within the larger context of the restructuring of global (or glocal) capitalism in which control over the means of communication has become more centralised while processes of production and distribution of information and cultural commodities have been decentralised.

Even while content distribution is considered decentralised when considering the gatekeeping of production, trends have shown that with more individuals assuming the role of a citizen journalist, traditional media companies are now seeing user-generated content for hyperlocal news. Hyperlocal news could be as specific as an area code, zip code or city block. Online subscribers would then *add* this region or area based on content or geographic interest. Hyperlocal news has been seen already, from hospital radio stations, company newsletters, and college newspapers. However, now the user can select hyperlocal content from around the world, in their local neighborhood, and even future vacation destinations.

Super Mario Forever is an example of Citizen Media meets Gaming. Forever, a ROM hack of the original Super Mario Bros., is notorious for being incredibly difficult. The hack's popularity originated in a video posted on tudou.com. From there it spread to various gaming forums and eventually was uploaded to YouTube. Its fame was escalated further when a man narrated over the top of the video and released it as Super Mario Frustration. Some fans of Frustration have made the same Mario game so easy that the games play themselves without any human intervention at all. These days, game developer Nintendo seems to have really emphasised the capacity of the 3DS for connectivity.

What this proves is that citizen media exists in various originating media. From old Nintendo games being brought into the Web atmosphere of now by citizen gaming enthusiasts, we also see examples of Benjamin Franklin being the publisher/printer/postmaster of his early newspapers juxtaposed with the contemporary example of the Tiziano Project, which has the mission of providing digital media production equipment in war-torn or underrepresented areas in need of media exposure. In this case, solely *ci*tizen media exposure delivers the story to the masses.

Although it might sound simple, the risks are high as well. This acts as a threat to an age old practice, but also provides a higher level of usage as social utility. This is also considered to be a form of entertainment and instrumental surveillance for a number of people, if not as infotainment.

Results

Each group decided to post its news story on Wordpress.com. The main reason cited was that Blogger.com required a Google-based Gmail electronic mail account, and the students refused to open a new account to gain access to Blogger. According to the students' notes, those with iPhones and Android operated phones completed the assignment without any major problems. The WordPress website has a mobile application that can be downloaded for the iPhone, Android, and Blackberry operating systems. The students who used the mobile applications for their iPhones and Android phones stated they were able to complete the assignment in an efficient manner. The photos they took on the assignment were easily uploaded to their WordPress sites. Once the photos were uploaded, they were able to write their stories on the mobile web site as a traditional newspaper article. Their biggest complaint at this point was using their thumbs to write the story on the cell phones' screen-based keyboard.

The student who used a Windows-operated phone did not encounter any difficulties in completing the assignment but could not download the WordPress application. Instead, the student completed the assignment using WordPress's standard website via his cell phone. Two students indicated difficulties with the assignment because of the phone they used. One used a Blackberry Pearl without success. He borrowed a friend's iPhone to complete the assignment. The student indicated that after the WordPress application was installed, he could not upload a photo from the assignment. That process locked up his phone. No other student had a Blackberry, but the course instructor owned a Blackberry Curve and had similar difficulties accessing WordPress on his phone as he tested out the assignment.

The second student who encountered difficulties used the Sanyo Instinct, which uses Sprint's own operating system for internet access. While the student could access the internet from her phone, she could not download WordPress's application nor could she access the standard web site directly from her phone. Her assignment could not be completed solely from her phone. She was only able to use the phone for photography. She used a tape recorder for the interviews and a desktop computer to upload the story to WordPress.

Future research

Since this was a pilot project, the next step in this research is to assign more projects to the students using cell phones as the basis for mobile journalism. Ideally, the students would produce another newspaper style article and also work on a television style broadcast or audio podcast assignment utilising video recorded from their cell phones. Mobile applications now exist for video editing, such as Splice, VidTrim, Vignette, and Videocam Illusion. Citizen journalists will also convert a phone into a teleprompter for reading during live smart-casts from their phone by using live apps such as Report-IT Live for IP audio podcasting, an app that can arrange pre-recorded packages along with the live broadcast. Citizen journalists needing live streams for a video report will be utilising such apps as Qik. Future experimentation is ongoing at Kennesaw State University.

Since WordPress worked well as a platform for uploading the news stories, it might be used again or the professor might design a specific course-based web site specifically designated for the assignments where the students could upload to the site from the scene of the news story. The iPhone and Android-based phones would be used again. Since WordPress has a mobile application for Blackberry, any future assignments should include a Blackberry even though the mobile application did not work well with either the Blackberry Pearl or Curve. Other Blackberry models could be experimented with as well.

Summary

During the Nixon–Kennedy debates, the public caught its first glimpse at how the new medium of television would change the substance of politics: television would increase our focus on the interpersonal skills of our politicians and diminish our focus on the issues. Parkridge 47's YouTube political ad framing Hillary Clinton as an Orwellian autocrat on behalf of Barack Obama was a testament to the power of citizen journalists in cyberspace. We could also say that the inherent hypermediocrity of social networking is transforming media further into a democracy of trash, with cultural and media ghettos throughout cyberspace and most notably within the worlds of 2.0 applications. With endless streams of citizen-produced media messages consumed by many and by none at all, fascinance could be achieved whether or not the message is consumed by others. This is within the citizen media world. Both presentation and democracy are the issues. It is important to note that these projections used to be exclusively for the elite celebrity or VIP; now it is a cultural democracy where these traits are meticulously calculated and performed online and possible for all.

References

Bettig, R., *Copyrighting Culture* (Boulder, CO: Westview Press, 1996).
Briggs, M., *Journalism Next* (Washington D.C.: CQ Press, 2010).
Farhi, P., 'The Twitter Explosion'. *American Journalism Review*, June/July (2009), 27–31.
Goggin, G., 'Adapting the Mobile Phone: The iPhone and its Consumption'. *Continuum: Journal of Media and Cultural Studies* 23/2 (2009), 231–244.
McNeill, S., *Digital Symbiosis* (San Francisco, CA: National Social Science Press, 2010).
Perigoe, R., 'Ten-Year Retrospective'. *Canada and the United States in the Age of Digital Journalism* 10/2 (2009), 247–253.

7   Harnessing Visual Educational Resources
    to Better Realise Pedagogical Objectives

We reside in an image-rich world, and we are intrigued, fascinated, and otherwise impacted by what we see. High definition adds vibrancy, and new media increases circulation. Visual content can be harnessed to enliven our classes, provide illustrative examples, and enhance learning. Part of our pedagogy, of course, is what to *do* with this visual content. In other words, how do images fit into our lesson plan? What instructional goals do we wish to accomplish and how might images, still and moving, help us achieve those goals?

A liberal arts education emphasises the ability to think critically and to engage in complex reasoning. Nurturing these skills has always been important, and perhaps now more than ever. These abilities have declined among American students – largely due to a lack of emphasis in contemporary higher education (Arum & Roksa, 2011). (I only hope Ireland and other countries are doing better and can help lead the way!)

Using images is a means to reach our students, engage them, and help them develop higher-order thinking. In these ways, visual content can prove invaluable in our lesson plans. Fortunately, many authors have provided insights and tools for doing so. In what follows I examine some of their approaches and other possibilities for using/discussing visual content in the classroom to help our students achieve *visual literacy*. In doing so, I hope to make clear that visual literacy is an important element in one's education.

The centrality of visual literacy

Understanding how information literacy is defined and discussed can help us recognise what constitutes visual literacy. Visual literacy is commonly thought of as being able to think critically about the images one encounters and the meaning they suggest or would impart/convey (Felton, 2008). If we understand it as a type of information literacy, though, we recognise it also involves an ability to *use* visual information effectively. Effective use entails more than producing the desired results; it also means using information responsibly. Responsible use pertains to accuracy and truthfulness, acknowledging any biases or agenda, revealing sources, and respecting others' intellectual property by adhering to all guidelines pertaining to copyrighted material and fair use (American Library Association, 2000).

Given the common ability and means to produce our own visual content, it is essential that we include responsible use/production as part of our understanding of what it means to be visually literate. We need to think critically and responsibly about verbal/visual content we encounter as well as any we might produce – holding ourselves accountable as both a consumer *and* producer of messages. We have this responsibility as a professor in the classroom, bringing in visual content or supervising students who do. We have this responsibility as a citizen who would post/publish content online or elsewhere. For instance, we have witnessed the impact of postings from protestors in Egypt, Iran, and elsewhere and from victims of disaster – such as tsunamis, floods, or nuclear accidents. Their pictures and words can be quite moving and impactful.

The rhetorical tradition also emphasised accountability for producers and receivers of messages and can further inform our understanding of visual literacy. If we are to have a system of government where citizens have some say in the policies that impact them and affect the country at large, information must flow freely and citizens must be literate – able not only to read but to think critically about what they are reading. Since much of the information we receive today is visual, we must be able to *read* not only verbal text but also visual text. We must nurture our own abilities as well as those of any we would educate.

Our high-tech world has only intensified our exposure to and reliance upon visual information, making visual literacy all the more important in our lives (Rakes, 1999). Visual information impacts our understanding of policy and which policies we will support. It impacts our evaluation of leaders and which leaders we will endorse. Visual information impacts our views of products and services and who will get our business. It impacts how we see ourselves and how we view and conduct our relationships with others, and the advent of online dating and social networks underscore how visual information has become increasingly important in relational development. Visual information impacts all facets of life. It is powerful, exerting much influence. It is something we must attempt to understand and respect.

Educators must especially be appreciative of visual information and its power. Studies have helped us glimpse the basis of this power. For well over a decade we have been aware of the efficiency of visual information. Research reveals that 'human brains extract valuable information from audiovisuals more quickly and more easily than from purely verbal information' and do so with 'a more error-free grasp of information' (Graber, 1996, p. 85). These findings continue to hold up (see Hockley, 2008; Stenberg, 2006). For example, listeners who see a statistical trend via a graph are more likely to understand it – and more immediately – than if left to chart it mentally on their own (Shah & Hoeffner, 2002; Edell & Staelin, 1983). Research makes it quite evident that using visual information along with verbal information bolsters understanding as well as improves retention and recall (Hodes, 1994; Chanlin, 1997; Rakes, 1999).

Having students create their own visuals is a good way to help them become good producers and consumers of visual information. When creating, they can learn basic elements involved in visual communication (Rakes, 1999). Learning these basics can also provide them with tools to critique visual messages. The arrival of PowerPoint to our classrooms made this quite clear. As we taught students to use it effectively they were also more able to better evaluate how well their peers used the program, both in terms of design properties and images used. Teri Sosa (2009) reminds educators of the importance of helping students learn more than design principles for their visual communications, insisting that we teach students to think critically about the visuals they use or that they encounter. In this way, we can nurture creative as well as critical abilities.

Other authors have likewise noted the relationship. After elaborating six goals of visual literacy, Landra L. Rezabek (2005) observes, 'in a world saturated by visual images' it is vital that we learn 'to read and write using visuals.' Doing so not only allows us to communicate better, but it also 'helps us to ... discern and discriminate when visual messages are being used to promote and persuade' (p. 20).

The use of visual content to promote and persuade has prompted the interest and concern of scholars who note how visual content, especially photographs, can stir our emotions and disarm us intellectually (Messaris, 1994; Hoffman, 2000). In an especially compelling essay, Peter Goin (2001) observed how a photograph is somewhat fact and somewhat fiction. Goin notes how with the advent of photography, photographs were considered 'faithful witnesses', a 'mechanical reproduction' and 'nothing more' (p. 363). He notes how that perception lingers, pointing to academic journals where photographs are often paraded as fact with 'the myth of objectivity ... hardly debated' (p. 367). Goin would have us contemplate the way we use the visual content, especially when it comes to seeking truth. He explains:

> According to scientific method, facts can and should be verifiable. And photographs contain elements – such as optical accuracy – reminiscent of fact. Truth and fact, though, are not the same. Truths are culturally derived and do not depend on the same standard of 'objectivity.' Truths imply wisdom and discovery, human emotion and shared values. We know that a photograph can represent a fact. But a photograph can also represent a truth that transcends fact. (p. 368)

It is up to us to recognise the boundaries and help our students see them as well. As Goin notes, 'The simple and elegant rectangle [of a photograph] is a window through which we view ... already a context being defined' (p. 368).

Students need to be smart about images as well as how they are tagged. Visual and verbal content often are used in tandem to influence. As Sheng Kuan Chung (2005) observes, 'through visual and textual manipulation, media advertising not only persuades people to buy the advertised product but also constructs false or questionable realities, beliefs, and values in relation to that product' (p. 19). Chung goes on to describe an assignment in which students deconstruct cigarette advertisements to expose what lies beneath the pictures and text. Students then redesign the ad to suggest an alternative reality – the downside to smoking.

Chung's approach makes good sense. Other authors have likewise noted how images and words in a message must be considered together as we glean meaning. Swedish professor and scholar Rune Pettersson (2009), for instance, offers that 'we need to consider combined verbal and visual messages, not only text and not only visuals, when we study communication and communication-related issues' (p. 38). Scholars of communication studies agree with Rune, as well as with his suggestion that to do so with the proper sophistication requires an interdisciplinary approach. Cara Finnegan (2010), a professor of communication studies at the University of Illinois, for example, notes that studying visual modes of public address is 'to do interdisciplinary work' (p. 252). To understand better the value of an interdisciplinary approach, let us now examine the work of scholars of communication studies.

Approaches to cultivating visual literacy

Scholars in communication studies offer insightful analyses drawing upon their expertise as well as utilising the work of scholars outside of their field. The examples are many, but two stand out as especially useful for our purposes – one a book-length work and the other an essay in a recently published handbook of rhetorical studies. These works can help us acquire a higher level of visual literacy and see how to likewise assist our students' development.

Icons and ideology

In *No Caption Needed*, published in 2007 by the University of Chicago Press, Robert Hariman and John Louis Lucaites help us understand the rhetorical dimension of photographs and their potential power. They note that 'like all public address' photographs 'make some beliefs and actions more intelligible, probable, and appealing, and others less so' (p. 8).

The authors begin with a 'close reading of the patterns of visual display and audience identification in the image itself.' They then trace and examine the 'official, vernacular, and commercial appropriations' of the image. This approach allows the authors to expose the image's 'distinctive forms of appeal' and 'role in public culture' (p. 29). They consider and interpret each photograph in terms of aesthetic familiarity, civic performance, semiotic transcriptions, emotional scenarios, and contradictions and crises. These dimensions provide – in full or in part – an analytical framework we can take into the classroom, and the authors illuminate how to do so in a series of chapters where they apply their approach to a specific iconic photograph.

In one chapter, for example, the authors examine a widely recognised and remembered photo taken during nationwide protests against the Vietnam War, and more specifically against President Nixon's decision to invade Cambodia. When national guardsman opened fire on protestors at Kent State University on 4 May 1970, killing four and wounding nine, newspaper photographer John Filo (then a senior at Kent State) was on the scene, camera in hand. Filo took a picture of a young woman kneeling by one of the victims shot dead by the guardsman. Hariman and Lucaites describe her as 'screaming in pain, incomprehension, and outrage at those who ... shot the ... student' (p. 139). The photograph was widely reproduced, including the high honor of the *New York Times*' front page, above the fold. Filo won a Pulitzer prize for his photo.

The authors note how the photograph functioned, ultimately, as a clarion call for peace. They explain how male figures in the photograph stand 'alert, calculative, focused on the enemy.' The kneeling woman, in contrast, 'is breaking the political standoff [between the National Guardsmen and the protestors] by crying out (as mothers cry out for peace).' The peace desired is one that 'would end both war and demonstrations' (p. 142).

The authors note that in American culture public displays of emotion typically prompt concern. 'When public life appears emotional,' they write, 'it is assumed to be imperiled: either the politician is exhibiting a loss of the self-control essential for responsible administration of the state, or the public audience is succumbing to those irrational impulses that can lead to demonstrations, riots, and the breakdown of the social order' (p. 137). The photograph operates within these parameters. The authors hold that the girl becomes a civic model because she is capable of spontaneous, profound, authentic grief and rage on behalf of a fellow citizen and at the same time 'the fact that the girl is kneeling rather than in an upright and more belligerent stance suggest that her outcry is occurring within an established order of public representation' (pp. 145–146).

To sum up, they note that 'citizenship itself has to be exercised if it is to be secure, and that exercise will take the form of an emotional demand that the state stop waging war against its own people.' But, 'on the other hand,' they observe, 'the demand must occur within a context of self-restraint; one breakdown in public order cannot be repaired by another' (p. 147).

The explication of their approach, coupled with various instances of its application across time, makes Hariman and Lucaites' book an excellent resource for scholars and educators, alike. We can gain fresh insights from their work to enhance our own critical abilities as well as help us sharpen those of our students. Another work worthy of our attention is an essay by Cara Finnegan, who has long pursued a research program in the area of visual communication. Her essay is titled 'Studying Visual Modes of Public Address: Lewis Hine's Progressive-Era Child Labor Rhetoric' and it appears in *The Handbook of Rhetoric and Public Address*, published in 2010 by Wiley-Blackwell.

Finnegan's work: recognising visual discourses

Finnegan (2010) presents a 'critical perspective on the study of visual modes of public address,' offering 'not a complete guide to visual methodologies' but 'starting points for those who wish their explorations of public address to include visual discourses.' These starting points consist of 'five approaches to analyzing visual images in terms of their production, com-position, reproduction, circulation, and reception.' She notes that 'together, these constitute a "perspective" ... a *way of seeing* the role of visual images in public culture and the assumption that visual modes of public address shape and frame our experience of public life' (p. 251).

Her assumption is well warranted. She observes, quite correctly, that 'the history of American public address is very much a visual as well as a textual/oratorical history' (p. 251). Various social movements have been propelled forward by visual images, from the civil rights movement in the 1960s to contemporary concerns over global warming.

Finnegan examines an instance of visual discourse from early twen-tieth-century America to support her observation. Prior to analysing the visual artifact as a component within a rhetorical campaign, Finnegan explains, in detail, each of the five approaches: production, composition, reproduction, circulation, and reception. *Production* considers *where* an image came from and *why they appear* where they do. It attends to the technology that was available and used, the genre to which it would belong (e.g. photojournalism, advertising), and the agent or agency that created the visual content in terms of what was typical of their work, what their motives might be, and what forces might impact their production (p. 253).

Composition pertains to using 'specific analytical tools' that 'enable the critic to get at both content and form, which work together to construct potential meanings in a work' (pp. 253–254). Content is 'what the image shows or depicts' and to discern content may require 'additional research' as 'social, cultural, and historical knowledge often comes into play' (p. 254). Finnegan explains that considerations of content also 'may involve exploring how the gaze is activated'. For example, 'images in which the gaze is directed at the viewer ... create "a visual form of direct address" ... [as in the] classic example ... [of] the Uncle Sam recruiting poster, "I Want YOU"' (p. 254).

Formal characteristics include such compositional elements as 'color, light, and spatial organisation'. Finnegan notes that much can be suggested with colour as well as light, as well as with the arrangement of the vari-ous elements within an image, such as how they appear in relation to one another. Angles can also impact meaning. Horizontal angles, for example, can be used to 'activate various senses of involvement between the viewer and the subject of the image' and vertical angles can 'suggest power differences' (p. 255).

Reproduction is concerned with an image's place among other discourse – which can include 'other images as well as written texts, headlines, or captions' – as well as their role within a particular message of which they are a part (p. 256). This aspect of the analysis should also take into account the degree to which the visual content (and its use) was usual or unusual for its time as well as where a viewer would have encountered the image.

Considerations of *circulation* entail tracking the 'movement of discourse' so to 'say something about audiences' potential exposure to an image.' Circulation also involves noting where an image appeared true to its original form and where it appeared in modified form and, thus, was appropriated to another rhetor's *ends* (p. 258).

Reception involves an assessment of audiences' 'responses to a work' (p. 258). To calculate effect(s), Finnegan notes that we 'typically study response empirically, intertextually, or using some combination of these.' For the former we can rely on such sources as 'newspaper or magazine articles, letters to the editor, critical reviews, or material located in letters or diaries.' Intertextual material that a critic can consult consists of 'how audiences interpret or remake the work for their own rhetorical purposes' (p. 259). For example, in America images of the iconic, on-screen cowboy John Wayne (who died in 1979) are used to remind us that we are tough and resourceful and must be ready and willing to fight evil doers, even when the odds are against us.

Finnegan follows her elaboration of the five approaches with a demonstration of how they apply, examining the visual rhetoric of child labor reform during America's Progressive era. Her study of Lewis Hine's photography and its accompanying written text led her to conclude that 'Hine's photographic-text assemblage, titled *Making Human Junk*, served not as a stand-alone visual argument but as a summary statement punctuating broader arguments about child labor, national health, and the value of children and childhood' (p. 252). To substantiate her thesis, she 'mobilises some of the tools' she has described to 'illustrate how some of the approaches may be combined in a single case study.' Specifically, she utilises 'elements of composition, production, and a single reproduction of the Hine's image' (pp. 259–260).

These few elements, used in combination, allow Finnegan to make her case convincingly. Compositional factors, such as the gazes of the children who are pictured, make a *demand* on the viewer (p. 254). The pictures are accompanied by short bursts of text clarifying the children's plight. Composed in this manner, the observer is all but supplied an answer for the rhetorical question appearing at the bottom of the poster, 'Shall industry be allowed to put this cost on society?'

Knowing other of Hine's work regarding the issue of child labour, as well as others' discourse on the subject, also illuminates the poster's 'particular rhetorical force'. Understanding these aspects of reproduction, Finnegan is able to explain how the artifact 'summarised the anti-child labor position in ways that connected it to broader arguments linking the health of the child to the health of the nation' (p. 262). Some of those connections were especially impressive. One spokesperson espousing a similar view was President Theodore Roosevelt. He did so in a 1911 speech titled *The Conservation of Childhood*, four years prior to Hine's *Making Human Junk*. Knowing how Hine's discourse fit with other discourse of its day allows us to see that he tapped into the rhetorical force known as the *Bully Pulpit* – a phrase coined by President Roosevelt to characterise the potential power of the office of president.

Through Finnegan's work we can see how Hine also had a pulpit of his own. The poster's reproduction and circulation further illuminate its potential power. Finnegan explores the widespread availability of the poster, especially in downsized form in booklets at the 1915 World's Fair as well as in the February issue of *Child Labor Bulletin*. She discusses placement within those pages. In the section prior to the reprinted poster, Hine had offered statistical evidence for his claims and cited numerous reputable sources such as 'the Federal Bureau of Labor, state legislative initiatives ... and newspapers from around the country.' He also had provided other 'visual ... evidence' (p. 263). This material helped prepare the reader for the poster that followed. The images and captions provided in the poster brought all together in abbreviated form, providing a summary of sorts.

The rhetorical question prompted deeper reflection upon what should be done and why.

Tracing reproduction and circulation reveals further, that Hine 'wrote captions like an investigative reporter', and he 'was not simply an illustration photographer who provided photographs to editors and writers to use as they wished; he was an active participant in shaping the format in which his photographs were reproduced' (p. 262). Knowing these details allows Finnegan to observe that visual modes of public address have been present in America throughout its history and are not, as some scholars have suggested, relatively insignificant until contemporary times (p. 251).

Finnegan's approach obviously has much merit, as does that of Hariman and Lucaites. As Finnegan notes, what she offers are 'starting points', acknowledging that she does not have a comprehensive method or the last say on the matter. Hariman and Lucaites (2007) have suggested similarly that their analytical framework is not 'the last word' (p. 19), and they note further that they 'are not valorising icons in order to minimize the use of less popular images' (p. 28). Images do not have to become icons to influence, especially in this age of new media where virtually any visual-verbal message can *go viral*.

An approach-in-progress: the case of copycat shooters in our midst

Chances are, you have seen the images of young men with guns and the panic they have stirred, the carnage left in their wake, and the ceremonies convened for those who are left to somehow carry on. It is an all-too-common scenario. The case of senseless shootings as reported in the news makes for an especially provocative study. When we apply what we know from rhetorical studies coupled with what we can apply from other fields, we can see how the shootings 'make sense' to the perpetrators. We can also detect how news agencies can become complicit in the acts of violence that they report; what they report today can influence events they will report on tomorrow. Visual literacy helps us understand the connection.

The work of scholars from communication studies and other fields can assist our critique. Hariman and Lucaites' discussion of *identification* and *emotional/motivational impact* can yield good insights. Their approach can be made crisper when we supplement it with other works from their field and from psychology, sociology, and journalism. Finnegan's concepts of *production, composition, circulation,* and *reproduction* are also quite applicable and revealing. Armed with these and our own critical abilities, much can be discovered about the perpetrators of violence and the role played by those who *report* it.

Identification as influence

One of the many forms of rhetoric is *identification*. As an element of rhetoric, it occurs when people allow perceived similarities between themselves and someone else to influence their opinion or affect their actions (Woodward, 2003; Harte, 1977). Identification helps explain the power of verbal and visual discourse. As Hariman and Lucaites (2007) observe, such discourse can 'activate strong emotional identification or response' (p. 27). Identification can have a positive effect, such as building community. For example, during World War II, a workplace poster of Rosie the Riveter was an effective means of positive identification. The image of this beautiful and strong woman, flexing her bicep, persuaded women to roll up their sleeves and work harder than ever to keep things moving on the home front while most men were away fighting (Kimble & Olsen, 2006). This constitutive function is something Hariman and Lucaites have noted, observing that 'photojournalism provides resources for thought and feeling that are necessary for constituting people as citizens and motivating identification with and participation in specific forms of collective life' (p. 13).

Identification does not always yield such laudable outcomes. One instance in which identification can have a negative effect is copycat shootings. Not long ago, Littleton, Colorado and Conyers, Georgia were merely two peaceful, unassuming towns. Things changed in 1999 when both towns gained widespread attention due to deadly school shootings (Sullivan & Guerette, 2003). When two students in Littleton, Colorado went on a shooting rampage in their high school, killing thirteen and wounding another twenty-four, television crews arrived on the scene to capture images of students fleeing as gunfire still erupted inside the school during the forty-nine-minute ordeal. The crews from Denver's television, radio, and newspaper media soon had company. Reporters from near and far, this ilk and that, raced to the scene, producing a full-blown media frenzy that lasted for over a week (Shepherd, n.d.; Toppo, 2009).

The incident at Heritage High School in Georgia, occurring on the one-month anniversary of Columbine, prompted onlookers to wonder if it were mere coincidence or something more. It was, indeed, something more. The Conyers shooter told authorities that the media coverage of Columbine provided him with the idea. The extensive coverage, including detailed information about the shooters, allowed Thomas Solomon, Jr. to identify with the two shooters and begin planning his own 'massacre'.

When the media covered the shooting in Littleton on Tuesday, 20 April 1999, they did more than simply inform the public of what had happened; they covered the story to the extreme (see Maguire, Weatherby, & Mathers, 2002). They provided detailed information about the shooting, repeatedly broadcasting the clips of high school students running frantically from the building, a bloodied student dropping headfirst from a second-floor window into the outstretched arms of an officer standing atop an ambulance, and live interviews with students who had just escaped. Tears poured down the face of one girl in a live report as she recalled how one of the shooters had 'put the gun in my face and started laughing' as she begged him not to shoot her. He told her 'it was all because people were mean to him last year' (90ttoo b, 2010).

The reports grew more and more elaborate. Television and print media soon supplied viewers with grainy images of the perpetrators taken by school surveillance cameras. In those images, the attackers strolled calmly, guns in hand, making their way through the school as they carried out their plan. These images and others appeared along with detailed information about the two shooters' and their lives, including photographs of the two, which they aired simultaneously, positioned side-by-side. At one point, one network glorified the two with a background that resembled a wild-west, wanted poster. Videos taken by the two as they planned their 'mission' also found their way on air. One video featured an angry rant and another provided footage of them shooting guns in the woods. In short, the coverage was nothing short of spectacular, a spectacle to behold.

All of this information, visual and verbal, hit the airwaves and newsstands for everyone to see – and everyone did see, including Solomon. The coverage allowed Solomon to see the similarities between himself and the Littleton shooters. All three were white males. All three had been made to feel second-rate by their classmates at school. And all three held grudges against those who had put them down (Hemenway, 2002).

Critics point to identification as playing a key role in motivating Solomon. Mercer L. Sullivan and Rob T. Guerette, highly regarded experts on crime, conclude that when Solomon recognised these similarities and witnessed how the Littleton shooters took care of their problems he felt justified in taking care of his problems the same way. He had commented to classmates that he wished the shooting had happened at their school and that he understood the shooters' desire to bring guns to school and open fire. He admired the Littleton shooters so much that he even chose the one-month anniversary of their shooting (and deaths by suicide) as the date for his own reenactment. The only obvious difference in the shootings was that the Littleton shooters committed suicide to complete their mission. Solomon lived to go to trial because he was unable to go through with his own suicide and ultimately surrendered (Sullivan & Guerette, 2003).

These are not the only two school shootings to have occurred in the United States. Every time a school shooting occurs and the media proceeds to cover it in detail, someone out there is given the opportunity to identify with the shooter(s) and plan his own means of similar retaliation against classmates who have made him feel inferior and/or plan an act of terrorism grand enough that the world will see and remember (Cullen, 2004; Toppo, 2009). There is no such thing as bad attention when one craves attention.

Recognition as motivation

Some copycats are obviously turned on by the notoriety. Such was the case with the Virginia Tech shooter. He fit the profile of 'woe is me' and 'REVENGE!' as well as 'wanting attention'. More than anything, it seems, he wanted revenge of legendary proportion, and grabbing media attention was just the ticket. To ensure he would get noticed, he mailed his video to *NBC News*. He knew they would find the content irresistible and air it for all to see. As in the case of Columbine's attackers, his rant would be broadcast as well as pictures of him posing with his guns and with a hammer. He would live on with his image and story online, in magazines, and in books, too. Various media would continue to reproduce and circulate the images he, himself, had provided. His fame and legacy would be, to some extent, autobiographical.

Similar motivations apparently animated the gunman who shot US Representative Gabrielle Giffords in early 2011. Giffords had convened an informal public forum on 28 January at a Tucson, Arizona supermarket. In the aftermath of the shooting, investigators found handwritten notes the gunman had left, telling of how he had 'planned' his 'assassination' (Johnson, Gillum, & Welch, 2011). The shooter, Jared Lee Loughner, was subdued by three fellow citizens who were able to wrestle him to the ground and eventually disarm him (Hopper, Dolak, & Sher, 2011). In his mug shot, he smiles proudly. In his court room appearances he likewise beams. And when asked to state his name for the record, he spoke up for all to hear, signalling no remorse, only great self-satisfaction (Kieffer, 2011).

Production, composition, circulation, and reproduction

Yes, we have seen 'the pictures'. We have experienced those taken by reporters and cell phone video by those unfortunate enough to be on the scene. We have seen audiovisuals supplied by the perpetrators themselves. And we have seen the dramatic black and white video from surveillance cameras. When it comes to *production*, the sources are many, and the information is authentic and genuine, supplied to us in all its honesty by news sources we trust to tell us the facts. We experience the content during live broadcast, repeat broadcasts, and afterwards, on-demand as they live on to tell the story. They live on in perpetuity on online sources like YouTube. *Circulation* is immediate and *reproduction* never-ending.

Images like these can play a significant role in motivating those similarly inclined. It may very well be that Hariman and Lucaites (2007) are correct when they posit that 'social actors are more and more likely to be thinking, feeling, and acting on the basis of what they have seen rather than only heard or read' (p. 5). It may be that visuals are especially powerful. Finnegan's notations regarding *composition* help explain why. In the videos the perpetrators recorded they fix their gaze upon the viewer, directly addressing whoever is watching (p. 254). Such is the case with Columbine's Eric Harris who looms in near the camera for an 'in-your-face' effect. His positioning of himself, looking down into the camera, also imparts that he is looking down upon the viewer. The angle is one that conveys his superiority. The Virginia Tech shooter, Seung-Hui Cho, likewise directs his gaze upon his viewer while delivering his 'manifesto'. In another video, recorded inside an automobile, he is calmer and sometimes looks away from the camera as if to punctuate his dislike for us, his viewers. In these moments, his refusal to look at us is as if to say we disgust him; we are unworthy of his eyes. He stares us down as he would gun us down, when posing with a gun levelled directly at the viewer.

While the average viewer may find the behaviour and the gaze disturbing, those similarly inclined may find it bold and take some degree of inspiration from it. The visual content may 'speak to them' in ways it does not to us. Whether it is television reports, newspaper photos of the perpetrators, or the videos the perpetrators have themselves made, the images can be powerfully intimate. As Hariman and Lucaites (2007) observe, 'photojournalism ... because of its conventional (and somewhat unavoidable) focus on individuals in tightly framed scenes on the scale of a family photo album ... reproduces a preoccupation with personal experience and the self-interested pursuit of happiness.' They explain further that:

'Any particular photo equips the viewer to act as a citizen, or expand one's conception of citizenship, or otherwise redefine one's relationship to the political community' (p. 18). The angry diatribes recorded on video by Columbine's Harris, Virginia Tech's Cho, and Arizona's Loughner may not make sense to us, but they may make some sense to others, who like themselves, are angry at society for whatever reason. Furthermore, these visual-verbal displays can activate emotional response (see Friedman et al., 2010). Again we can turn to Hariman and Lucaites who observe that 'the photograph's focus on bodily expression not only displays emotions but also places the viewer in an affective relationship with the people in the picture' (pp. 35–36). That affective relationship, as we have noted above, is one of *identification*.

All the world's a stage: contemplating labels and narratives

What we know about *labelling* can also enhance our visual literacy, helping us better understand how visual and verbal content work in tandem to influence. Images are powerful, and so is the language we choose to suggest meaning for an image. In the early days of Columbine, journalists heralded what happened as a 'massacre' and its perpetrators as the 'Trenchcoat Mafia'. The shooter in Arizona received the recognition he desired, being referred to by reporters as an 'assassin'. He had used that word to describe who he would be, and he achieved his goal. Language plays a central role in establishing one's identity. How we label ourselves and our actions influences our behaviour. Loughner's ambition came down to one word.

The power of labelling has been recognised widely – including in the social commentary of theatre. Playwright Stephen Sondheim, for instance, has commented on the power of labels and their role in establishing our identity. In his musical, *Assassins*, there is an exchange near the end of the play between John Wilkes Booth (who shot President Lincoln) and Lee Harvey Oswald (who was accused of shooting President Kennedy).

BOOTH: Lee, when you kill a president, it isn't murder. Murder is a tawdry little crime; it's born of greed, or lust, or liquor. Adulterers and shopkeepers get murdered. But when a president gets killed, when Julius Caesar got killed – he was assassinated. And the man who did it ...

OSWALD: Brutus.

BOOTH: Ah! You know his name. Brutus assassinated Caesar – what? – two thousand years ago, and here's a high school drop-out with a dollar twenty-five an hour job in Dallas, Texas, who knows who he was. And they say fame is fleeting ...

When we label ourselves, we envision who we are – the role we are playing in the theatre of life. We envision a storyline for the character we have assumed. To understand the power of whom we cast ourselves to be and in what storyline, we can turn to what scholars refer to as *narrative theory*. The stories we encounter, such as those we are told as we are growing up and those that we encounter in books and on the news, 'remind us of who we are and who we have been and who we may become' (McClure, 2009, p. 190). They can address us as a people and as an individual – and as we have discussed already, visual content may be especially intimate and affective, perfect for appealing to us on an individual level.

Recent work in narrative theory helps us understand what potential perpetrators of violence may gain from the stories of violence they encounter in the media (and in preserved form in books, newsmagazines, and online). What they glean may make sense to them in ways that escape our sensibilities, such as the rants made against society, the government, or a particular public figure. Even if the verbalised content does not strike a cord rationally, it might emotionally (Friedman et al., 2010). And it may simply be the images of the perpetrator's actions, with no words needed, that engender identification. Whatever the case, be it one or all of these, the impressionable person is primed to *go off* and by doing so, fits in with the infamous few with whom they identify; they become part of that *club* (McClure, 2009).

Conclusion

In light of what we know from Communication Studies, Psychology, and other fields, we can better critique media reports; we can improve our visual literacy and that of our students. We can build a better understanding of visual literacy if we consider it as part of information literacy and view it in light of the rhetorical tradition, both of which emphasise accountability. Our enhanced understanding of visual literacy allows us to question whether the media have been responsible in their reporting of verbal and visual information. They know how to be effective. The old adage, *if it bleeds it leads* would seem to be a guiding principle, sure to generate interest and shore up profits. Such gains come at a high cost, though – more lives, more victims, more suffering.

Now more than ever, students need to develop information literacy, including visual literacy. If we are to equip students for the media rich world in which we reside, we will have to help them develop their abilities as effective producers and consumers of both images and words. To do so requires an interdisciplinary approach. The field of communication studies, especially rhetorical studies, helps us hone our critical understanding and skills as responsible producers and consumers of visual and verbal content. Other fields can likewise help us acquire visual literacy – psychology, sociology, and journalism as well as those who study the technical aspects of video and photography and graphic design. Old and new media, alike, are important because both are utilised. Informed in this manner, we can further understand the various implications of the discourse we experience, in all its complexity – verbal and visual.

I have illuminated some of what is available to help us achieve this pedagogical objective and the importance of doing so. Like Finnegan, what we seek is *perspective*. It is what we want students to develop. We aim not to tell them *what* to think but help them learn *how* to think. All we have, after all, are 'starting points', but thanks to her and others we have good places to start. We have the insights of scholars from across the disciplines to illuminate what people need to do as teachers, citizens, and reporters.

These insights can inform our work as professors and the work we would have our students do.

At the same time, several other provocative questions exist, suitable for probing/ investigation by students and scholars alike. For example, are males more stimulated by such imagery? Some studies suggest so (see Verona & Curtin, 2006). Might we apply what we learn more broadly, such as with how we cover acts of terrorism, gang activity, or any other news making events by those who seek glory through acts of violence? What influence might we, the viewing public, have for the content reported and how it is reported?

These are a few of the many questions that remain – important questions. Visual educational resources can help us pose the questions and to do so true to their form – rich and provocative! Viewed and discussed in the classroom, they can yield yet more questions and insights, beyond those we introduce, stimulating perhaps even the most apathetic of students, ones who have previously seemed uninterested (see Seglem & Witte, 2009). Such content can prompt our students to think more deeply and pursue more rigorously. As they do so they can sharpen their visual literacy and contribute to our own.

References

American Library Association, *Information literacy competency standards for higher education* (Chicago, IL: The Association of College & Research Libraries, 2000).

Arum, R. & Roksa, J., *Academically adrift: Limited learning on college campuses* (Chicago, IL: University of Chicago Press, 2011).

Chanlin, L., 'The effects of verbal elaboration on student learning.' *International Journal of Instructional Media* 24 (1997), 333–339.

Chung, S., 'Media/visual literacy art education: Cigarette ad deconstruction.' *Art Education* 58/3 (2005), 19–24.

Cullen, D., 'The depressive and the psychopath: At last we know why the Columbine killers did it'. *Slate*, 20 April 2004. Retrieved 22 March 2011 from <http://www.slate.com/id/2099203/>

Edell, J. & Staelin, R., 'The information processing of pictures in print advertisements.' *Journal of Consumer Research* 10 (1983), 45–61.

Felton, P., 'Visual literacy.' *Change* 60 (2008), 60–63.

Finnegan, C., 'Studying visual modes of public address: Lewis Hine's Progressive-Era child labor rhetoric' in S. Parry Giles & M. Hogan, eds, *The handbook of rhetoric and public address* (Oxford, UK: Wiley-Blackwell 2010), 250–270.

Friedman, R., Deci, E., Elliot, A., Moller, A., & Aarts, H., 'Motivational synchronicity: Priming motivational orientations with observations of others' behaviors'. *Motiv Emot* 34 (2010), 34–38.

Goin, P., 'Visual literacy.' *Geographical Review* 91/½ (2001), 363–369.

Graber, D., 'Say it with pictures'. *Annals of the American Academy of Political and Social Science* 546 (1996), 85–96.

Hariman, R. & Lucaites, J., *No caption needed: Iconic photographs, public culture, and liberal democracy* (Chicago, IL: The University of Chicago Press, 2007).

Harte, T., 'The concept of identification in the rhetorical theories of Kenneth Burke and Eric Hoffer.' *Communicator* 7 (1977), 64–69.

Hemenway, D., 'Lethal violence in the schools.' *Journal of Health, Politics, Policy, and Law* 27 (2002), 267–272.

Hockley, W., 'The picture superiority effect in associative recognition'. *Memory & Cognition* 36 (2008), 1351–1359.

Hodes, C., 'Processing visual information: Implications of the dual code theory.' *Journal of Instructional Psychology* (1994), 21, 36–43.

Hoffmann, G., 'Visual literacy needed in the 21st century'. *ETC* 57/2 (2000), 219–222.

Hopper, J., Dolak, K., & Sher, L., 'Heroes of Tucson shooting: Something had to be done.' *ABC News.* Retrieved 22 March 2011 from <http://abcnews.go.com/US/heroes-rep-gabrielle-giffords-shooting-tucson-arizona-subdued/story?id=12580345>

Johnson, K., Gillum, J., & Welch, W., 'Rep. Giffords still critical after deadly shooting spree.' *USA Today.* Retrieved 22 March 2011 from <http://www.usatoday.com/news/washington/2011-01-08-gifford-shooting_N.htm>

Kieffer, M., 'Suspect in Tucson shooting pleads not guilty.' *The Arizona Republic.* Retrieved 22 March 2011 from <http://www.usatoday.com/news/nation/2011-03-09-loughner-plea-tucson_N.htm>

Kimble, J. & Olsen, L., 'Visual rhetoric representing Rosie the Riveter: Myth and misconception in J. Howard Miller's We Can Do It! poster'. *Rhetoric & Public Affairs* 9/4 (2006), 533–569.

Maguire, B., Weatherby, G., & Mathers, R., 'Network news coverage of school shootings.' *The Social Science Journal* 39 (2002), 465–470.

McClure, K., 'Resurrecting the Narrative Paradigm: Identification and the case of Young Earth Creationism'. *Rhetoric Society Quarterly* 39 (2009), 189–211.

Messaris, P., *Visual literacy: Image, mind, and reality* (Boulder, CO: Westview Press, 1994).

Pettersson, R., 'Visual literacy and message design.' *Tech Trends* 53/2 (2009), 38–40.

Rakes, G., 'Teaching visual literacy in a multimedia age.' *Tech Trends* 43/4 (1999), 14–18.

Rezabek, L., 'Why visual literacy: consciousness and convention.' *Tech Trends* 49/3 (2005), 19–20.

RogueTribeMediaWorks, 'Columbine High School – I Will Remember You.' Retrieved 22 March 2011 from <http://www.youtube.com/watch? v=_fHg8cQd4wQ& feature=related>

Seglem, R. & Witte, S., 'You gotta see it to believe it: Teaching visual literacy in the English classroom.' *Journal of Adolescent & Adult Literacy* 53/3 (2009), 216–226.

Shah, P. & Hoeffner, J., 'Review of graph comprehension research: Implications for instruction.' *Educational Psychology Review* 14 (2002), 47–51.

Shepherd, A., 'The Columbine shooting, live television coverage.' Retrieved 22 March 2011 from <http://www.columbia.edu/itc/journalism/j6075/edit/ readings/ columbine.html>

Sosa, T., 'Visual literacy: The missing piece of your technology integration course.' *Tech Trends* 53/2 (2009), 55–58.

Stenberg, G., 'Conceptual and perceptual factors in the picture superiority effect.' *European Journal of Cognitive Psychology* 18 (2006), 813–847.

Sullivan, M. & Guerette, R., *Deadly lessons: Understanding lethal school violence* (Washington, DC: National Academies Press 2003).

Toppo, G., '10 years later, the real story behind Columbine.' *USA Today*, 4 April 2009. Retrieved 22 March 2011 from <http://www.usatoday.com/news/nation/200904-13-columbine-myths_N.htm>

Verona, E. & Curtin, J., 'Gender differences in the negative affective priming of affective behavior.' *Emotion 6* (2006), 115–124.

Woodward, G., *The idea of identification* (Albany, NY: State University of New York Press, 2003).

90ottooa, 'Columbine shooting: The final report 1/5.' Retrieved 9 July 2010 from <http://www.youtube.com/watch?v=oVh_Cq7h_gI>

90ottoob, 'Columbine shooting: The final report 2/5.' Retrieved 9 July 2010 from <http://www.youtube.com/watch?v=5R8ouTxQg6c&NR=1>

MARGARET FARREN AND YVONNE CROTTY

8 Leadership in ICT in Education: Our Story at Dublin City University

This paper reports on the development of information and communications technology (ICT) in education at Dublin City University (DCU) in the context of evolving government policy in promoting ICT in education over the past two decades. It uses this historical account to trace the evolution at DCU of a distinctive approach to ICT in education and training at Masters degree level. This approach can be characterised as a shift from imparting knowledge about computing technology and uses to the practical examination and development of innovative approaches to ICT in the educational process; and reflecting on the implications of these creative approaches for professional development in a range of workplace contexts.

Irish Government policies in ICT in education

In the 1990s the Irish Government gave priority to extending and improving upon the number and quality of graduates who could take up paid employment in the emerging computing industry in Ireland. This led to a substantial increase in the number of places on computing courses at third-level education. The same concern with catering for the computing industry's recruitment needs, but over a longer timescale, led to the establishment of the National Centre for Technology in Education (NCTE) in the late 1990s to foster the application of ICT at primary and post-primary levels. Major advances have taken place in the use of computers at both primary and post-primary levels. The NCTE played a role in these developments, and in helping plan further major investments.

The role of the private sector

In 1980 Computer Studies was introduced as an optional module in Leaving Certificate mathematics. Later in 1985, a Computer Studies course was established at Junior Certificate level (NCCA, 2004) as a non exam based subject. In 1995, the Irish Government's White Paper, 'Charting our Education Future', concerned with educational policy at large, failed to recognise fully the importance and the implications of introducing Computing as a subject into post-primary education. Its only reference to Computing at post-primary level was the declared ambition to achieve competence and understanding in practical skills, including computer literacy and information technology in the junior cycle. This weak reference to the educational dimensions of an industry that was rapidly growing and exercising a profound influence on the development of the country's economy caused concern to various bodies.

Due to the efforts of Professor Michael Ryan of the School of Computer Applications at DCU, several positive developments emerged. For example, among those who believed decisive new steps should be taken was Mr Donal Daly, of the Irish software company Expert Edge. He had seen the pioneer Tech Corps in operation in Massachusetts, USA, and its effects on the school system there. This initiative involved companies helping their local schools by providing computing expertise on a part-time basis, and in some cases providing the computers as well. He brought the idea back to the Irish industry body, the Irish Software Association (ISA), who received it positively and drafted a proposal for an 'Irish Tech Corps' (ITC).

Subsequent to this exchange of views, Mr Paddy Moore, Chairman of the ISA, discussed with DCU the possible involvement of DCU's School of Computer Applications with the 'Tech Corps' scheme and found there was an obvious fit with DCU's own planned intentions. A joint proposal for an 'Irish Tech Corps' (ITC) was drafted, agreed by the School and the ISA, and submitted to funding agencies and the Department of Education in 1996. The Department of Education and Science (DES) was supportive of the proposal but wished to exclude schools that were deemed by the initiators of the scheme to be unable to benefit from the initiative. It was decided to proceed on the basis of non-Exchequer funding only. Over the following three years, the ITC set up networks of sixteen computers in each of forty-six schools, roughly half of them primary, half post-primary. The computers were typically three years old and transferred from organisations that were replacing equipment. Technical, pedagogic, and administrative support was provided. There was no direct cost to the State.

By the end of the pilot project, forty-six schools had been equipped with computer networks and selected software packages. An internet link was provided by Telecom Éireann (TE). The systems were set up in such a way that minimal technical support was required. In general, the configurations worked well. A set of workshops on the use of the systems was devised and these were well attended. Overall, the systems had a greater impact at primary level than at post-primary. A key idea from the ITC was teachers from different schools meeting in networks to share experiences. It became clear that curriculum pressures at post-primary level and the lack of computer-based resources for many subjects limited the use of the facility, whereas a wealth of material was available at the primary level and was used enthusiastically. In parallel to the ITC was the Information Age Towns/Schools Project (1997) which was funded by TE and included installing an internet access point and computers in each school and providing computers into homes and providing training to parents in designated Information Age towns: Ennis, Kilkenny, Killarney and Castlebar.

Government's decisive shift toward promotion of computer education

Meanwhile, Government policy was swinging strongly in favour of more decisive approaches to the promotion of the ICT in schools. In 1997, the Minister for Education and Science, Mícheál Martin, TD, launched the Schools IT 2000. This initiative was to be implemented by the NCTE which was established in early 1998. It represented a bold initiative by the Irish government to promote ICT in schools in Ireland. It highlighted the need for more teacher training, more funding for computers, more technical support, and encouragement to make use of ICT in education (DES, 1997). The main objective was to ensure that all pupils should have the opportunity to achieve computer literacy and to equip themselves for participation in the information society, while teachers were to be supported toward the development and renewal of their professional skills, so as to enable them to utilise ICTs as part of the learning environment. It acknowledged that a special effort by Government was needed to educate teachers in making use of ICT in their day-to-day teaching. A key aspect of the Schools IT 2000 was the Schools Integration Project (SIP). It involved pilot projects in a number of 'lead' schools in Ireland working in partnership with education centres, businesses, industry, third-level institutions and the community to develop and share 'best practice' in the use and integration of ICT in teaching and learning. Some of the largest funding in the State's history to that date was for SIP. The project details can be accessed at <http://www.sip.ie>.

The role of technology in teaching and learning was highlighted again in another Irish Government policy document. The 'Blueprint for the Future of ICT in Education' (DES, 2001) set out a three year strategic action plan for ICT in primary and post-primary schools. It outlined the main thrust of DES's ICT strategy that included expanding ICT capital provision for schools, increasing access to and use of internet technologies, further integrating ICT into the school curricula, and improving the professional development of teachers.

The Irish Government's policy for the development of ICT in education was further elaborated in the 'Statement of Strategy 2005–2007' (DES, 2004) document, which referred to the need for education to support a knowledge- and innovation-based society and lifelong learning. The emphasis on computer literacy skills is clear in the following statement: 'we encourage pupils to achieve computer literacy and acquire the necessary skills for participation in the Information Society' (2004, p. 36). There was also reference to key challenges in the changing teaching environment. These included:

- the changing face of delivery of education, including changes in the practice and profession of teaching to reflect today's information age.
- the role of the teacher: less focused on the provision of knowledge and more concerned with the teaching of learning skills.
- the changing environment requiring ongoing training, support and development.

(DES, 2004, p. 14)

The initial drive of ICT policy was focused on equipping schools and the metric used was lowering the pupil to computer ratio. The second and third policy became more focused on usage of equipment.

The drive towards uses of ICT in schools has come not only from Government policies and reports, but also from public agencies and businesses, such as the Higher Education Authority (HEA) and Discover Science. Industry's interest in promoting computer education was a powerful influence. ICT Ireland is the representative lobby group for the knowledge sector within IBEC (Irish Business Employers Confederation). Dr Kevin Marshall, Academic Programme Manager of Microsoft Ireland and the chairman of the ICT Ireland group, stated that the aim is to ensure that 'we have a coherent, costed and forward thinking ICT policy for schools, in order that we can meet the challenges of the knowledge economy' (Marshall, cited in O'Brien, 2006).

The views of the National Council for Curriculum Assessment (NCCA) are particularly relevant to the mainstreaming of developing interest in the effective use of ICT in schools. The revision of the junior cycle curriculum, and later the senior cycle and primary curricula, began with the formation of the NCCA in 1987. The revised primary school guidelines were issued in 1999 without any reference to ICT. However, a later supporting document, 'Information and Communications Technology (ICT) in the Primary School Curriculum', was developed by the NCCA and launched by the Department of Education and Science (DES) in 2004. Over the past decade the NCCA has published reports and consultative documents in the area of ICT in schools. The NCCA commissioned a team from the University of Limerick to explore 'the possible form, content and perceived impact of the introduction of a new computer-based subject to the Leaving Certificate (established)' (2004, p 6). This report, 'Computers and Curriculum: Difficulties and Dichotomies' (2004), brought to a close the idea of Computing as a Leaving Certificate subject and it was left as an optional subject for Transition Year and the Leaving Certificate Vocational Programme. Other reports included: 'Curriculum Assessment and ICT in the Irish Context: A Discussion paper' (2004) and the ICT Framework, 'A Structured Approach to ICT in Curriculum and Assessment Revised Framework' (2007). The aim of the ICT Framework was to realise the integration of ICT across the curriculum. It is clear that the NCCA recognised the need for teachers to be knowledgeable about how ICT could be used in appropriate ways in teaching and learning, and they describe the teacher as 'a gatekeeper of his/her students' classroom learning – including learning with ICT' (NCCA, 2004, p. 9). A corollary of statements of this kind could be that teachers are expected to have adequate pedagogical support in using ICT in education.

In 2008 further Government reports on ICT in education were published. These included the 'ICT in Schools: Inspectorate Evaluation Report' (DES, 2008) and the Strategy Group's report, 'Investing Effectively in Information and Communications Technology in Schools 2008–2013', carried out at the request of the Minister for Education and Science (DES, 2008). The reports acknowledged that there was a need at post-primary level to focus on the general application of ICT in teaching and learning. However, it was recognised that there was a need to provide teachers with the appropriate ICT infrastructure and supports to facilitate greater ICT integration in learning and teaching. It was also found that a quarter of teachers rated themselves at the 'intermediate' or 'advanced' level in terms of IT skills. One of the key investment priorities recommended in the reports was in the professional development of teachers to ensure the integration of ICT in teaching and learning. It is in the context of these reports that the NCTE produced a handbook for principals and coordinating teachers called 'Planning and Implementing e-Learning in Your School', along with an e-Learning Roadmap, with the purpose of assisting schools to develop strategies and action plans to integrate ICT into learning and teaching across the curriculum. The e-Learning Roadmap allowed a school to review its current state of ICT use and where it would like to go under the following headings: ICT Infrastructure, e-Learning Culture, Professional Development, ICT in the Curriculum, Leadership and Planning. Industry continued their interest in promoting ICT in education with the joint Industry-Government publication entitled 'Smart Schools = Smart Economy' (DES, 2009), which marked the start of industry's involvement in the policy formation of ICT in schools. The publication called for the 'holistic integration' of ICT into the curriculum and assessment procedures (2009, p. 9) and recommended that the Teaching Council focus on the ICT professional development needs of teachers in the development of its strategy for the Review and Accreditation of initial teacher training programmes. It is interesting to note that this latter issue was addressed in the 'Initial Teacher Education: Criteria and Guidelines for Programme Providers' (Teaching Council of Ireland, 2011), which specifically refers to ICT in teaching and learning as a mandatory component of all initial teacher education programmes in Ireland.

There are still challenges in integrating technology into classroom practices, despite reports that governments and other stakeholders in OECD countries have dedicated large budgets to ICT projects in schools (Enochsson & Rizza, 2009). Research shows that although increasing numbers of teachers and student teachers are becoming personal users of ICT, and the availability of technology is increasing, this knowledge does not simply transfer into teaching practices (Ottesen, 2006; Player-Coro, 2007). While the very important issue of integrating ICT into the curriculum moved centre stage in government policy, the characteristics of Computing as a subject have in some measure been lost sight of. In Northern Ireland, Computer Studies has been a subject at GCSE and A-level for the past two decades. ICT and Computer Studies have been subjects at GCSE level. There are hopefully new developments with the Framework for Junior Certificate (2012) developed by the NCCA, which focuses on key skills with ICT at the core. NCCA will initially develop eight short courses for the junior cycle but schools are also encouraged to develop their own short courses. The Framework for Junior Cycle will commence in 2014 with Digital Media Literacy and Computer Programming to be among the first short courses to be offered. Although ICT is integrated into the curricula, the assessment remains the same. Perhaps there will be no change in assessment until e-Portfolios are introduced into the Junior Cycle Framework.

Dublin City University's Centre for Teaching Computing (CTC)

The role of DCU's School of Computer Applications in setting up the Irish Tech Corps (ITC) in collaboration with the Irish Software Association and the impact that this has had in the schools sector has already been referred to. This initiative coincided very well with DCU's distinctively education-orientated approach to the handling of Computer Studies in the institution generally. In 1992, DCU had set up a Centre for Teaching Computing (CTC) as a joint venture with the University of Ulster, to support Computing academics throughout Ireland, in the shared development, evaluation and dissemination of teaching materials and methodologies. Professor Michael Ryan was Head of the School of Computer Applications in DCU at that time and the Centre for Teaching Computing (CTC) developed under his direction with the guidance of Dr Micheál O 'hEigeartaigh. The Centre organised workshops and conferences for higher education staff and annual conferences on subjects concerned with ICT in the curriculum. This was the first centre that was established in Ireland to support the use of technology in the context of teaching and learning in higher education.

Margaret Farren joined the Centre for Teaching Computing in November 1997. Previously she had taught Computer Studies to A-level, Business Studies on BTEC (British Technical Education Council) courses and Computer Studies and Information Technology to GCSE level at a sixth-form college in London and at an International School in Brussels. The strength of the GCSE Information Technology curriculum was that it valued the process of inquiry. It provided the opportunity for students to explore and experiment with ICT and to carry out project work in areas of interest and relevance to them. It also enabled the teacher to apply an interactive approach to IT teaching in the classroom.

In 1998, the staff in the CTC organised a conference jointly with the Association for Computing Machinery (ACM) on 'Teaching Computing, USA', which took place in DCU. During its lifetime, the CTC also organised conferences for primary and post-primary teachers, e.g. the Socrates–Comenius Conference on 'European Linkage in Teaching Computing at Primary and Secondary Level', jointly organised by DCU and the Computer Education Society of Ireland (CESI). CESI had organised its own annual conference since 1973 and since that time it has given an organised voice to the innovators of ICT in education. The establishment by the Government of the NCTE in early 1998 on the DCU campus was welcomed by the Irish Tech Corps.

After the establishment of the NCTE, the School of Computer Applications in DCU continued to link with schools and a university-school collaborative project called Setanta (<http://webpages.dcu.ie/~farrenm/SetProject.htm>) was established in 1999 between the School of Computer Applications and St Aidan's secondary school in North Dublin. It involved close partnerships between pupils and teachers in St Aidan's school and students and lecturing staff in the School of Computer Applications. The idea was to develop an intranet with learning resources appropriate for teaching and learning in post-primary schools around Ireland. It aimed to develop a model for a school-based intranet for the teaching of post-primary subjects and to develop courseware for use in Irish post-primary schools. Some of the courseware developed as part of the Setanta project included an Interactive Maths Tutorial, as well as a Virtual Art Museum (VAM) for use in the teaching of Art at Leaving Certificate level (Farren, Mooney, & Pentony, 2001). The Setanta project later evolved into one of the SIP projects.

Third-level qualification in Computer Applications for Education

A Masters degree in Computer Applications for Education was established in DCU's School of Computer Applications in 1996 as a two-year part-time programme. It was the first Masters degree programme in Computer Applications for Education in Ireland. The programme consisted of the following modules: Computer Programming, Algorithms, Computer Software Installations, Network Information Management, Computer Networks, Computer Architecture and Operating Systems, Quantitative Methods and Simulation, Multimedia and Information Retrieval Systems, Computer Applications in Education and Human Computer Interaction. From a glance at these modules it can be seen that the programme was mainly geared towards technical understanding of ICT rather than being about ICT as applied to education. The teaching and research interest of the majority of academic staff in the School of Computer Applications was in the technical aspects of computing rather than computer applications for education. It is clear now that this technical approach to ICT was important but it underestimated the necessity for teachers to examine appropriate pedagogical uses of ICT in day-to-day teaching and learning. By the time the masters degree closed in 2002 over 100 teachers had received the MSc in Computer Applications for Education. Teachers who graduated from the programme have become champions in the use of technology in their own schools and some led developments in technology-in-education initiatives that have enabled the wider teaching community in Ireland to explore the benefits of technology in education. The assumption of the MSc in Computer Applications for Education programme was that the teachers being trained would teach Computing as a subject. It was also assumed that if they were to make use of computers in other areas of the curriculum they would already have the pedagogical understanding of how to make full use of ICT. The programme closed at a time when there were calls for the professional development of all teachers in the pedagogical uses of ICT in the classroom, the development of appropriate third-level certification and accreditation structures, and the promotion of postgraduate research (NPADC, 2001).

Margaret Farren's move from the School of Computer Applications to the School of Education Studies in 2002 paralleled the shift to mainstreaming ICT in education that was beginning to happen as a result of the development of Government policy. A two-year part-time Masters in Education and Training Management with a focus on leadership had been established in the School of Education Studies since 1995. In her move to the School of Education Studies, Margaret began to integrate an ICT strand into the existing Masters in Education and Training Management programme. This brought an ICT dimension into the Masters programme and an ICT research dimension to the School of Education Studies. In 2006 the ICT strand was renamed e-Learning, emphasising the developing trends in education on learning facilitated and supported through the use of ICT. Participants on the MSc in Computer Applications for Education in the School of Computer Applications (1996–2002) focused on computing as a body of knowledge and sought to master computer systems and procedures. Participants on the MSc in Education and Training Management (e-Learning) (2002–present) in the School of Education Studies are offered a different approach to teaching, learning, and research (e.g. Moodle virtual learning environment is one of the tools used to assist participants to collaboratively explore the values embedded in their practice). They also have the opportunity to engage their imagination and creativity in developing multi-modal forms of representation in their practice-based research.

Since 1993, with the establishment of the Self-study of Teacher Education Practice Group of the American Educational Research Association (AERA), higher education educators have been exploring the epistemological implications of self-studies (researching one's own practice) for the generation of educational knowledge. The *International Handbook of Self-Study of Teaching Practice* (Loughran, Hamilton, La Boskey, & Russell, 2004) provides clear evidence of how self-study is influencing teacher education in the academy and other social formations. According to Pithouse, Mitchell and Weber (2009), 'the very process of self-study itself changes its practitioners and their situations. Seeing things differently, self-study can prod us to take action.' These authors include action research, narrative inquiry, arts-informed inquiry, auto-ethnography, and life histories as approaches to self-study research. The idea of practitioners generating knowledge has not been given serious weight in the academy. Schön (1995) referred to the power of the disciplinary in-groups that have grown up in the academy around the dominant epistemology. The increasing flow of literature on practitioner research approaches influenced Margaret's choice of research methodology for doctoral research. In researching her own practice she clarified the meaning of the values of a web of betweenness and pedagogy of the unique as they emerged in the course of her practice (Farren, 2006). Yvonne Crotty began lecturing in the School of Education in 2003. She started to teach on the Masters programmes in 2005 and in 2007 as Co-ordinator of the eLearning programme, she set about revising the modules. Yvonne opened up opportunities for participants to develop their multimedia skills and make use of multi-modal forms of representation in their research. Yvonne Crotty's interest in the use of multi-modal forms of communication and expression to represent educational knowledge and her belief in the power of visual methods led to her doctoral research, in which she used multi-modal forms of communication to express her practice-based research and clarify what it means to have an educational entrepreneurial spirit (Crotty, 2012). The direction taken by Margaret and Yvonne in their doctoral research studies has influenced the philosophical and educational foundation of the MSc in Education and Training Management (e-Learning) programme.

MSc in Education and Training Management (e-Learning strand)

We will now focus on the specifics of the Masters programme. This programme was originally designed in 2002 to meet the professional development needs of practising teachers who were keen to learn how to integrate technology into their subject area. Over the past decade the programme has attracted professionals from different sectors of education (primary, post-primary, and tertiary), and other areas, e.g. corporate training, industry including technology, pharmaceutical, creative arts, banking, non-government organisations (NGOs), government departments, community organisations, and state agencies. What unites participants is their interest in improving their own practice and developing creative approaches to the use of ICT in the particular learning environments in which they work.

The programme is offered through a blended approach, whereby participants learn in both online and face-to-face settings. The modules are constantly being updated to meet the evolving needs of professionals in the workplace. There are currently six modules on the programme: Visions for Emerging Technologies, e-Learning: Culture and Organisations, Emerging Pedagogies, Multimedia and Educational Innovation, Digital Creativity in the Workplace, Entrepreneurial Education and Training and Collaborative Online Learning Inquiry.

As educators, we believe that dialogue is fundamental to the teaching and learning process. Throughout the programme, participants develop their own sense of being as they learn in relation with others. This relational quality of learning underpins the notion of a web of betweenness (O'Donohue, 2003; Farren, 2005), bringing us back to the intuitive worldview of the Celtic Imagination and capturing the idea that each person's uniqueness enriches the community: 'True community is an ideal where the full identities of awakened and realised individuals challenge and complement each other' (O'Donohue, 2003, p. 25). ICT, far from displacing the educator, opens up new creative possibilities, provided that they see learning as a collaborative process, not only involving teacher/student dialogue but with a wider dimension of student/student dialogue moving toward a web of betweenness that ICT can facilitate (Farren, 2005, 2006, 2008). Like Max van Manen, we do not consider pedagogy to be found in observational categories, but rather, like love or friendship, in the experience of its presence – that is, in concrete, real-life situations (1991, p. 31).

Throughout the course of the masters programme, professionals from a range of workplace contexts are supported to develop their own capacity as learners and encouraged to observe and reflect on what is happening in their own pedagogical practice and in their relationship with others. The idea of pedagogy of the unique (Farren, 2005) expresses the belief that each participant on the programme has a particular and distinctive constellation of values that motivate their research enquiry and that set a distinctive context within which that enquiry proceeds. Yvonne draws on her fifteen years experience as a secondary school teacher to show how collaboration, cooperative and project-based learning is essential to her pedagogy. (Crotty, 2005, 2011, 2012). Her research emphasises the importance of creating 'safe environments' to ensure meaningful, enjoyable, creative learning abounds. The Masters programme has been a 'conversion experience' (Carroll, cited in Rohr, 2006, p. 139) for these professionals as they examine their own value system and provide practice-based accounts of research.

In order to confront Schön's warning about the need for scholars to make their practice into appropriately rigorous research (Schön, 1995, p. 34) and to ensure that research demonstrates 'academic rigor and practical relevance' (Schneberger, Pollard, & Watson, 2009), we draw on Winter's (1989) six criteria for judging action research accounts: dialectical critique, reflective critique, collaboration resource, risk, plural structure, theory, practice and transformation. These criteria emphasise dialogue, reflection and action, collaboration, listening to other points of view and taking risks in bringing new ideas into action. All these help to foster transformative learning. We also take account of Smith's point (1989, 1993, cited in Sparkes, 2002, p. 221) that judgement in qualitative inquiry should take place through debate, discussion and the use of exemplars. As for methods of establishing social validity, we include the application of Habermas's (1976) four criteria of comprehensibility, truth, rightness and authenticity.

The following are examples of action research enquiries carried out by previous participants:

The use of an inquiry-based learning approach to improve practice and encourage higher order thinking among students of mathematics in a post-primary school.
Caitriona Rooney, post-primary school teacher

Scaffolding online professional development in a training context.
Elspeth Hennessy, Education Officer, Professional Services Membership
Association

Facilitating professional development through a vodcast, video and e-learning course within a nursing context.
Sinead Murphy, clinical nurse facilitator

The production of a digital video artefact to promote greater understanding among youth workers of their own learning to learn competences?
Shane Crossan, manager of a community-based youth servicee

Reflecting back and looking forward

As ICT reaches into every branch of human and non-human information
exchange, one may rightly ask where the bounds of any subject described
as Computing can be set. The ForFas reports on Irish Government policy
would have strongly advised Government to fund ICT in education. The
Expert Group on Future Skills Needs (EGFSN-Forfás, 2008) reported that
the demand for ICT skills in Ireland would exceed the domestic supply. In
January 2012 the 'ICT Action Plan: Meeting the High Level ICT Skills
Needs of Enterprise in Ireland' was launched. It outlined the immediate
introduction of graduate conversion courses (Level 8) to meet the ICT
needs of industry. Government policy and indeed business thinking over
the past two decades have focused on computer literacy and the integration of ICT into teaching and learning across the curriculum. However,
Computer Studies has been a subject at GCSE and A-level in Northern
Ireland for at least two decades. The 'Review of the ICT Skills Demand in
Ireland' document published by the Joint Committee on Jobs, Enterprise
and Innovation in October 2012 put forward a number of key recommendations to bridge the gap between the needs of the ICT industry and the
capacity of the Irish workforce to meet those needs. One recommendation
was that the DES should include Computer Science and /or Programming

in the school curriculum. The need for post-primary schools to move from 'application usage' to 'application development' (p. 19) was noted in the report. As already mentioned, the NCCA are now developing short courses in Digital Media Literacy and Computer Programming and plan to introduce these courses in the junior cycle in 2014.

Various initiatives and policies over the last two decades have led to progress in understanding what ICT can contribute to teaching and learning. Much has changed since the Masters in Computer Applications for Education programme in DCU's School of Computer Applications (1996–2002), when it was assumed that teachers would have sufficient pedagogical knowledge and would only require technical skills in order to integrate ICT in their teaching. It was also envisaged, at that time, that the programme would enable teachers to teach Computing as a subject. In the end Computing was not introduced into the post-primary school curriculum. The MSc in Education and Training Management (e-Learning) programme (2002–present) is enabling educators to engage learners in the creative uses of ICT, in addition to helping teachers, among other professionals, to reflect on their pedagogical practice and offer practice-based accounts of how they are learning to live their values of humanity as fully as they can within their workplaces and communities. Our experience in ICT in education and practitioner research approaches has led to invitations to participate in a European Seventh Framework project, 'Pathway to Inquiry Based Science Education' (2010–2013), and a Competitiveness and Innovation Framework project (2013–2016), 'Inspiring Science', with a focus on mainstreaming e-Learning in national policies for the modernisation of education and training, and the professional development of educators.

Of particular relevance to our work as higher education educators charged with the development of professionals from a range of workplace contexts is the ICT Action Plan's reference to up-skilling the current workforce in ICT skills (DES, 2012, p. 16). Through the MSc in Education and Training Management (eLearning) and our research programmes we are enabling professionals from a range of workplace contexts to develop skills in the use of digital technology and multimedia; gain knowledge of the effective design and use of collaborative online technologies for teaching, learning and creative inquiry; and engage in systematic action reflection cycles of expressing concerns, producing action plans, acting and gathering data, and evaluating the effectiveness of changing practice. In this way we are embedding the learning experienced in the workplace into the curriculum in higher education. We have also spearheaded a unique initiative in collaboration with the Global eSchools and Communities Initiative (GeSCI) which enables African leaders to gain a Graduate Diploma in Leadership Development in ICT and the Knowledge Society from Dublin City University (<http://www4.dcu.ie/cwlel/Global-eSchools-Research.shtml>). Extending our work and research to the African continent is further evidence of the flourishing of a web of betweenness that ICT can facilitate.

In order to bring the various European and international research projects together we have established the Centre for e-Innovation and Workplace Learning: <http://www4.dcu.ie/cwlel/index.shtml>. The Centre is supporting practitioners from a range of workplace contexts to make explicit the values underpinning their pedagogical practices and to carry out actions based upon wise and considered practice. The Centre is contributing to developments in ICT in education, especially in light of the possibilities of next-generation approaches to the application of ICT and their incorporation into education and training contexts.

References

Carroll, J.E., 'Sustainability and Spirituality' in R. Rohr, *Contemplation in Action* (Crossroad Publishing Company: New York, 2006).

Crotty, Y., 'Through the enlightened eye and I – am I bringing creativity and visual literacy into higher education?' *Education Journal of Living Educational Theories* 4/1 (2011) 1–36.

Crotty, Y., 'How Am I Bringing an Educational Entrepreneurial Spirit into Higher Education?' PhD thesis, Dublin City University (2012). Retrieved 1/01/12 from <http://yvonnecrotty.com/?page_id=102>

Crotty, Y., 'How do I create a visual narrative that contributes to my learning and the learning of others?' Masters dissertation, Dublin City University (2005).

Department of Education and Skills, Ireland, *ICT Action Plan: Meeting the High Level ICT Skills Needs of Enterprise in Ireland* (2012). Retrieved 1 September 2012 from <http://www.education.ie/en/Publications/Policy-Reports/ICT-Action-Plan-Meeting-the-high-level-skills-needs-of-enterprise-in-Ireland.pdf>

Department of Education and Science, Ireland, *Smart Schools = Smart Economy. Report of the ICT in Schools Joint Advisory Group to the Minister of Education and Science* (2009). Retrieved 10 July 202 from <http://www.education.ie/en/Publications/Education-Reports/Smart-Schools=Smart-Economy.pdf>

Department of Education and Science, Ireland, *Investing Effectively in Information and Communications in Schools (2008–2013)*. Retrieved 10 July 2012 from <http://www.education.ie/en/Publications/Education-Reports/Investing-Effectively-in-Information-and-Communication-Technology-in-Schools-2008-2013.pdf>

Department of Education and Science, Ireland, *ICT in Schools: Inspectorate Evaluation Studies* (Dublin: Brunswick Press, 2008).

Department of Education and Science, Ireland, *Statement of Strategy 2005–2007*. Retrieved 10 July 2009 from <http://www.education.ie/servlet/blobservlet/strategy_statement_05_07.pdf>

Department of Education and Science, Ireland, *Information and Communications Technology (ICT) in the Primary School Curriculum. Guidelines for Teachers* (2004). Retrieved 10 July 2009 from <http://www.ncca.ie/uploadedfiles/ECPE/ICTEnglish.pdf?>

Department of Education and Science, Ireland, *Blueprint for the Future of ICT in Education (2001)*. Retrieved 15 July 2009 from <http://www.ncte.ie/cao/documents/d247.PDF>

Department of Education and Science, Ireland Schools, *IT 2000: A Policy Framework for the New Millennium* (Dublin: Stationery Office, 1997).

Department of Education and Science, Ireland, *Charting our Education Future. White Paper on Education* (Dublin: Stationery Office, 1995).

Enochsson, A. & C. Rizza, 'ICT in Initial Teacher Training: Research Review'. *OECD Education Working Papers* 38 (2009). Retrieved 10 September 2012 from <http://dx.doi.org/10.1787/220502872611>

EGFSN-Forfas, *The Expert Group on Future Skills Need* (2008). Retrieved from <http://www.forfas.ie/publication/search.jsp?ft=/publications/2008/Title,2000,en.php>

Farren, M., 'e-Learning and action research as transformative practice.' *Innovate: Journal of Online Education* (2008). Retrieved 10 July 2009 from <http://

innovateonline.info/pdf/vol5_issue1/e-Learning_and_Action_Research_as_ Transformative_Practice.pdf>

Farren, M., 'How am I creating a pedagogy of the unique through a web of betweenness with a new epistemology for educational knowledge?' Action Research Expeditions (December 2007).

Farren, M. 'How am I Creating my Pedagogy of the Unique through a Web of Betweenness?' PhD thesis, University of Bath (2006). Retrieved 18 July 2012 from <http://www.actionresearch.net/living/farren.shtml>

Farren, M., with Mooney, M. & Pentony, D., 'Setanta: A University-School Collaboration Project' in D. Twomey et al., *Proceedings of Computer Education Society of Ireland National Conference. Challenges for Learning in a Digital Age* (2002). Retrieved 20 July 2009 from <http://odtl.dcu.ie/wp/2001/odtl-2001-01.html>

Habermas, J., *Communication and the evolution of society* (London: Heinemann, 1976).

Joint Committee on Jobs, Enterprise and Innovation, Ireland, *A review of the ICT skills demand in Ireland* (2012). Retrieved on 12 December 2012 from <http://www.oireachtas.ie/parliament/media/committees/jobsenterpriseandinnovation/Report-on-ICT-Skills--1-October-final.pdf>

Loughran, J., Hamilton, M.L., LaBoskey, V. K. & Russell, T.L., eds, *The International Handbook of Self-Study of Teaching and Teacher Education Practices* (Dordrecht: Kluwer Academic Publishers, 2004).

McNiff, J., Lomax, P., & Whitehead, J., *You and Your Action Research Project*, 2nd Edition (London: RoutledgeFalmer, 2003).

National Centre for Technology in Education, *Developing an eLearning Plan* (2009). Retrieved 10 June 2009 from <http://www.ncte.ie/courses/Developingane LearningPlan/>

National Council for Curriculum and Assessment, *ICT Framework: A structured approach to ICT in Curriculum and Assessment. Revised Framework* (2007). Retrieved 12 June 2009 from <http://www.ncca.ie/uploadedfiles/publications/ict%20revised%20framework.pdf>

National Council for Curriculum and Assessment Curriculum, *Assessment and ICT in the Irish Context: A Discussion Paper* (2004). Retrieved 12 June 2009 from <http://www.ncca.ie/uploadedfiles/Publications/CompCurrReport.pdf>

National Council for Curriculum and Assessment, *Computers and Curriculum: Difficulties and Dichotomies* (2004). Retrieved 5 June 2009 from <http://www.ncca.ie/uploadedfiles/Publications/CompCurrReport.pdf>

National Policy Advisory and Development Committee, *The Impact of Schools IT 2000* (2001). Retrieved 10 June 2009 from <http://www.ncte.ie/npadc/ncte_report.pdf>

New Media Consortium, *The Horizon Report* (2005). Retrieved 5 July 2012 from
    <http://net.educause.edu/ir/library/pdf/CSD3737.pdf>
O'Brien, C., 'Integrating computers into the classroom.' *The Sunday Business
    Post* (2006). Retrieved 20 July 2012 from <http://archives.tcm.ie/business-
    post/2006/10/15/story18004.asp>
O'Donohue, J., *Divine Beauty: The Invisible Embrace* (London: Transworld, 2003).
Ottesen, Eli, 'Learning to teach with technology: Authoring practised identities'.
    Technology, Pedagogy and Education, 15/3 (2006) 275–290.
Pithouse, K., Mitchell, C., & Weber, S., 'Self-study in teaching and teacher develop-
    ment: a call to action.' *Educational Action Research* 17/1 (2009) 43–62.
Player-Koro, C., 'Why teachers use ICT in education'. *JURE* 27–28 (2007).
Schneberger, S., Pollard, C., & Watson, H., *Information Systems Management* 26/1
    (2009).
Schön, D., 'Knowing-in-action: The New Scholarship requires a New Epistemology'.
    Change (1995).
Sparkes, A.C., 'Telling Tales in Sport and Physical Activity (A Qualitative Journey)'.
    Human Kinetics (2002).
Teaching Council of Ireland, *The Initial Teacher Education: Criteria and Guidelines for
    Programme Providers* (2011). Retrieved on 5 October 2012 from <http://www.
    teachingcouncil.ie/_fileupload/Teacher%20Education/ITE%20Criteria%20
    and%20Guidelines%20Final%20July%202011.pdf>
Van Manen, M., *The Tact of Teaching: The Meaning of Pedagogical Thoughtfulness*
    (Albany: State University of New York Press, 1991).
Whitehead, J., 'Creating a Living Educational Theory from Questions of the Kind,
    How Do I Improve My Practice?' *British Educational Research Journal* 15 (1989),
    3–17.
Whitehead, J., 'An Epistemological Transformation in Educational Knowledge from
    S-STEP Research' (2009). Retrieved 21 September 2012 from <http://www.
    actionresearch.net/writings/jack/jwsstep130409sandiego.htm>
Winter, R., *Learning from Experience: Principles and Practices in Action Research*
    (Falmer Press Ltd, 1989).
Wroe, P., 'The drive is on to produce more Irish ICT graduates.' *The Sunday Business
    Post* (2012).

9 An Epistemological Transformation in Educational Knowledge from S-STEP Research

Since the establishment of Self-Study of Teacher Education Practices (S-STEP) in 1993, S-STEP researchers have made a significant contribution to the knowledge base of education.

I shall start the conversation with some evidence that S-STEP researchers have answered Schön's (1995) call for a new epistemology. I shall claim that this new epistemology can be made explicit from the explanations given by S-STEP researchers for their educational influences in their own learning, in the learning of others and in the learning of the socio-cultural formations in which we live and work. I call these explanations living educational theories (Whitehead, 1989, 2009).

I began my research programme into educational theory at the University of Bath in 1973 with the desire to rectify a mistake in the dominant discipline's approach to educational theory. In this approach it was believed that educational theory was constituted by the disciplines of the philosophy, psychology, sociology and history of education. It was also believed that the practical principles I used as a teacher to explain my educational influences in my own learning and in the learning of my pupils were at best pragmatic maxims that had a first crude and superficial justification in practice that in any rationally developed theory would be replaced by principles with more fundamental theoretical justification (Hirst, 1983, p. 18).

I would like to dwell on the significance of working with a view of educational theory that would replace the practical principles of educators with principles from the disciplines of education. This was the view of educational theory my tutors worked with in my continuing professional development programmes for an Academic Diploma in the philosophy and psychology of education, and then for a Masters degree in the psychology of education, between 1968–72 at the University of London, Institute of Education. During this time I was working full time as a Science teacher and then as a Head of a Science Department in a London comprehensive school. The tension that moved me from being a teacher of Science in a school to being an educational researcher and educator in a university was focused on the mistake in educational theory, of believing that the practical principles that educators used to explain their educational influences in learning should be replaced by the principles from the disciplines of education. By a practical principle I mean the reasons I give to explain why I am doing what I am doing. For example, at times in my working life I have felt my freedom being constrained in a way I felt to be inappropriate and not justified by other principles. Hence I explained my activities in terms of me seeking to live my value of freedom more fully. In explaining why I was doing what I was doing, I used the practical principle of freedom (Whitehead, 1993). My understanding of a discipline of education is of a form of knowledge such as the philosophy, psychology, sociology and history of education in which each discipline can be distinguished from another because of the conceptual framework it uses to explain phenomena and the methods of validation it uses to evaluate the validity of claims to knowledge made from within the conceptual framework.

I want to be clear that my tension with the discipline's approach to educational theory included my pleasure in knowing that my cognitive range and concerns were being extended by my understandings of the theories of the philosophy, psychology, sociology and history of education. The pleasure in extending these understandings continues to this day. This pleasure was held together with the dismay of being subjected to a mistaken view of educational theory that sought to replace the explanatory principles I used to give life its meaning and purpose in my work in education, with the conceptual frameworks and methods of validation of the disciplines of education. In other words, the explanations I gave for my educational influences in learning could not be subsumed under any disciplines of education taken individually or in any combination. However, insights from the disciplines were helpful in the creation of my own living educational theory.

Hence my passion for the self-study of teacher-education practices (S-STEP) in educational research. It is S-STEP research that will not permit this replacement. S-STEP research insists on including the explanatory principles that practitioner-researchers use to give their lives meaning and purpose, in their explanations of educational influences in learning. This is, of course, not to deny the significance of theories from the disciplines of education. S-STEP researchers include insights from the theories of the disciplines of education where these are useful in strengthening the validity of their explanations of educational influences in learning. To distinguish the explanations of S-STEP researchers for their educational influences, from the explanations derived from the propositional theories of the disciplines of education, I call the former living educational theories.

In claiming that S-STEP researchers have brought about an epistemological transformation in educational knowledge (Bruce-Ferguson, 2008; Whitehead, 2008a & b; Laidlaw, 2008; Adler-Collins, 2008; Huxtable, 2009) I want to focus on the inclusional units of appraisal, the standards of judgment and the logics of this new epistemology.

Unit of appraisal

The units of appraisal are the explanations produced by S-STEP researchers for their educational influences in their own learning, in the learning of others and in the learning of the socio-cultural formations in which we live and work. You will find some thirty research degrees at <http://people. bath.ac.uk/edsajw/living.shtml> with this unit of appraisal.

Because the unit of appraisal is an individual's explanation of educational influence in learning and each individual is responsible for the creation of their own living educational theory I want to clearly distinguish the propositional theory from the dialectical theories and from the living theories. Propositional theories are general explanations that are usually communicated in the form of linguistic abstractions and statements. The propositional theory is not a living form; it is usually subsumed under the general concept of a person and the living is eliminated from the discourse. An example of this can be seen a key text from the 1960s and 1970s, *Ethics and Education* by Richard Peters.

Peters (1966) would ask what was implied for a person seriously asked a question of the kind 'What ought I to do?'. In answering the question, the living in the answer was transformed and eliminated in the general concept of a person.

In dialectical theories the nucleus of the 'I' is contradiction in the sense of holding together two mutually exclusive opposites, such as in the experience of being free and being not free, at the same time. Contradictions are the nucleus of dialectics.

In living theories informed by inclusionality the 'I' is not experienced or understood as a discrete body that can be contained in a propositional form or represented with contradictions as its nucleus. In inclusionality the 'I' is experienced and understood as a unique confluence of dynamic relationships (Rayner & Jarvilehto, 2008).

I hope that the distinctions between propositional, dialectical and inclusional experiences of the 'I' help to clarify that the unit of appraisal I am working with is an individual's explanation of their educational influences in learning in which the 'I' is experienced and understood as an inclusional 'I'.

Standards of judgment

When we judge the validity of a claim to educational knowledge or a belief we hold about the world, we use standards of judgment. In the creation of a new epistemological for educational knowledge I want to suggest, following Laidlaw (1996), that we use living educational standards of judgment. Living educational standards of judgment are values laden. By this I mean that we cannot distinguish something as educational without approving it in the exercise of a value-judgment. The practical principles we use to explain our educational influence are also values-laden for the same reason.

As we reflect on the nature of our explanatory standards of judgment in our explanations from an epistemological perspective, we need to understand the values that constitute as educational our explanatory principles and standards of judgment. The distinction I make between an explanatory principle and a standard of judgment, from an epistemological perspective, is that my explanatory principles are the principles I use in the creation of my living educational theory. As I reflect on this claim to knowledge, from an epistemological perspective I explicate the explanatory principles as the principles I use to evaluate the validity of my claim to knowledge.

When I think of the values that help to constitute my practices as educational I am thinking of values as flowing with energy that is motivational. I mean this in the sense that I explain my actions in terms of my values. If, for example, I am feeling the denial of values such as freedom, justice, love and compassion, I work towards the greater realisations of these values and explain my actions in terms of the expression of living more fully these embodied values in practice. The meanings of the embodied values are clarified in the course of their emergence in practice and in the form of their communication the meanings of the embodied values as distinct from their expression in practice are transformed into the living standards of judgment of a claim to educational knowledge, in the living educational theory.

Logics

Following Marcuse (1964, p. 104) I understand logic as a mode of thought that is appropriate for comprehending the real as rational. Logic is focused on the way we make sense of something. It is the way we form meaning into comprehensible expressions.

The last 2,500 years have seen a conflict between propositional and dialectical logicians. Drawing on Aristotle's logic, propositional thinkers have claimed that two mutually exclusive statements cannot be true simultaneously. Dialectical thinkers have claimed that contradictions are the nucleus of dialectics. Propositional thinkers reject dialectical claims to knowledge as being without the slightest foundation. Indeed, they are based on nothing better than a loose and woolly way of speaking (Popper 1963, p. 316). Dialectical thinkers claim that propositional thinking masks the dialectical nature of reality (Marcuse, 1964).

The new epistemology for educational knowledge created from S-STEP research includes a living logic that can draw insights from ideas formed with both propositional and dialectical logic without being drawn into their rejections of the rationality of the other.

My own thinking has often moved on through my imagination as I encounter a tension, conflict or contradiction. My understanding of a living logic moved on from a tension in the work of Ilyenkov (1977) on dialectical logic. At the end of his inspiring work on dialectical logic Ilyenkov was left with a problem he could not answer before he died: If an object exists as a living contradiction, what must the thought be (statement about the object) that expresses it? In the introduction to his book on dialectical logic Ilyenkov expressed his commitment to write logic. I think that the commitment to write logic, rather than to study his living logic in his practical life, ensured that he would be caught within the writing of propositional and dialectical statements in a way that left him with no way of answering his question, apart from trying to write an answer.

I now want to break with the propositional and dialectical thinking in my paper and focus on visual representations of educational practice and the explanations of educational influences in learning of S-STEP researchers from which a new epistemology for educational knowledge has been created with living explanatory principles, standards of judgment and living logics.

I'll begin by referring to a video clip of my own educational practice as an S-STEP researcher in a PhD supervision, available on <http://www.youtube.com/watch?v=w2kdOfRKFYs>. In this brief clip of a supervision session with Jacqueline Delong before the successful completion of her doctorate, at the end of a week of supervision, we are talking about an improvement in the abstract to the thesis, when there is a pooling of our life-circulating/life-affirming energy and understanding in a spontaneous expression of laughter over a point Jacqueline raises about me not having responded to her work in terms of wisdom.

I see being expressed in this video clip something that is omitted in propositional and dialectical discourse. I am thinking of the meanings of the expression of flows of the embodied energy and values that constitute the energy-flowing and values-laden practical principles that educators express in their educational practices with their students. I want to be clear here. I am claiming that visual narratives of the educational influences in learning of educators can communicate the meanings of these energy-flowing and values-laden explanatory principles in explanations of educational influences in learning. You can access Jacqueline Delong's (2002) thesis at <http://www.actionresearch.net/delong.shtml>.

You can also access a 2009 AERA paper by Delong on building a culture of inquiry through the embodied knowledge of teachers and teacher educators in aboriginal and non-aboriginal contexts (Delong, 2009) at <http://www.jackwhitehead.com/delong/jdAERA09Paperfinal.pdf>.

I think that I might also be able to communicate the significance of visual narratives in communicating the meanings of energy-flowing and values-laden explanatory principles in an epistemology for educational knowledge through comparing two of my publications on living educational theory some twenty years apart and looking at the points about visual narrative in a living theory methodology.

The first is the most influential of my publications on the generation of living educational theories in the *Cambridge Journal*. You can access the text, dating back to 1989, here: <http://people.bath.ac.uk/edsajw/writings/livtheory.html>.

The second is the March 2009 paper on action research on living theories in the journal *Action Research*: <http://www.jackwhitehead.com/jack/jwartheory0309.pdf>.

The third is in the first issue of the *Educational Journal of Living Theories* on a living theory methodology at: <http://ejolts.net/node/80>.

I want to focus on the significance of live urls in living theories. This evolution of living theories is shown in the theories being generated by researchers at Nelson Mandela University (Wood, Morar, & Mostert, 2007). These researchers are exploring the implications of asking, researching and answering their questions concerning the movement from rhetoric to reality as they enquire into the role of living theory action research in transforming education. Wood et al. demonstrate an understanding of the importance for the action researcher of exploring the implications of seeking to live their ontological values as fully as possible in their professional practice.

The significance of these living theories that have been generated by action researchers from an inclusional perspective is that they have established a new epistemology in the academy in terms of living units of appraisal, standards of judgment and logics. The importance of understanding a unit of appraisal is that this is whatever is being judged in terms of its validity. The standards of judgment are what we use to do the judging. The importance of logic is that it is a mode of thought that is appropriate for comprehending the real as rational.

In distinguishing the new epistemology for educational knowledge through its units of appraisal, living standards of judgement and living logic I have found most helpful Rayner's (2006) ideas on inclusionality. For Rayner,

> At the heart of inclusionality, then, is a simple but radical shift in the way we frame reality, from absolutely fixed to relationally dynamic. This shift arises from perceiving space and boundaries as continuous, connective, reflective and co-creative, rather than severing, in their vital role of producing heterogeneous form and local identity within a featured rather than featureless, dynamic rather than static, Universe. (p. 72)

Rather than thinking of standards of judgment in terms of propositional or dialectical statements, the new epistemology is understood in terms of relationally dynamic standards of judgment that are continuous, connective, reflective and co-creative. Such standards of judgment can be understood in relation to answers to particular kinds of educational questions, such as those asked by Claire Formby, Marie Huxtable and Christine Jones.

Claire Formby has asked, researched and answered:

> How am I integrating my educational theorizing firstly with the educational responsibility I express in my educational relationships with the children in my class, but also with the educational responsibility I feel towards those in the wider school community? (Formby, 2008, <http://www.jackwhitehead.com/tuesdayma/cfee3draft.htm>)

And also:

> How do I sustain a loving, receptively responsive educational relationship with my
> pupils, which will motivate them in their learning and encourage me in my teaching?
> (Formby, 2008, <http://www.jackwhitehead.com/tuesdayma/formbyEE300907.
> htm>) (Whitehead, 2009, p. 93)

What has emerged from asking, researching and answering such questions,
especially the latter question, is the inclusional standard of judgment of
a loving, receptively responsive educational relationship. The question
continues to exist as a living contradiction in experiencing the negation of
educational values, sometimes internally and sometimes in the sociocultural formations in which the question is asked. For example, such a living
contradiction exists between the educational assessment of the teacher in
relation to her pupils talents, and the application of Standard Assessment
Tests to the pupils. The standard assessment tests are applied by government
agencies with an oppressive intensity that contradicts the emancipatory
intent of the educator exercising evaluative judgments in relation to the
pupils' learning, with educational intent. The answers to Formby's questions integrate insights both from propositional theories that are useful and
from critical evaluations of national policies that are influencing practice.

Before considering the influence of the politics of educational knowledge on the legitimation of the new epistemology, I want to draw attention to the significance for the new epistemology of accounts produced by
Marie Huxtable and Christine Jones, two friends and colleagues who work
respectively as a Senior Educational Psychologist and Inclusion Officer
in Bath and North East Somerset – the equivalent of a North American
School Board.

Marie Huxtable's (2009) multi-media account of improving practice
and generating knowledge can be accessed at: <http://www.jackwhitehead.
com/huxtable/mariehuxtablepaper170309.htm>. In this paper Huxtable
analyses the educational influence of Sally Cartwright in working with her
seventeen-year-old students on their extended projects. These are projects
in which students ask and answer questions of interest to them and which
can be accredited in examinations that count in selection for university. The

account includes video clips of both Cartwright and her students in public presentations of their extended projects. Huxtable explains her educational influence and support with Cartwright in terms of the energy-flowing and values-laden standards of judgment that she uses to give meaning and purpose to her life and work in education. The living standards of judgment are inclusional in the sense that they are relationally dynamic and receptively responsive to the educational needs of both teacher and students. They also include insights from both propositional and dialectical thinkers in the generation of the living theory.

The MA dissertation Christine Jones has submitted for examination provides an answer to her question: 'How do I improve my practice as an Inclusion Officer working in a Children's Service?' You can access the dissertation at: <http://www.jackwhitehead.com/cjmaok/cjma.htm>.

If you browse down the contents you will come to the heading 'Contents of CD Rom – Video-clips'. I do hope that you will access the first brief clip on Jones speaking to colleagues about a childhood memory. As you watch this clip and hear what she is saying, I think you may empathise with the feeling of humiliation that she felt on being reprimanded by the teacher. I think you might also appreciate the nature of the energy-flowing and values-laden response from Jones as she explains how this formed her desire to be a teacher.

To conclude this paper on an epistemological transformation in educational knowledge I want to focus on the politics of educational knowledge, because of the influence of power relations in the sociocultural formations of universities that are influencing the legitimation of the new epistemology.

The politics of educational knowledge

The influence of the politics of educational knowledge in legitimating what counts as educational knowledge in universities and other organisations has a long history. Galileo was shown instruments of torture to make him recant something that he knew to be true in relation to the earth's movement around the sun. This knowledge contradicted the view propagated by the Catholic Church that the sun moved round the earth as the centre of the universe. It took over 300 years for the Church to publicly acknowledge its mistake.

In 1983 Paul Hirst acknowledged the above mistake in the discipline's approach to educational theory in thinking that the practical principles used by educators to explain their educational practices would be replaced in any rationally developed theory by principles with more theoretical justification.

In 1991 a research committee in a UK university asked a self-study researcher, who had included I in the title of his work, to remove this personal pronoun from the title. Following internal and external pressure, self-study researchers were permitted to include I in their research titles.

In 1980 and 1982 I experienced the rejection of two of my doctorates from the University of Bath with the statement from the University Registrar that the University Regulations did not permit me to question the competence of my examiners under any circumstances. This kind of regulation was common in UK universities at this time. The regulations were changed in 1991 to permit questioning of examiners' judgments on the grounds of bias, prejudice or inadequate assessment. Again, this change required external pressure from European legislation.

As I have said above, and I think it bears repeating, propositional thinkers can reject dialectical claims to knowledge as being without the slightest foundation (Popper, 1963, p. 316). Dialectical thinkers claim that propositional theorists are masking the contradictory nature of reality. The rejection by proponents of these logics of the rationality of the other's position still continues to fuel the paradigm wars. Hence it is to be expected that introducing a third logic of inclusionality, in a new epistemology of educational knowledge, will be met by a mixture of bemusement, curiosity, hostility and outright rejection by those in positions of power in the academy to decide what counts as valid educational knowledge.

I make this last point to emphasise that the generation and legitimation of living educational theories takes place in contexts that have been influenced by different historical traditions and sociocultural influences and that these contexts are in a continuous process of transformation. It may feel at a particular moment in time that a particular set of power relations will continue to exert their influence. Yet from a historical perspective we can see that such power relations exist in a transition structure that is in a continuous process of transformation. What gives me hope today is the pooling of our life-circulating energy and values-laden living theories as we persevere in enhancing the flow of our energy, values and understandings that carry hope for the future of humanity and our own.

This chapter is dedicated to the memory of Sally Cartwright who died aged 53 in January 2013 and whose educational values continue to inspire.

References

Adler-Collins, J., 'Creating new forms of living educational theories through collabo-rative educational research from Eastern and Western Contexts. A response to Jack Whitehead.' *Research Intelligence* 104 (2008), 17–18.

Bruce-Ferguson, P., 'Increasing Inclusion in Educational Research: Reflections from New Zealand.' *Research Intelligence* 102 (2008), 24–25.

Delong, J., 'How can I improve my practice as a superintendent of schools and create my own living educational theory?' Retrieved 31 March 2009 from <http://www.actionresearch.net/delong.shtml>

Delong, J., 'Building a culture of inquiry through the embodied knowledge of teach-ers and teacher educators in aboriginal and non-aboriginal contexts.' Retrieved 31 March 2009 from <http://www.jackwhitehead.com/delong/jdAERA09Pa-perfinal.pdf>

Hirst, P., ed, *Educational Theory and its Foundation Disciplines* (London: RKP, 1983).

Huxtable, M., 'How do we contribute to an educational knowledge base? A response to Whitehead and a challenge to BERJ.' *Research Intelligence* 106 (2009).

Huxtable, M., 'Improving Practice and Generating Knowledge.' Retrieved 24 March 2009 from <http://www.jackwhitehead.com/huxtable/mariehuxtablepa-per170309.htm>

Ilyenkov, E., *Dialectical Logic* (Moscow: Progress Publishers, 1977).

Jones, C., 'How do I improve my practice as an Inclusion Officer working in Children's Services?' Retrieved 22 March 2009 from <http://www.jackwhitehead.com/cjmaok/cjma.htm>

Laidlaw, M., 'How can I create my own living educational theory as I offer you an account of my educational development?' Retrieved 22 March 2009 from <http://www.actionresearch.net/moira2.shtml>

Laidlaw, M., 'Increasing Inclusion In Educational Research: A Response To Pip Bruce Ferguson And Jack Whitehead.' *Research Intelligence* 104 (2008) 16–17.

Marcuse, H., *One Dimensional Man* (London: Routledge and Kegan Paul, 1964).

Peters, R.S., *Ethics and Education* (London: Allen and Unwin, 1996).

Popper, K., *Conjectures and Refutations* (Oxford: Oxford University Press, 1963).

Rayner, A., 'Inclusional Nature: Bringing Life and Love to Science.' Retrieved 22 March 2009 from <http://www.inclusional-research.org/inclusionalnature.php>

Rayner, A. & Jarvilehto, T., 'From Dichotomy to Inclusionality: A Transformational Understanding of Organism-Environment Relationships and the Evolution of Human Consciousness.' *Transfigural Mathematics* 1/2 (2008), 67–82.

Schön, D., 'The new scholarship requires a new epistemology'. *Change* 27/6 (1995), 26–34.

Whitehead, J., 'Creating a living educational theory from questions of the kind, How do I improve my practice?' *Cambridge Journal of Education* 19/1 (1989), 41–52.

Whitehead, J., *The Growth of Educational Knowledge: Creating your own living educational theories* (Bournemouth: Hyde Publications, 1993).

Whitehead, J., 'Increasing Inclusion in Educational Research.' *Research Intelligence* 103 (2008), 16–17.

Whitehead, J., 'An Epistemological Transformation in what counts as Educational Knowledge: Responses to Laidlaw and Adler-Collins.' *Research Intelligence* 105 (2008), 28–29.

Whitehead, J., 'Using a living theory methodology in improving practice and generating educational knowledge in living theories.' *Educational Journal of Living Theories*, 1/1 (2008), 103–126.

Whitehead, J., 'Generating living theory and understanding in action research studies.' *Action Research* 7/1 (2009), 85–99.

10 The Research Journey – Immersion into the Virtual World

This is an account of my own journey into a Second Life (SL) environment as a third-level teacher, prior to bringing my own teaching group into a similar environment. The research methodology employed in this study is ethnography and therefore focuses on a discrete location and cultural group, concerned with a range of actions within that setting. In essence, ethnography attempts to explain and answer *'what is going on here?'* The process of understanding 'first-hand' the virtual world of SL involved extended participant observation. *Being there* entailed an extensive journey of immersion into the virtual world, which can be described as a rite of passage. This journey had distinct stages of immersion comprising separation, transition and transformation. A variety of data collection methods was employed to contribute to a comprehensive description of the actions within the virtual world setting. The data collection techniques employed included participant observation, textual chat log transcript collection, field notes, unstructured interviews, teacher reflective journals, student reflections on lesson activities and in-world photography.

The journey of immersion into the virtual world

Three stages emerged during the journey of immersion into the virtual field. These stages are identified as separation, transition, and transformation. As this research field is a virtual space, immersion refers to prolonged 'mental absorption' (Carr et al. 2006, p. 54) through a virtual body within a virtual space. First, separation refers to the movement from the offline world into the virtual world. Second, transition refers to the period of adaptation and adjustment to the virtual environment. Third, transformation refers to the final process of learning and my teaching activity in the virtual environment.

Stage one: separation

In this research, I described the journey from the physical world into the virtual as a territorial rite of passage, akin to crossing a new frontier or threshold. In children's literature, the movement from one world to another is a perilous journey, from safety to the unknown. The frontier line has symbolic significance; a secret untended garden (Burnett, 1911), an open window (Barrie, 1911), a wardrobe (Lewis, 1950), a doorway or gate (Tolkien, 1954). Within each story, the protagonist pauses briefly at the threshold line to consider the possible consequences of their actions, simultaneously looking back at the known and forth into the unknown. In crossing the threshold, the protagonist sets out on a journey of 'becoming' anew. In each instance, s/he returns transformed; physically, emotionally, psychologically or spiritually. In this research, the frontier line was not marked by rocks or sacred spaces but by a computer screen.

In early September 2008, I took the first step in this rite of passage and landed on Welcome Island in Second Life (SL). Welcome Island is designed as a tutorial space through which a new resident must pass. It provides the opportunity for the practice of communication and locomotive skills before venturing further into the virtual world. It is, in a sense, a neutral zone (van Gennep, 1906, p. 18) in which the new resident remains until they have mastered basic skills. Those who join SL begin their virtual life as a newbie, the official SL term for a new member. The newbie could be compared to Turner's neophyte: 'they have no status, property, insignia, secular clothing, rank, kinship position, nothing to demarcate them structurally from their fellows. Their condition is indeed the very prototype of sacred poverty' (Turner, 1979, p. 8).

In the virtual world, the newbie finds he or she is separated from the ordinary, experiencing a sense of wonder and bewilderment within this new environment. Newbies are easy to spot. Not yet adept at editing their appearance, their form takes the shape of the cookie-cutter avatar. The cookie cutter is a generic avatar which gives away the newbie. The newbie is bound to bump into many doppelgangers and cries of *Look, it's my twin* are regular. Not yet familiar with the method of dressing their avatar, newbies can be spotted wearing their suitcases rather than the clothing. This period of initiation is a passage through which every resident must pass. All newbies, therefore, begin their SL experience as equal in confusion and disorientation.

Stage two: transition

I began my virtual world journey by choosing a generic female avatar from the prepared options. As my SL skills base developed, I experimented with my avatar identity. One day I would choose a female avatar, the next I would choose a male avatar, all of different shapes and sizes. The following excerpt recounts an early SL experience as a buxom female avatar and illustrates how identity choice can have consequences for one's SL experience:

> During my excursions today, I was approached by a tall, dark and (virtually) hand-some male avatar with obvious amorous intent. 'Hey babe, wanna (*sic*) have some fun' he typed into the public text chat box. Uncomfortable with the attention, I politely responded 'No, thank you' and walked away. Persistent in his endeavours, he ran alongside me 'You look hot!' he typed and motioned his avatar to whistle. I collected my thoughts, laughed to myself and typed 'Thank you.' Delighted that this might indicate an invitation to more, the amorous avatar moved in closer. Within an instant, I morphed my avatar appearance – shifting from slim avatar to a tiny balloon-like man, reminiscent of Humpty Dumpty. 'You are mad!' he typed as he backed off at speed. I chuckled to myself and waddled on. (Field note excerpt, 2008)

This experience concurs with Taylor's findings that suggest online 'body choice may support stereotyping' (2002, p. 56). For a period after this event, I chose to engage in my virtual world activities through a fox avatar. The choice of avatar body had a two-fold purpose. First, as the fox avatar was relatively unusual it acted as a conversation opener facilitating engagement with other SL residents. In this way, the avatar acted as a research tool (Martey & Shiflett, 2012). Second, it helped to avoid unwanted flirtatious attention and enabled me to *'get on with the job'*. In this way, the avatar was employed as a prop 'for the presentation of the researcher self in the social arena' (Martey & Shiflett 2012, p. 118).

Adaptation to SL is a challenging and experiential learning process. SL ability development is a gradual process, with success dependent upon the amount of time spent 'in-world'. For full participation in the environment, the basic skills of movement and communication are essential. Such skills are more common than one would first imagine. Most SL residents are familiar with basic computer gaming procedures, and the general principles of ICT. SL skill development thus becomes a 'reformation of old elements into new patterns' (Turner, 1979, p. 9). I began by learning practical virtual locomotive skills, how to walk, run and fly. I learned how to communicate within SL through local text chat and voice chat. Chat abbreviations and emoticons frequently saturate in-world non-verbal communication. Additionally, as communication is synchronous, researchers suggest that avatar body language allows another level of expression (Ventrella, 2011). As an ethnographer and resident in the community, it was imperative that I learned to employ and 'read' this language. Additionally, as I intended to set up home in SL, I studied the fundamentals of Linden Scripting Language (LSL). Again, through a process of assimilation of prior knowledge with new, I came to an understanding of the unwritten rules and etiquette of SL. I devoted the majority of year one to what Agar describes as 'wandering around doing nothing' (1982). This time provided the opportunity to immerse myself and explore 'what is going on here'. This time, however, was not without its tests.

An avatar in 'Steampunk' clothing was strolling around the empty University campus. Despite my regular visits to this campus, this was the first time I had seen someone here. She had long black hair tied back in a pony-tail. A red fascinator was perched on her head. She wore a red full length 'lady of the manor' gown with a voluminous skirt. Over this, she wore a black tailcoat. On her feet were short shoe-boots. The elaborate outfit told me she was certainly not a 'newbie'. Glad to see company (and wondering where she purchased her outfit), I introduced myself through public text chat and motioned my avatar to wave Hi. In an instance, she ran at me, her long red dress swoshing out behind her. She made contact and bumped my avatar backwards. Thinking this was accidental, I attempted to side-step out of her way. She turned and followed, this time making contact on purpose, propelling my avatar backwards. A moment of panic, what is she doing? 'Hey' I typed. I took my hands away from my keyboard and watched with bewilderment and bemusement as my avatar was pushed along at speed. What to do? Not quite sure ... Is it someone I know? I checked her SL profile. This was not a mischievous friend. Annoyed with the treatment of my avatar, I logged off. Twenty minutes later I logged back in. As the SL programme loaded, I felt as though I was peeping around a corner. A quick 'pan camera' action indicated she had left the scene, to be on the safe side I teleported out of there. I had been 'griefed'. (Field note excerpt, 2009)

Throughout the initial transition period, I encountered breakdown and breakthrough experiences. In the world of ritual, such marginal experiences contribute to the feeling of being 'betwixt and between' (Turner 1979, p. 95). The marginal position is precisely that, an experience of being on the threshold between the community and isolation. Events contributing to 'breakdown' moments included unwelcome attention and, as illustrated in the field note, some intermittent encounters with 'griefers'. Most frequently 'breakdown' experiences occurred as a direct result of spending weeks, and in some cases months, in virtual isolation roaming what seemed like a barren post-apocalyptic landscape of virtual wilderness. For the novice ethnographer and new SL resident, such limbo experiences could be described as liminal moments (van Gennep, 1906):

> During the liminal period, neophytes are alternately forced and encouraged to think about their society, their cosmos, and the powers that generate and sustain them. Liminiality may be party described as a stage of reflection. (Turner 1987, p. 14)

Breakthrough came as a result of sustained engagement with the environ-ment. I learned of, and encountered, a variety of residents and groups that have settled in SL. These groups ranged from faith-based communities (Church of Latter Day Saints, SL Evangelists, Unitarian Church of Second Life) and fantasy identity-based communities (Steampunk, Furries, Tinys) to everything in-between.

Establishing identity

By 2009, I had established my research would focus on an exploration of teaching and learning in Second Life. With this in mind I felt it was neces-sary to re-create a researcher's identity, a professional avatar that would be believable as a researcher and as a teacher. The reconstruction of self-identity within the virtual world is beyond a mere appropriation of another avatar, but rather emerges as a direct result of reflection on my role as a learner. In this process, the researcher tries something, withdraws, reconsiders, and tries something else (Turkle, 1997, p. 67). Avatar selection is crucial to 'a user's projected identity, whatever they choose it to be' (Ducheneaut et al., 2009, p. 1159). Modifying avatar appearance is straightforward; we can slip on a new skin with relative ease. At this point in my research, however, the construction of a digital self was more nuanced than the mere appropria-tion of another avatar. Avatar construction commenced with reflection on my role as a researcher, and a learner. Consequently, the construction of a professional avatar could be considered a deliberate attempt at impression management, a performance of the self (Goffman, 1959). The language of performance, however, is problematic. It suggests a deliberate production and 'acting out' of a fiction. A fiction implies the use of the imagination but also elements of fabrication. Clearly the creation of an avatar is an exercise in production. Nonetheless, to knowingly 'act out' a false representation of the self could be construed as deceptive. Given my professional context, the choice of my avatar was pedagogically driven. Specifically, this involved the creation of a believable and accurate representation of my corporeal self with a virtual realm. In this way, I do not consider my avatar as a mask or performance tool. Rather, it is a presentation, perhaps even a dimension, of the already established *self* within the virtual world.

O'Brien (1999) argues that 'gender is one of the first means by which persons introduce and represent themselves to others in electronic communities' (p. 86). We are not 'magically freed from our bodies when we go online' (Martey & Consalvo, 2011, p. 178). Gender choice can provide us with a method to assess and categorise the other in a personally significant way. Presenting my professional self in the virtual world in a gender ambiguous form, such as the fox avatar, or in a highly sexualised manner might have had a negative impact on both my virtual world identity and possibly my real-world professional identity. Further to this, I did not want to create further distance between my students and myself in my subsequent Second Life learning environment. As a result, my persistent avatar choice is in human female form. Additionally, it has some resemblance to my corporeal characteristics (colour of hair, eye-colour). While I do not consider my avatar an idealised version of my corporeal self, it is certainly enhanced with clever (invisible) lighting attachments and make up.

Avatar clothing has both an aesthetic and functional role. However, it also has a social role as it contributes to impression management. In sum, clothing relates a 'specific expression of self' (Martey & Consalvo, 2011, p. 168). My avatar clothing selection adheres to a professional dress code; a suit jacket, blouse, knee length skirt and low heeled shoes. In short, my digital representation communicates to others that I am a professional engaged in formal activities. In this way, my avatar is an authentic representation of my offline persona. For this reason, over the course of this research I maintained this avatar appearance. As my avatar identity was persistent for the duration of the study, I was easily recognisable to my peers and students.

Finding a home

Next, in order to establish a *sense of place* within SL, I created a home followed later by the development of a virtual campus. It is necessary here
to clarify what exactly is meant by place. Place is broadly defined as 'a
meaningful location' (Creswell, 2004, p. 7). In addition, place is generally understood to have three key elements: location, locale, and a sense
of place (Resor, 2010, p. 186). The location of my SL residence is fixed to
a SLURL, while the locale is *Calaveres*, a suburban housing development.
A *sense of place*, however, is more difficult to determine. As employed by
geographers, *a sense of place* is defined by the non-material, that is, 'the
subjective and emotional attachment a person has to a place' (Resor, 2010,
p. 186). The difference between place and space then is *meaning*. Within the
virtual world this issue is compounded by the fact that *place* exists within
a *virtual* space. As a result, an SL *place* cannot be physically experienced,
however as meaning relates to the non-material, a virtual space can still be
experienced as *meaningful*. The establishment of a *sense of place* refers to
the process of creating a virtual *home* that later acted for a period of time
as a classroom base for students.

Stage three: transformation

Transformation, in this case, refers the final stage in the journey of immersion into the virtual world. In this stage, I became first a student and then
a teacher within SL. While I refer to this as a final stage of immersion, I do
not intend to suggest that this is the final phase of learning in and about
SL. As SL is a virtual world, it is continually evolving and therefore learning is a continual process.

　　To understand the potential of the environment (for teaching and
learning) one should first consider becoming a student within that

environment. The rationale for becoming a student in SL is based on the belief that we can learn *by observing teaching in action* and *learn through participation* (Lortie, 1975). First, we can learn by observing teaching in action. Specifically, we can learn how teaching occurs in SL through observation of teaching in the virtual classroom. In this research, I focused on the observation of key skill sets set out by my teacher education module descriptors. These skill sets include:

(a) Teaching and learning process skills – specification of outcomes, lesson management, and assessment of lesson outcomes.
(b) Classroom management skills – responsiveness to students, how to approach discipline and pupil management.
(c) Teacher communication skills – employment of teaching tools and delivery of lesson.
(d) Subject content engagement skills – how to motivate learners and present content in an engaging manner.
(e) Methodological skills – which methods can be employed and which work best from a students' perspective.

Second, we can learn through participation within a SL module. By becoming a learner in SL we learn by doing (Dewey, 1910; Lewin, 1936; Piaget, 1982; Kolb, 1984; Gardner, 1985). We learn the following: classroom communication skills (how to respond – text or chat), classroom etiquette, teaching methods that are engaging for the students, how to overcome challenges (technical or locomotive) and what it feels like to be a student in SL (creation of identity, being part of a class community, learning from one another). This interplay between *observation* and *participation* permits the SL student (and researcher) a unique lens into pedagogical practice in the virtual world. This approach concurs with best practice in online learning which affirms that teachers should experience 'technology from a learner's point of view before deciding whether and how to use it' (JISC, 2009, p. 4).

  To learn from the inside, I searched for a suitable module to participate in as a student. By 2010, I had firmly established connections within the environment. Through continual engagement with the Second Life educators' list (SLED), I became aware of a relevant module, Is One Life Enough, offered by a neighbouring third-level institute. I participated in this module as both a student and researcher.

To continue my immersion into the environment, I designed and sought approval for the module *Religion in Cyberspace*. The design of the module was informed by my personal experience within the SL environment and my experience as a student within the module Is One Life Enough. The SL based module *Religion in Cyberspace* is offered as a third year undergraduate Religious Studies optional module in the college. This module is the field in which I conducted the corpus of my research. In this phase of the research, I assumed the role of teacher and researcher within the environment.

Concluding remarks

At this point, a justifiable question is posed: How do you know you achieved immersion into the virtual world? I return to the role of the ethnographer to answer this question. The ethnographer aims 'to do field research by doing and becoming – to the extent possible – whatever it is they are interested in learning about' (Emerson et al., 1995, p. 2). This paper provides a descriptive account of '*doing and becoming*'. Three key stages of immersion experienced during the rite of passage into the virtual world were identified. They comprise separation, transition and transformation. First, separation refers to the movement from the offline world into the virtual world. Second, transition refers to the period of adaptation and adjustment to the virtual environment. Third, transformation refers to the process of *both* learning and learning to teach within the SL environment. Within each stage, distinct sub-stages of development are highlighted. As a result of the rite of passage into the virtual world, I moved out of my comfort zone, from security into the unknown. In an effort to understand teaching and learning in SL, I stepped away from the role of teacher and assumed the role of student. Liminal moments, moments of darkness, questioning, and reflection, interspersed the journey.

References

Agar, M.H., 'Toward an ethnographic language.' *American Anthropologist*, 84/ 4 (1982), 779–795. Agar, M.H., *The professional stranger: an informal introduction to ethnography* (US: Elsevier, 1986).

Aldrich, C., *Learning online with games, simulations, and virtual worlds* (US: Josey-Bass, 2009).

Barrie, F.H., *Peter and Wendy* (UK: Hodder and Stoughton, 1911).

Barthes, R., *The pleasure of the text* (New York, Hill and Wang, 1975).

Bell, M., 'Towards a definition of virtual worlds.' *Journal of Virtual Worlds Research* 1/1, 1–5.

Boas, F., *The mind of primitive man* (UK: Macmillan, 1911).

Boellstorff, T., *Coming of age in second life: an anthropologist explores the virtually human* (Oxford: Princeton University Press, 2008).

Burnett, F.H., *The secret garden* (UK: Heinemann, 1911).

Carr, D., Buckingham, D., Burn, A., & Schott, G., *Computer games: text, narrative and play* (UK: Polity Press, 2006).

Castranova, E., *Synthetic worlds: the business and culture of online games* (Chicago: University of Chicago Press, 2006).

Creswell, T., *Place: A Short Introduction* (Malden: Blackwell Publishing, 2004).

Dewey, J., *How we think* (Boston, MA: D.C. Heath and Co., 1910).

Emmerson, R., Fretz, R., & Shaw, L., *Writing Ethnographic Fieldnotes* (Chicago, IL: University of Chicago Press, 1995).

Gaible, E. & Burns, M., 'Using Technology to Train Teachers: Appropriate Uses of ICT for Teacher Professionals'. Retrieved June 2010 from <http://www.infodev.org/en/Publication.13.hmtl>

Gardner, H., *Frames of Mind: The Theory of Multiple Intelligence* (New York, NY: Basic Books, 1985).

Goffman, E., *The presentation of self in everyday life* (New York: Doubleday Anchor Books, 1959).

JISC, *Responding to learners: a guide for practitioners* (2009). Retrieved July 2010 from: <http://www.jisc.ac.uk/media/documents/publications/lxp2.pdf>

Kellaghan, T., 'Preparing Teachers for the 21st century. Report of the Working Group on Primary Education.' in A. Burke, ed., *Teacher Education in the Republic of Ireland* (Armagh: The Centre for Cross-Border Studies, 2004), 19–28.

Kolb, D.A., *Experiential Learning: Experience as the Source of Learning and Development* (Englewood Cliffs, NJ: Prentice-Hall, 1984).

Lacey, C., *The Socialization of Teachers* (London, UK: Methuen, 1977).

Lee, H., *To Kill a Mockingbird* (Philadelphia, PA: Lippincott, 1960).

Lewin, K., Heider, F., & Heider, G.M., *Principles of Topological Psychology* (New York, NY: McGraw-Hills, 1936).

Lewis, C.S., *The lion, the witch and the wardrobe* (UK: Geoffrey Bles, 1950).

LindyMac's Blog. Retrieved June 2012 from <http://www.blog.lindymckeown. com/?p=95>

Loughran, J.J., *Developing a Pedagogy of Teacher Education: Understanding Teaching and Learning about Teaching* (New York: Routledge, 2006).

Loughran, J.J., *Developing Reflective Practice: Learning about Teaching and Learning through Modelling* (London, UK: Falmer Press, 1996).

Loughran, J., 'Enacting a Pedagogy of Teacher Education' in T. Russell & J. Loughran, eds, *Enacting a Pedagogy of Teacher Education: Values, Relationships and Practices* (London: Routledge, 2007).

Malinowski, B., *Argonauts of the western Pacific: an account of native enterprise and adventure in the archipelagoes of Melanesian New Guinea* (Abingdon: Routledge, 1932).

Martey, R. & Shiflett, K., 'Reconsidering self and site: methodological frameworks for virtual world research.' *International Journal of Communications* 6, 105–126.

Mead, M., *Coming of age in Samoa: a study of adolescence and sex in primitive societies* (Harmondsworth: Penguin, 1977).

Odysseus Tempest's Blog. Retrieved June 2010 from <http://odysseustempest.word-press.com/>

Resor, C.W., 'Place-Based Education: What is Its Place in the Social Studies Classroom?' *The Social Studies* 101/5 (2010), 185–188.

Taylor, T.L., 'Living digitally: embodiment in virtual worlds' in R. Schroeder, ed., *The social life of avatars: presence and interaction in shared virtual environments* (London: Springer-Verlag, 2002), 40–59.

Tolkien, J.R.R., *The Lord of the Rings* (UK: Allen and Unwin, 1954).

Turkle, S., *Life on the Screen: Identity in the Age of the Internet* (London, UK: Weidenfeld & Nicolson, 1996).

Turner, V., *The ritual process: structure and anti-structure* (New York: Cornell Paperbacks, 1979).

Ventrella, J., *Virtual body language: the history and future of avatars how non-verbal language is evolving on the internet* (US: Eye Brain Books, 2011).

Wang, T.J., 'Educating avatars: on virtual worlds and pedagogical intent', *Teaching in Higher Education* 16/6, 617–628.

Woods, P., *Inside Schools: Ethnography in Educational Research* (New York, NY: Routledge & Kegan Paul, 1986).

FAWEI GENG, CARL MARSHALL AND ROWAN WILSON

11 A Case-Study on Podcasting Impact at the University of Oxford

Audio and video podcasting at the University of Oxford has been taking place at the level of individual departments and academics for many years. Some units, such as the Oxford Internet Institute, have had mature programmes of podcast publication in place since 2005. Due to Oxford's devolved nature, however, there was initially no centrally coordinated effort to draw together these materials and offer them from a single location.

In 2008 Apple Inc invited Oxford to join the European launch of their already extremely successful iTunes U educational podcasting platform. In response to this request a team based at Oxford University Computing Services (OUCS) formed to draw together the infrastructure required to present the various audio and video via the iTunes U portal. As the deadlines for joining the platform were tight, pre-existent solutions were reused as much as possible. OUCS had already developed an RSS (Really Simple Syndication) publishing platform in-house for use by University departments, societies and individuals, and this was expanded to support the supplying of RSS feeds listing podcasts to Apple's iTunes U portal. Using this system – called *OxItems* – staff from all around the University could add feeds of audio and video items to a queue, to be assessed by the team within OUCS for publication within Oxford's iTunes U presence.

The terms under which Oxford could join Apple's iTunes U platform were examined and eventually approved at the highest committee level within Oxford. As part of this approval, the team within OUCS was – with the help of support staff within the departments themselves – responsible for obtaining signed agreements from contributing academics concerning the provenance and propriety of the material in their contributions. This was seen as a necessary step in managing the risks of publishing such a wide array of material, but added an administrative step to the technical process.

In short, the collection investigated by this project consisted[1] of approximately 2,650 media files (podcasts) of mostly academic related content (lectures, interviews, discussions, workshops, etc); comprised of two thirds audio (MP3), one third video and some electronic books and pdf publications. These are arranged into 323 RSS feeds (groups of related material), and presented via five centrally maintained portals and several other external portals. The collection has grown during the project lifetime (October 2010 to March 2011) with over 400 new items added and thirty new feeds created.

Areas of concern

By the time of the launch of iTunes U in the UK in late 2008, Oxford had built a workable technical and administrative process for podcast publication via iTunes U, but one that had some shortcomings. Of particular relevance to this project were the following:

Remoteness of contributors. Technical support staff in departments were often responsible for both the recording of podcasts and the inputting of metadata (information about the podcasts) into the *OxItems* system. Without this effort from local staff, the iTunes U project would have been impossible, but one negative consequence of this was that the team within OUCS were often not in direct contact with the academic contributors and therefore often unaware of feedback on the podcasts from external users, students and the contributors themselves, as well as lacking advance warning of upcoming materials.

Scattered hosting. Again, to aid initial setup, the decision was taken at the beginning to devolve responsibility for hosting podcasts to the departments

---

1   Valid at time of writing, March 2011.

and colleges sponsoring them. While some podcasts were hosted within systems managed by OUCS (providing support where departments were unable), many were hosted on web servers managed by independent departments. This made the collation of a complete set of access statistics from local web servers for the entire collection of iTunes U impractical, though that situation has improved over time.[2]

Split collection interfaces. Again, to aid initial setup, the decision was taken at the beginning to devolve responsibility for hosting podcasts to the departments and colleges sponsoring them. While some podcasts were hosted within systems managed by OUCS (providing support where departments were unable) many were hosted on web servers managed by independent departments. This made the collation of a complete set of access statistics from local web servers for the entire collection of iTunes U impractical, though that situation has improved over time.[3]

From the beginning it was clear that for reasons of interoperability the work being put into the creation of the centralised podcasting listing could not be presented solely through Apple's iTunes U interface. The iTunes client only runs on the Windows and Mac OS platforms, potentially excluding visitors who do not use either and those who choose not to, or do not have access to, iTunes. Therefore a simple web page interface to the RSS feeds was created. This took the form of an exhaustive listing of podcast feeds and their contents generated as a single page. This answered the interoperability need but clearly presented scalability issues in the long term, as well as creating the necessity to maintain two separate means of accessing the collection. However, other portals for distributing Oxford's podcasts have also arisen – notably the Mobile Oxford portal (<http://m.ox.ac.uk/>) created by the JISC Erewhon project – thus increasing the complexity of monitoring usage.

2   See project blog post 'Fishing with a broken net' – <http://bit.ly/gUDKEN> – for more details on further developments.
3   See project blog post 'Fishing with a broken net' – <http://bit.ly/gUDKEN> – for more details on the current situation.

168 FAWEI GENG, CARL MARSHALL AND ROWAN WILSON

The rise of Open Educational Resources

In 2009, the podcasting team at OUCS gained funding from the Higher Education Academy and JISC for the OpenSpires project as part of the Open Educational Resources (OER) programme pilot phase. OpenSpires aimed to make a significant number of Oxford podcasts available under an open content licence, specifically the Creative Commons Attribution-Non Commercial-Sharealike licence. The project was successful in revising the technical and administrative processes within the team in order to embed OER release. Work on the OpenSpires project brought with it a new focus on use and reuse of our resources, and as a result a greater interest in user tracking.

Against this background the JISC-funded Listening for Impact project has, over the period October 2010 to March 2011, attempted to:

- address the lack of systematic analysis of the impact of our podcasts offered on our public-access University of Oxford podcasting sites and via Oxford on iTunes U.
- develop and instigate practical approaches to embedding academic podcast resources within the teaching and learning virtual environment at Oxford and the wider subject community.
- collect and evaluate data to demonstrate the impact of the Oxford Podcast collection, which will strengthen the case for continued sustainability for the podcasting service, the Oxford Podcast collection and consequently, the OpenSpires OER collection at Oxford (the OpenSpires OER collection is a subset of the Oxford Podcast collection).
- research and contribute towards the knowledge of embedding online collections in academic disciplines by a case study of impact and user engagement.

Marketing and promotion[4]

Making high quality materials freely available drew great attention from the media and general public when supported by a well organised professional press release and marketing campaign. After launching Oxford on iTunes U in October 2008, Oxford podcasts attracted a great deal of attention from the media including newspapers, radio, and TVs.

> 450 hours of free podcasts, lectures, films and admissions guides up on the iTunes U academic portal, available to anyone who wants to download them.[5]

> We hope that this service will make Oxford's diverse range of audio and video material more widely accessible to applicants, alumni, supporters of the university, and the intellectually curious.[6]

> ... for the first time this brings everything together on one, easy to use website, that is really easy for people to navigate. It gives people a real sense of breadth and depth of the activities that are going on at the university.[7]

A global audience of learners[8]

Oxford's podcasts inspired, engaged and motivated learners and teachers around the world. Materials were also reused by teachers in other organisations. Podcasting on iTunes U by Oxford academics attracted listeners from around the world including Sweden, Norway, Brazil, USA, Canada,

---

4   Tools to monitor this impact: Google Alerts; LexisNexis searching.
5   Source: <http://www.digitaltrends.com/international/oxford-v-cambridge-on-itunes/>
6   Source: <http://www.guardian.co.uk/education/2008/oct/07/elearning.students>
7   Source: <http://www.oxfordmail.co.uk/news/3748048.Get_lectures_on_your_iPod/>
8   Tools to monitor this impact: email collection, surveys, interviews.

China, Korea, and New Zealand. From the feedback sent to a number of academics – including Marianne Talbot (whose global No. 1 podcast reached >5000 downloads per week) – it was clear that listeners come from a wide range of backgrounds: professionals (teachers, writers, lawyers, and orthopaedic surgeons), students, retired lifelong learners. Some listeners were motivated by the podcasts to write to their creators.

Motivating distance learners:

> I have recently enrolled in an Open University in Australia with the plan to complete a BA in Philosophy, but the first unit I have had to complete is a Study Skills unit which has been so boring and mundane I have been questioning whether to continue or not. Your enthusiasm for philosophy is infectious and put me back on course to continue my studies. Thanks again. (Student comment)

Supporting existing students:

> I have finished watching your 6 episodes about Critical Reasoning for Beginners to gain solid basic ideas for preparing my GMAT test and for personal life. The episodes do help me a lot in understanding logical thinking ... (Student comment)

Helping teachers in their professional development:

> Thank you for offering online your lectures on introductory quantum mechanics, and thank you for providing a PDF copy of your text. The text is a marvelous [*sic*] resource, and your lectures are exceptionally lucid and compelling. I am learning a great deal and enjoying them very much. I teach high school science and maths, and I hope I can pass along to my students (at least some of) these ideas with the same excitement and clarity. (High school teacher)

Reuse in the classroom:

> I hope you'll be pleased to hear that your podcasts on approaches to Shakespeare are being very much appreciated. As head of More Able and Talented at a large state school, I am constantly looking for resources to improve our teaching and your podcasts are giving us just that opportunity. Members of the English department are now using Wittgenstein's Dabbit illustration in the way you did and finding it to be a very effective approach and our more able students are being encouraged to listen to the podcasts both to improve their understanding of the plays and to encourage them to believe that the Oxford is not a rarefied and unattainable target,

but operates at a level they will find accessible. Beyond that I and an increasing number to whom I have been recommending the site have really enjoyed the lectures. (Head teacher)

Podcasting can provide learners with opportunities to be in control of their learning. Listening to podcasts can be seen as a passive form of learning. However, feedback to this project indicates that it does offer listeners the chance to be in control of where, when and how they learn.

I have downloaded and am listening to your series of lectures on philosophy. I play them in the car as I drive to and from work and as a result of your lectures, my journey takes a lot longer as I slow right down to make the journey last a lot longer. I have the audio version, so there are gaps as you demonstrate things, but when I get home I can check the video version on line. Can I just say how utterly engrossing they are – and how completely stimulating. I completed my undergraduate studies a great number of years ago, but listening to you lecture makes me yearn for study. (Email feedback from a listener to the 'Philosophy for Beginners' series)

I have quite a bit of work to do to understand some of the trickier derivations – fortunately, I have a 'pause' button and much more time than your students do. (Email feedback from a listener to the 'Quantum Mechanics' podcast series)

Internal audiences[9]

Compared to the current Oxford students, prospective and new students have a different focus and interest in podcasting. In October 2010, 676 students who had just started their studies at Oxford and who would not have received any internal marketing material yet completed a podcasting-related survey. A few interesting points are summarised as follows:

9   Tools to monitor this impact: electronic survey; manned survey point at Freshers' Fair.

- Around 90 per cent of the respondents had heard of iTunes U.
- Around half of the respondents had downloaded podcasts that were aimed at potential admissions to Oxford. Around 70 per cent had downloaded podcasts related to their primary subject of interest.
- Podcasts related to admissions and university life were among the most popular.

Two quotes from the survey:

> I found the ones from the admissions offices really helpful. As an international student they were a really good way for me to learn about the admissions procedure as it's not as easy for international students to come to the open days as it is for UK residents.

> The social anthropology dept. did a series of interviews of current students about life as a grad student at their dept, which was really helpful ... I don't know if I will use it now that I'm here, but a few students have been asking about whether lectures will be on iTunes U so perhaps in a few years it will be expected? I hope not ... I still believe in education taking place in the classroom, particularly for students AT the institution ...

This survey showed that the collection was reaching a key external audience – people new to Oxford – in a format and manner that appealed to them and met their needs. This survey can be run longitudinally to monitor changes in usage.

Current Oxford students are becoming increasingly aware of Oxford podcasts and they value relevant content delivered in a format that aids revision. A survey was sent out to three different departmental groups, but at various stages of the project's life: November 2010, December 2010 and February 2011. This survey was not repeated with each group; nevertheless it does seem that more and more students are aware of the Oxford podcasts. For example, the percentage of students who listened to podcasts from the Oxford podcasting portal (podcasts.ox.ac.uk) increased from 7 per cent (November 2010 group) to 33 per cent (February 2011 group). The proportion of students who had not listened to any Oxford podcasts reduced from 44 per cent to 16 per cent.

Three student surveys were undertaken by the project covering a broad range of topics and indicators. For example, they indicated that the main reasons current Oxford students listened to Oxford podcasts were: they allowed them to 'catch-up' if a lecture was missed; they stimulated the student's interest in a subject; and they were an aid to revision. The features that made podcasts more attractive to current Oxford students were: lectures/talks were related to their own course/subject; there are resources associated with podcasts: e.g. transcripts, slides, or brief description; the podcast can be played in-line, i.e. in the location where it is discovered.

Surveying students and other audiences not only helps to gather feedback but also is a way of raising awareness of our service.

> I never knew they existed, but will definitely use them from now on.

> Although I have not listened to any OU podcast, this is a laugh because I wasn't sure where to look.

On reflection, it seems that the two main factors that make our podcasts popular are the content itself in a repeatable/reusable format, and how the content is explained and presented. In other words, if a lecturer knows how to explain the topic in a clear, logical and sometimes entertaining matter, this is a more important factor in keeping students engaged and motivated than cosmetic presentation.

Tools, techniques and technologies

Web log analysis is complex but rewarding. The methods commonly recommended to analyse and report on content usage (Log analysis and similar, such as promoted by the TIDSR toolkit) are very difficult to apply to situations where there is a high level of demand for the material. The collaboration with Apple drives traffic enormously but also complicates analysis of usage because of the volume of access data that traffic generates (around 1–2 million accesses daily). Commercially or freely available tools to help with this analysis were deemed inadequate after testing with Oxford's set-up. The necessity to process multiple log files covering the same period and to generate reports on separate feeds and items quickly, led us to determine that a flexible Stats system based on a SQL database was necessary. We describe this in more detail on the 'Outcomes' section below. Our initial Rapid Analysis Report suffered from this lack of usable tools combined with a large rich source of data. Unfortunately the quantity of passive tracking data has continued to grow during the project and technical speed limitations have meant that absorbing and analysing this data has been curtailed due to limited time. Therefore, this report looks at information from our new tools, but only for data harvested from our central hosting, and only for the period of 7 November 2010 to 28 February 2011.

Reconciling the various data sources continues to be challenging, though the Listening for Impact work has significantly advanced this activity. Further data importing and development of this Stats system is set to continue after the project concludes as the value of having this data available to be flexibly queried has been firmly established within the Podcasting Service. The ability to generate reports on individual podcasts or series is extremely helpful in answering common questions from contributors and demonstrating the impact on podcasting activity both for individual academics and the University as a whole.

Oxford podcasts are popular globally and that popularity is growing. Using the data supplied by Apple and the size of our log files over time[10] we can see that our volume of traffic and downloads has mushroomed during the course of this project, and one of our aims has been to try and understand why. Unfortunately the conclusive answer to this has eluded us as it lies too far back in our richer data to be queried at time of writing. However, earlier sampling combined with a plot of Accesses by Geography supports our hypothesis that Apple's launch of iTunes U into the Chinese educational sector at the start of September 2010 led to a rush of interest in our material similar to the rush we experienced at our European launch two years earlier, albeit six times larger. This is borne out by the rise in, and high levels of traffic from China and related countries accessing our materials, compared to the situation before the launch. We also believe that other engineering changes Apple made to the iTunes U store at the same time also benefited our exposure by making the portal more accessible to general web users and searching.

Apple's promotional activities continue to be the primary driver for downloads of our content (over 50 per cent of accesses can be shown to have come from iTunes U), with items they have promoted leading to (high) appearances in their global Top 100 download chart, which have then largely been sustained by continued exposure through that channel. Whilst increasing traffic through other promotional means (such as our social media experiment described in finding 12 on the following page) is possible, nothing competes with the scale of interest generated by Apple's marketing. Indeed, a recent example ('Love and other things') shows that gaining a place in their Top 100 listing alone is not enough to sustain success.

The general wisdom of statistical analysis that recommends analysing trends, not absolutes, applies here. Trends show our podcasts are continuing to increase their distribution and the average rate of downloads continues to increase even after two and a half years of publishing. One factor we cannot account for is market share or almost anything that would allow us to compare against other institutions, as almost no other publishers share comparable information, and the one or two that do use differing methodologies.

Over 1 in 7 (15 per cent) accesses of our material are initiated directly from mobile devices. Analysis of our web logs shows that 15 per cent of our accesses are initiated from Apple mobile devices (iPod, iPhone and iPad). This is significantly higher than the average share for mobile browsers in general web traffic, which is currently around 4 per cent according to monitoring site Statcounter.[11] Also notable is that our mobile traffic is over-whelmingly from Apple devices, with negligible levels of access from other popular devices such as Android smartphones and tablets or Blackberry.

11   <http://bit.ly/gGge7f>

Again, Statcounter[12] would suggest that this differs from trends for the web in general over the same period, where the split of traffic between the Android browser, the Blackberry browser, Apple Mobile Safari, Opera Mobile and Mini and others is far more balanced. It seems extremely likely that the project's close association with Apple and the presence of the iTunes client by default on every Apple mobile device are resulting both in greater numbers of accesses from mobile devices and a skewing of mobile accesses towards Apple platforms.

In analysing the breakdown of accesses to our content, first by platform and then specifically from internet enabled mobile devices, we can see that Apple platforms feature more highly than normal compared to regular website browsing – almost 35 per cent of accesses compared to 6 per cent shown by Statcounter for OS comparisons.[13] This Apple influence is even higher when you discover that 55 per cent of our podcasts are accessed via Multimedia Player applications (opposed to 40 per cent via a traditional web browser) and that 99 per cent of those Multimedia application accesses are via Apple supplied software. In relation to access from mobile device platforms, we have found that there are 15 per cent iOS accesses, with the combined accesses of all the other mobile platforms equating to less than 1 per cent of the total Apple device accesses.

Promotion via social media is time consuming and the benefits appear limited. As part of our investigation into publishing our content in other channels, the project team composed a series of tweets highlighting selected podcasts. Details of the methodology and outcomes can be found in the project blog post 'Can you hear me tweeting?'.[14] To summarise, the results in terms of traffic driven to the resources highlighted were surprisingly modest. The Twitter identity '*@oxfordpodcasts*' had in excess of 1,500 followers over the course of the experiment, yet the number of click-throughs to the tracked URLs was below twenty in every case.

12   <http://bit.ly/gRy5Oi>
13   <http://gs.statcounter.com/#os-ww-monthly-201009-201102>
14   <http://bit.ly/hf7asW>

We attribute this to two factors. Firstly, our use of Twitter was relatively unsophisticated, essentially treating it as a broadcast channel without social and interactive components. Secondly, the eclectic mix of material that emerges from the Oxford podcasting portal may also work against the formation of a cohesive community of followers; many may be interested in Oxford podcasts as a concept, but each individual podcast is likely to be of interest to only a small subset of the followers.

In an informal comparison with the click-through rates obtained by another project located within OUCS – the JISC-funded advisory service on free and open source software OSS Watch – we found that despite having only one third the number of followers, Twitter notifications of OSS Watch blog posts were receiving thirty to fifty times the number of click-throughs achieved by *oxfordpodcasts*. We speculate that the differences could be explained by the two factors mentioned above. It is also worth noting that OSS Watch tweets will tend to be retweeted by followers far more than those of *oxfordpodcasts*, often with relevant hashtags appended. This is likely to greatly increase the visibility and reach of the individual tweets.

Requirements for change

In undertaking this project, the team was already aware of some issues with both the arrangement of the current podcasting portal and its integration with other services. Feedback from students and academics had highlighted the facts that the Oxford podcasting portal's search functionality was poor, that we lacked an individual landing page for each podcast series (making linking to podcast series problematic and rendering the indexing of our material by external search engines non-optimal) and that there was no easy way to integrate podcasts into our Sakai-based Virtual Learning Environment *WebLearn*. Rectifying these issues became a matter of priority, and over the course of this project they have all been addressed.

In gathering opinions on the podcasting service over the last six months, we have also received a lot of feedback about the podcasts themselves. The nature of the podcasting activity within Oxford means that the team within OUCS can only pass on requirements concerning the material itself to academics; we do not commission the material, so there is a limit to how much specification we can undertake. Nevertheless the opinions we have gathered will inform the advice we give to contributing academics in the future. Below we reproduce quotations from this feedback sorted into broad categories:

Students asked for more podcasts in more subjects:

> Please podcast all lectures sometimes we have essay crisis, cannot come to lecture, but we really want to go!

> I appreciate my lecture being made into a podcast. I hope other lectures will be [*sic*] into podcasts too!

Students asked to include associated learning materials with the podcasts:

> More description of their content so can see what it is before downloading/listening.

> Slides must be available online, esp for courses like Quantum Mechanics.

Suggestions were made for the improvement of podcasts:

> Clearer audio, more lectures recorded.

> On occasion, the audio quality is poor, which makes the podcast very difficult to listen to.

Other suggestions were made on how to make the podcasts more appealing:

> Keep it short.

> Make it more interactive.

> videos will be nice.

> not just of the curriculum lecture courses but maybe alongside that you could have a couple of extra-curricular ones that talk about some of the more interesting (but perhaps beyond the scope of the course) or more current issues on the subject.

Challenges encountered and lessons learnt

The podcasting activity within the University of Oxford publishes large quantities of material while employing a relatively small team of people. As detailed above, the drawing together of disparate publication mechanisms to create a unified presence happened in a relatively short time and relied on pre-existent systems that were in the main created for other purposes. The throughput of podcasts began high and has remained so, with no opportunity for significant downtime for revision of service architecture. For these reasons making changes to the current system is extremely challenging.

The changes which the 'Listening for Impact' project has enacted reside in two distinct locations: *WebLearn*, the Sakai-based virtual learning environment for the University and the *Podcasting Portal* itself <http:// podcasts.ox.ac.uk/>. WebLearn has stable release cycles and therefore planning and implementing changes has been relatively pain-free. The podcasting portal, on the other hand, does not have a stable release cycle. As noted above, its history as a simple aggregation of all the podcasting feeds makes it difficult to sustain in the long term, and so a full replacement is being developed behind the scenes, and has been for some time. This replacement, based on the open source web portal software Drupal, is now available alongside the original podcasting portal (<http://beta. podcasts.ox.ac.uk/>). The replacement portal answers many of the criticisms of the original portal, and will allow a more systematic approach to revision in the future.

The latter stages of this replacement project coincided with the Listening for Impact requirement for alterations to the podcasting web presence, and so it seemed sensible to make the changes in the new version. However, the fact that those alterations (as well as many other tweaks) are embodied in a distinct version of the podcasting portal has some consequences. Firstly, the comparison of access data between the old and new portals is made extremely complex by changes in fundamental structure. This means that it will be some time before we can fully assess the benefits of the changes made. Secondly, the 'soft launch' of the new portal and its consequent parallel availability with the old portal further complicates analysis of change and ties the exposure of the Listening for Impact modifications to the timetable for the replacement portal.

The presentation of our podcasts via the Apple iTunes U portal has meant that we experience extremely high levels of interest and access from around the world. While this is gratifying and greatly supports the argument that University of Oxford podcasting is a high impact activity, it has some challenging practical implications. As mentioned in the findings above, the sheer quantity of accesses creates enormous log files, which in turn take time (four to eight hours each) to process for analysis and reporting. Even these do not in all likelihood represent the totality of the number of accesses to our material, as Apple employs proxying for highly-requested material, essentially directing some traffic away from Oxford and to a third party storage provider. We see evidence of this activity through requests from the storage provider to our web servers for the material, but we have no direct evidence of how many accesses these intermediary services are handling. Apple does provide a high level of statistics to us which relate to accesses initiated from the various iTunes clients on home computers, mobile devices and set-top boxes. Reconciling these statistics with our own internal recording mechanisms has been one of the aims of this project, and has been to a large extent successful. However the devolved nature of Oxford's podcast hosting means that a complete reconciliation remains impractical.

Another consequence of the association with Apple is the effect that their promotional choices have on consumption of our podcasts. While Oxford has control over the layout of our own podcast portal and the pages we manage within iTunes, Apple decides which materials it wishes to promote on the iTunes U landing page without direct communication with us. In our experience, podcasts promoted in this way experience a gigantic surge in traffic and remain popular even when the promotion has completed. While this may seem to be 'one of those good problems', it does mean that probably the most widely viewed public interface to our material is only partially under our direct control.

This in turn raises questions about how to manage institutional resources being devoted to promoting the service. As noted in the findings, the results of promotional activities undertaken by the team tend to be dwarfed by the results of Apple promotion and the resulting 'residence' in the Top 100 downloads charts of certain podcast series. In turn, these series become the 'news-worthy successes' of the project and this drives traffic to them even more. This 'feedback' effect is probably unavoidable, but does work against the presentation of the University's podcasts as all being equally valuable.

One key lesson is that tracking methods and feedback channels need to be considered as early as possible and integrated closely with user interfaces (e.g. the websites). As time passes without these processes in place, more and more historical data is lost and typically cannot be recovered, thus perspectives based on trends are hard to come by initially. For most typical websites, the freely available tools (such as Google Analytics) will often be adequate for basic reporting and are easy to incorporate. However, the more diverse and complex your systems are, the more effort and time will need to be expended to monitor effectively.

Outcomes and benefits

As a result of work undertaken by the Listening for Impact project, the University of Oxford now has a better understanding of the impact of the podcasting activity both within education and more generally. The project has generated tools for the analysis of impact that will continue to have use and provide benefit after the end of the project. These include *better processes for sampling user and contributor opinion*. As a result of the survey instruments and contact workflows generated by this project, it should now be considerably easier to sample and compare reactions to our activity. This in turn should make it easier to present the case for the service being a benefit to the institution as a whole.

Database tools for deep log analysis

The project team examined the set of available solutions for log analysis at the beginning of the project. Google Analytics was assessed and found to be a strong general solution for analysing accesses to page-based web resources. However for our purposes Google Analytics had a severe draw-back – its method of registering page accesses depends upon the execution of a javascript attachment to each monitored page. Most of the traffic from the Oxford podcasting site is in the form of direct requests for media items that cannot trigger the relevant Google Analytics javascript, making it at best only a partial solution to our problem. The team also considered log analysis and reporting tool Analog, which is available as open source software under the GNU GPLv2. This answered our requirements better, but is essentially geared to the creation of high level reports on specific aspects of web access activity (although it is fairly configurable). This kind of a solution could be extremely useful for monitoring trends in general aspects of our web traffic were it a single site, but it was not optimal for the rapid formulation and investigation of queries about use of arbitrary sub-sections of our resource. For these purposes a more flexible investigative tool was needed. Therefore we decided to create a database of log lines against which we could run arbitrary queries.

Using a popular open source database application in combination with processing and importation scripts written in Python, the project team created an extremely flexible database tool for querying and analysing web server access logs. Questions about access can be formulated as standard SQL queries and run against the database of log lines combined with some additional derived data such as approximate geographical location of the requesting IP address. This tool can be thought of as an adjunct to rather than a replacement for summary reporting tools such as Analog, in that it allows rapid formulation and investigation of hypotheses about our access data. This has proved invaluable for the Listening for Impact project, as we needed to dig deeply into our access data to make a baseline assessment of out impact. However the tool will also have more long-term uses. The wide subject spread of the podcasting resource means that it is difficult to predict what kind of questions we may want to answer about access in the future.

In terms of generalisable lessons for the sector, we would praise both Analog and Google Analytics as low cost and flexible reporting tools, despite the fact that in our case they had significant drawbacks. For lower traffic sites and sites with resources that can have the Google Analytics javascript additions attached directly to the resources whose popularity you wish to examine, those tools are ideal. For other projects with challenges similar to ours, we will be happy to discuss our work and share the scripts we have created to support database importation.

WebLearn and podcasting integration

WebLearn is Oxford's institutional VLE (Virtual Learning Environment). Since the major system upgrade in 2007 when Sakai (an open source platform which powers WebLearn) was introduced, it has seen a great uptake by academics, researchers and students across the University. It is now recognised as the main online platform for teaching and learning within Oxford. In the last few years, a number of departments (e.g. Chinese studies, Medical Sciences) have attempted to upload multimedia materials into their WebLearn site. As WebLearn is not considered to be the best place to store large multimedia files and has limited disc space, the process of introducing multimedia into WebLearn resources has been slow.

Since the launch of Oxford podcasting, a large number of media items have been produced, catalogued and made available to the public. The podcasts produced by subject experts particularly have proven to be extremely popular. Considering the central role played by WebLearn at Oxford and the richness and popularity of the podcasting resources, WebLearn and podcasting integration answered a clear and expressed need within the institution.

Drawing on the experience of working with academics who wanted to embed media items in WebLearn, the project team worked with the VLE developers at Oxford to adapt an existing WebLearn tool to facilitate the embedding of media items within the VLE.

Within a WebLearn site, the Oxford Podcasts tool allows a site owner to browse and search the Oxford podcasting portal site for relevant media items, or browse the feeds. Once an item has been identified, it can be embedded into the WebLearn site in the form of an in-line media player and the media item description. A WebLearn user can click on the media item to play directly in WebLearn.

Soon after the tool was released, it was publicised via a number of communication channels (mailing lists, OUCS website) to staff and students at Oxford. At the WebLearn user group meeting, the tool was introduced by a presentation comparing the old way of embedding media items in WebLearn with the new way facilitated by the tool. The institution's response was extremely positive.

Code for the adapted versions of the Sakai tools will be offered to the Sakai project for incorporation in future upstream releases.

Policy change on hosting of centrally-promoted media

The costs attributable to the complexities of data gathering from multiple distributed sources compared to the cost of hosting content centrally and the value of being able to report on usage has also led to a policy change within the Podcasting Service. In future all material published through University-maintained portals (i.e. Oxford on iTunes U and the Podcast Web Portal) will be hosted centrally, thus offering improved resilience and easier and data gathering and analysis.

Potential for use in REF impact statements

Now that we have better monitoring and analysis mechanisms in place, we are better placed to provide objective analyses of the public impact of the research-based podcasts we make available. Using the log analysis tools that this project has assembled we are now able to give individual academics accurate reports on the number and geographical provenance of accesses to their contributions, which in turn should provide important underpinning evidence for REF public impact case studies. We feel that these facilities are of strong utility now, and could be further developed in the future to encompass more detailed reporting, and also reporting on other technological aspects of research outputs such as development of on-line communities around digital resources. We hope that this will be of great use to Oxford in the coming years, and thereby raise awareness of the institutional benefits of maintaining and developing Oxford's podcasting service.

Recommendations

We would like to see UK institutions adopt a common reporting method on access to podcasts to allow comparison and mutual learning. We would be happy to share the code and database schemas behind our Stats application if other institutions feel they would benefit from them.

We are proposing a continual evaluation process to improve feedback from presenters and support staff to central service. This can be based on a reduced version of our last survey used as a twice yearly pulse check and folded into a client relations process.

We propose to continue the development on the Stats tool to allow for aggregation of data from multiple sources to be better linked to data about the podcast, thus enabling automatic searches related to departments, feeds, OER/Creative Commons content and more. We will also seek to improve reporting interface.

We would like to supply a survey template in the WebLearn institutional VLE or perhaps the SurveyMonkey external web-based surveying tool to allow academics to gather feedback from their students on podcasts they have contributed. This should also help to promote the awareness of podcasts amongst students.

Podcast contributors should be asked to also contribute hashtags that they feel to be of relevance to their topic to be used in social media promotion. We should also seek retweets from contributors for our promotional tweets, as a greater proportion of their followers are likely to find the material of interest.

RÜDIGER ROLF, NILS H. BIRNBAUM AND MARKUS KETTERL

12 Opencast Matterhorn in Production at the University of Osnabrück

The University of Osnabrück started to use Opencast Matterhorn version 1.0 in the winter semester of 2010/2011. The system was used to record sixteen lectures with the Matterhorn Capture Agent and nine other events (workshops, conferences, special events at the university). All recordings were also published by Matterhorn. In total there are more than 300 different recordings currently distributed with the present setup. The highly automated and flexible workflows that Matterhorn provides have been very helpful especially for frequent lectures. Nearly all events have been recorded and published without a technical assistant in the lecture room. Most lecturers were able to adapt to being recorded within the system very easily and event guest speakers could be recorded without any problems. As well as Matterhorn the media-management-system Lernfunk is used to connect the media from Matterhorn to the various distribution channels that the university provides (Webpage, iTunes U, LMS).

Organisation of lecture recordings at Osnabrück

The University of Osnabrück started with lecture recordings in 2002. Around this time more and more DSL internet connections were being established, so that distribution of video became affordable for the university and the students. There was also some funding for explorative eLearning projects, which allowed the university to build up a new institute (virtUOS – Center for virtual teaching and information management) to support lecturers in using various eLearning techniques. Since then virtUOS has been involved in several eLearning projects and activities. We support our lecturers in using eLearning tools, as well as offering consulting to other universities in this area. We are also involved in the ongoing development of open-source systems for eLearning.

First experiences with lecture recording were simple video recordings, but it soon emerged that displaying presentation slides in addition to the video was in high demand from both lecturers and students. Existing recording systems at this time used proprietary techniques and were quite expensive. They also required personnel for both the recording and post-production of the video. We knew that we could not afford the personnel and the license cost in the long term if more and more lecturers started recording. It seemed obvious that many of the processes during lecture recording should be automated.

Applying lessons learned

We decided to build our own software for lecture recording including our own ideas and research activities. The system is called virtPresenter. In its early versions the system used RealVideo for video-streaming and a combination of different web technologies for content replay. In addition, PowerPoint slides were converted to a fully vector based graphic format (SVG) for scalability and small content size, which was then a promising new standard for high quality graphics in the Web. Some versions later (applying lessons learned from everyday use) we switched from RealVideo and SVG to Flash-Video and Flash (Flex). This technology changeover turned out to be better supported, faster and much more reliable in the creation process and cross platform playback. We installed the necessary hardware for recording in lecture halls permanently. Pan-tilt-cameras were mounted on walls and separate computers that only recorded the video were placed in the rooms. The recording was started through a small plug-in for PowerPoint that remotely controlled the recorder, logged the presentation activities and submitted the presentation to a server that analysed and converted the PowerPoint slides to vector based Flash equivalents. The video was automatically converted from the high-quality recording codec to a streaming video format. Video and content segmentation was based on the time information extracted from the PowerPoint logs.

In our experience over the years, recordings in rooms that were not permanently equipped with hardware turned out to be much more problematic. At first, because of the personnel needed to set up the equipment, we could only record as many recordings as we had technicians available. If the technician was sick, the recording had to be cancelled in many cases. Another problem was that setting up the equipment in the fifteen minutes between two lectures caused errors – sometimes hard to predict (wireless microphones with empty batteries, computers that did not have an IP-address, etc.). Currently we restrict mobile recordings to video-only recordings with a camcorder. Further information and scientific publications regarding lecture capture and eLectures can be found on the virtUOS website.[1]

virtPresenter and its components were released as an open source project under the GPL licence but it was not widely adopted by others. The design and the setup of the system was complex and mainly based on the structures of our own university. In addition, due to money constraints we could not provide the required support to establish and maintain strong development partnerships. Due to these limitations we decided to get in touch with other projects and groups that had been active in this area as well, as described in the next section. It turned out that others were facing similar problems and future technology changeovers or adoption would have become very difficult and expensive if we had remained working independently in our own institutions.

---

1   <http://www.virtuos.uni-osnabrueck.de/Publikationen/HomePage>

Introduction to Matterhorn

In early 2008 the Opencast community was founded, based on an initiative from the University of California Berkeley and funded by the William and Flora Hewlett Foundation. Due to Opencast the developers of several open-source lecture recording systems from around the world gathered to create the vision of a next generation lecture recording system. The idea was to bring together the best of the current systems and visions for a future framework. The projects foundation would be based on a larger and experienced international community willing and capable to realise new ideas. The future system would be better designed, documented, extended – and maintainable. It also needed to provide a stable basis for all partners for everyday use and to allow improvement to the parts of the system needed for research activities.

Based on this idea the Matterhorn project was founded. Supported by a grant from the Mellon Foundation, thirteen partners started in mid-2009 to develop an enterprise lecture recording system that would fit the needs of a small college as well as the demands of a large university.

The idea of a recorder (the so called Capture Agent) in the lecture hall was taken to a new level. Like a VCR the recordings are scheduled. As well as the video the VGA-signal is captured too, so that any computer connected to the projector in the classroom can be captured. Because of these two changes the lecturer does not need to do anything to start the recording. S/he can totally focus on the lecture and need not get distracted by the technology. As a result of the screen recording the system is no longer restricted to a specific software element like PowerPoint or a specific operating system. The Core system performs the analysis, encoding and distribution of the media that the capture agent records. As well as the automatically recorded media, the system allows the uploading of media manually and offers an inbox for other systems to integrate with Matterhorn. The Core is able to execute user configurable workflows so that an adopting institution can modify Matterhorn to fit their needs. The analysis operations for OCR on the slides can be included or not, as desired, and the video formats can be selected based on the specific institution's policy. Matterhorn offers several workflow operations out-of-the-box, for instance, analysis of the ingested media, configurable video encoding, video trimming, vga-video analysis to detect slide changes in the video and extract text from these slides, distribution to YouTube and iTunes U. The service oriented architecture of the system based on Java, OSGI and further open source tools allows developers to add new operations in standalone modules without conflict.

Adopting Matterhorn – early pitfalls and shortcomings

With our involvement in the Matterhorn development, the virtPresenter system was rendered obsolete, as we did not have enough available personnel to maintain the old systems for everyday production as well. So we decided to be radical in our changeover and introduce Matterhorn with the first stable version 1.0 in the winter semester 2010 without any fallback.

Besides Matterhorn the Universität of Osnabrück operates the open source learning management system (LMS) Stud.IP, and Lernfunk, a content management system for lecture recordings. Like virtPresenter, Lernfunk has also been developed by virtUOS as a result of research activities in the area of enterprise-level lecture recording. Lernfunk connects the recording system with all distribution channels in a fully automated production process.[2] Stud.IP is used as the primary distribution channel for nearly 90 per cent of the recordings. Lernfunk manages the distribution of the recordings and delivers the necessary metadata to the LMS, iTunes U and the Lernfunk.de portal for public recordings. Therefore Lernfunk provides a couple of modules and plug-ins to connect the different recording and distribution systems with the Lernfunk system. Lernfunk uses web-services to import the metadata of the lecture recordings and store

---

2   <http://code.google.com/p/lernfunk>

them in its IEEE LOM and Dublin Core based database. Export-web-services and the RSS-generator provide the metadata for the CMS and the distribution channels.

Adjusting the infrastructure based on usage analysis

Adopting Matterhorn needs a couple of modifications in the aforementioned systems and the established processes, both in organisation and communication. For organisational processes an important difference between virtPresenter and Matterhorn is the steering mechanism for the recording and the capturing method of the presentation screen. Unlike virtPresenter, which uses a software client to start and stop the recordings, Matterhorn schedules the recording based on their start- and end-time. On the capture side, Matterhorn uses VGA capturing to record any content shown on the computer-screen.

With the time-based recordings we needed to become familiar with the typical behaviour of our lecturers. Usually a lecture in Germany is ninety minutes within a two-hour time slot. Typically a lecturer starts fifteen minutes later (c.t. = cum tempore) so that students have enough time for a break and to change rooms between lectures. But in a non-recorded lecture the lecture can begin whenever the lecturer thinks s/he is ready, and the lecture ends when the lecturer decides that s/he wants to finish. So we decided to start earlier and stop much later and evaluate these times after some weeks. Unfortunately the Matterhorn 1.0 version did not support trimming, so that these overhangs remained in the published video. With the 1.1 version, a few months later, trimming was introduced, so that students did not notice these overhangs anymore. After a few weeks we had analysed how lecturers delivered lectures and adjusted the recording times individually. In general no lecturer started earlier that s/he had informed us; most of them started two minutes after the announced time. Most lectures ended even before the ninety minutes limit, very few used the ten-minute headroom that we scheduled and only one lecturer exceeded even these ten minutes.

One problem with the scheduling approach as implemented in Osnabrück, on the other hand, was that lecturers sometimes failed to tell us when s/he changed the time of the lecture. Sometimes they decided to start earlier or later, so that the recording times did not fit exactly anymore and the technical staff missed parts of the lecture. With the trimming in Matterhorn 1.1 we decided to start the recording very early and record the maximum duration for those lecturers who tended to shift the beginning times of their lecture. The scheduled recordings highlighted that technicians had little contact with lecturers. In the first semester this was not a big problem as most lecturers were still familiar with the old system and knew the technical equipment in their lecture rooms quite well. In the second semester with Matterhorn, however, new lecturers came on board and more rooms became recording-ready.

At this stage lecturers had technical problems that were not Matterhorn-related and they had no one on hand to help them immediately. Some were not able to change the microphone battery, or connect their notebook to the projector. Attempts to train technical staff in the faculties for such support failed because technicians were not always available when lectures were timetabled. Another solution would have been to give the lecturers themselves training. Unfortunately, many lecturers either did not appreciate how such training could help them in their work, or decided too late before the start of the semester that they wanted to take advantage of training. As many lecturers have very tight schedules, there was no available time to provide training for them by the stage that they evinced an interest. When using our old software, virtPresenter, lecturers could not refuse training as software needed to be explained to them and the technical aspect of using microphones and projectors was part of this.

The VGA screen-capturing opened up possibilities for more teaching scenarios than our old PowerPoint-based approach. The lecturers could now use any operating system and any software they wanted. So now they could do live demos using their own subject-specialist software packages, show webpages, etc. Some of our rooms are equipped with Wolfvision

Visualizers[3] that can show anything that can be placed under the visualizer on the projector. The output of the visualizers is a VGA signal that we can also record with Matterhorn. This means that we do not even need a laptop presentation in the classroom anymore.

With the Matterhorn 1.0 capture agent especially, we encountered some problems connecting and re-connecting notebooks occasionally. Even with the 1.1 Capture Agent some resolutions and notebook models can be problematic. Colleagues from the University of Sasketchewan recommended the use of a VGA scaler to prevent this, but we have not been in a position to test this as yet. In general, lecturers at our university liked the simplified process for lecturing recordings of the Matterhorn infrastructure. If they wanted to be recorded they simply called the technician to schedule it. We were also able to record presentations of guest lecturers as no technical training was needed. Matterhorn worked quite well for recording conferences too. Unfortunately these were not always in rooms that had the fixed recording equipment.

One problem that we encountered was the reliability of Capture Agents. Many of these problems were not related to Matterhorn software and would have been preventable with more control. We had unexpected power breakdowns in some rooms and the relevant PCs had not been set up for an automated reboot. We had hard disk crashes, broken LAN cards, driver problems after updating the Ubuntu Linux on these machines and additional problems that can only be identified in real production. But strangely enough the main problem was that in general the automated recordings worked so well that we did not check the Capture Agents very frequently. Due to this many of these previously described minor errors led to a total loss of recordings. Currently we are trying to use XYMon[4] to monitor the Capture Agents and make sure that we notice upcoming problems before anything fails.

3   <http://www.wolfvision.com>
4   <http://xymon.sourceforge.net/>

Matterhorn workflow extension and customisation

In the adoption of Matterhorn we created our own workflows that produce the video formats that we want. We decided to create MP4/H.264 videos that could be used on mobile players such as the iPhone. In addition, we skipped the OCR because it did not function very well for German texts on the slides and was very time consuming in processing.

For Matterhorn 1.1 we encoded the videos in different qualities because students who had used Matterhorn in the previous semester reported that they sometimes encountered bandwidth problems on slow or shared DSL connections. The video quality now starts with a very low bandwidth demand that will even work on 3G connections. We published our current workflows and encodings in the public Matterhorn wiki.[5]

Besides the customisation of Matterhorn the CMS and LMS had to be enhanced to keep the automatic workflow that was established with the connection of virtPresenter and Stud.IP using Lernfunk. The Lernfunk CMS is built of three modules – the collection-module for the metadata import, the management-module which contains and UI for the database and the distribution-module which delivers the metadata to the distribution channels [5]. In addition Lernfunk delivers a couple of plug-ins for distribution systems such as our LMS Stud.IP, Wordpress and PMWiki. To execute the metadata import the Lernfunk import had to be added to the Matterhorn's workflow.

Lernfunk only needed minimal modifications to handle the new Matterhorn formats. The parser in the collection module got updated for the Matterhorn export format. While virtPresenter provides the metadata within a MediaRSS feed, Matterhorn delivers the metadata for the complete mediapackage in a JSON-Object. The distribution-module needed some minor updates in the embed code for the Matterhorn player that the web service delivers. The plug-ins for Stud.IP, Wordpress and PMWiki got an update to display the recordings and the metadata correctly. Besides

5   <http://opencast.jira.com/wiki/display/MH/Custom+Workflows+(Trunk)>

the general advantages of using a content management system such as increasing reliability and decreasing effort and costs for distribution, the Lernfunk System enables our university to operate different versions of Matterhorn. This was important because Matterhorn has currently no upgrade path between the 1.0 to 1.2 releases. Lernfunk allows us to run and manage the recordings from different versions of Matterhorn, virtPresenter and other lecture recording software. virtUOS provides two plug-ins to display Matterhorn recordings in Stud.IP. Besides the Lernfunk-Stud.IP plug-in virtUOS provides an additional one, that can be used without the CMS using only the Matterhorn REST endpoints for the integration. Both plug-ins provide a list of the recordings that are available for the course. The displayed information contains title, description and a link to the full recording for each media object and an embed-player that shows the Matterhorn recordings within the LMS web-pages. The University of Osnabrück uses the Lernfunk-Stud.IP plug-in which allows a much more fine grained control on the distribution settings than the current Matterhorn system.

Experiences and open issues

Adopting Matterhorn was the next step to decreasing the effort we have to spend in recording lectures. Based on our strategy to automate the whole production process, the alternation from virtPresenter to Matterhorn allows savings in the remaining manual tasks. Most time had previously to be spent on customer support. Due to the requirements of virtPresenter (Windows, .net-Framework, a defined version of PowerPoint), virtUOS had to provide a notebook for lecturers at most of the recordings. Besides the delivery and retrieval of the notebook in the lecture room, we had to ensure that lecturers sent us their lecture slides early enough to copy them onto the machine. With Matterhorn every lecturer uses their own notebook which saves a lot of administrative time. To date there have been no problems with operating system compatibility or VGA capture software.

Important features not yet available in Matterhorn are functions to monitor recordings and the sources and to give lecturers feedback that the system is properly recording. When we used the virtPresenter, the client gave lecturers and the technical team feedback if the system was not working as expected. Due to the recording-by-schedule approach in Matterhorn, this important feedback from the system is not available yet. So in some cases we had no recording because the recorder didn't start due to various reasons and nobody recognised it in time. Another problem is monitoring the video sources. The confidence monitoring was planned for the first release but was disabled because of high CPU and memory demands that led to system instabilities. Without a feature to check the sources, incorrect adjustments or defective sources in large scale installations are problematic. We are looking forward to the upcoming 1.3 release that will include this highly demanded confidence monitoring feature.

The more lectures we record the more we need a solid system. If students know that their lecture will be recorded, they can attend other courses live and watch the recordings of lectures they have missed. Lecturers don't want to hear about problems about recording, they want to know that their lecture is online and available as planned. Currently we still have a relevant percentage of recordings that get lost or are damaged. In the future we aim to have as near to a 100 per cent success rate as possible. We need wired microphones with a very wide recording angle in addition to the wireless microphones that are presently in use in our classrooms. We need a very high resolution camera[6] in addition to the regular camera and the VGA grabber, as a backup if VGA capturing should fail or if someone changes the camera to an unwanted position. There have to be some changes in Matterhorn to support such issues. Most of these can probably be done with simple changes to the workflows and not too many changes in the Java modules.

---

6   There are network cameras that record with up to 5 MP on a very low frame rate.

As we began to increase the amount of recordings we realised that we were finding it problematic to keep an overview on those recording events that had small problems or failed. All these problematic recording events demanded further action from our staff. The lecturer would have to be notified, the reason for the failure identified and fixed, timings in the videos would have to be edited etc. We started at first to write emails to notify colleagues when we noticed a problem. We then created a wiki page with all the glitches and their causes, in order to create a central reference resource. We are presently using TRAC[7] as a lightweight issue tracking system in order to get a better overview of the status of problematic recordings.

Matterhorn Outlook

One of the main problems of Matterhorn currently is that there is no upgrade path from one release to the next. The database and the search indexes are refactored from release to release to increase performance. Because of this, migration scripts are needed to transfer the recordings from one release to the next. None of the contributing institutions have committed themselves to providing these migration scripts yet. As soon as the data structures become more stable it will be easier to create these update scripts or hopefully update without any database changes.

Due to the rapid development of mobile devices, a request to adapt Matterhorn's recordings and user interfaces to mobile needs has featured greatly in recent times. The first mobile version of *Matterhorn2Go* has been released in the end of 2011 and is currently available for Android devices over the Android market.[8] The same version will also be released for Blackberry Playbook users and the Apple platform (iTunes store pending). The mobile version leverages Matterhorn's underlying media-analysis and

7   <http://trac.edgewall.org/>
8   <https://market.android.com/details?id=air.Matterhorn2GO>

segmentation features and makes them available for today's major mobile platforms and devices.

From a lecturer's perspective the adoption of Matterhorn makes recording easier. They can use their own computer and all the software they prefer for the lecture. We are now close to an ad-hoc recording service which is only limited by the equipment in the lecture room. To endorse this we are developing a Stud.IP plug-in that will add scheduling and distribution functionalities to the LMS itself. This will allow lecturers to schedule the courses independently using the LMS. This also implies full control in changing distribution channels or even retracting a recording. All these developments will hopefully increase demand for lecture recordings as it becomes more accessible to lecturers. The multi-distribution strategy, maintained by the Lernfunk CMS, the Matterhorn Engage Tools and the mobile app makes recordings more visible.

Conclusion

We recorded many more weekly lectures with Matterhorn than we did in the semesters prior to this with our old system. We were also able to reduce the administrative work in the process. But we learnt that even the best ideas for automation still need some administration and control of output. We would select and use Matterhorn again if we had to make the decision a second time (even without being part of the core development team). The tools have proven reliable in everyday use. It is still not 100 per cent mature but with every release the reliability increases and it becomes more usable. With the introduction of commercial recorders like those from Epiphan and NCast it gets increasingly easier to adopt the system and buy compatible hardware off the shelf.

Of course, a combination of good staff with expertise and good media skills are needed to get quality results.

References

Boiko, Bob, *Content Management Bible* (Wiley Publishing Inc., 2005 2nd Edition).

Ketterl, M., Mertens, R., Vornberger, O., 'Bringing Web 2.0 to Web Lectures', *International Journal of Interactive Technology and Smart Education (ITSE)*, 6/2 (2009), 82–96.

Ketterl, M., Schulte, O., Hochman, A., 'Opencast Matterhorn: A community-driven Open Source Software project for producing, managing, and distributing academic video', *International Journal of Interactive Technology and Smart Education* 7/3 (2010), 168–180.

Mertens, R., Ketterl, M., Brusilovsky, P., 'Social navigation in Web Lectures A Study of virtPresenter', *International Journal of Interactive Technology and Smart Education* 7/3 (2010), 181–196.

13   Best Practices for Bloggers:
Dimensions for Consideration

Blogs, as discussed in this writing, evolved from online personal diaries in which people posted running accounts of their lives. Blogging quickly broadened to include all manner of content. For example, the earliest recognised blog, Dave Weiner's 'Scripting News', running continuously since 1997, is a home for links, offhand observations, and ephemera (Rosenberg, 2009, p. 60). But it isn't until later that we called these early sites blogs. The quality that sets these sites apart from others is their ability to be easily and quickly updated. Publishing a page to the web is easy enough, but keeping it up to date is difficult. Unattended early web pages quickly deteriorated into collections of broken links and out of date information – a problem we still experience on the web today. Blogs, or Content Management Systems as the tools were called in the late 1990s, allowed for structured workflow in a production line, storing published content in a database.

Blogs are diverse in their subject matter. There are blogs about a broad range of topics using a range of tones and styles to give the site character. They have near universal reach across topics. There are personal diary blogs, political blogs, journalism blogs, expertise-based blogs, etc. Despite their broad ranging scope, blogs share some formal qualities and elements that make them stand out among other kinds of web sites. Blogs are web sites with regularly updated entries in the form of posts with the most recently updated information at the top of the page (Walker-Rettberg, 2008). Blogs are cumulative. They grow over time and require of the reader a sense of history and context for the content presented. Posts may contain text, links, images, and/or other media such as video clips, sound files, or Flash movies. Beyond the basic unit of the post, other blogging elements include post titles, timestamps, blogrolls, and 'about' pages. These formal qualities and elements compose a minimal definition of blogs. This definition is not exhaustive, nor is it exclusive. Jill Walker-Rettberg (2008) defines blogs as a medium itself, rather than a genre within the overarching single medium of the internet. For the purposes of this discussion we agree with this definition. Blogs are not simply a conduit for text, they are holistic new media artifacts whose design and layout, links and networks, say as much about the content as the postings themselves.

Bloggers choose to work within a set of technical affordances and constraints enabled by blogging software (Walker-Rettberg, 2008). From there, bloggers and their readers may recognise different genres of blogging in the medium. Each choice of medium, then genre, limits or directs the blogger toward certain style and content choices. There are many exceptions, and there are many opportunities to challenge these directions in blog style. But Dave Weiner, the godfather of blogging, identifies the common element of blogging: 'Almost all other elements can be missing, and the rules can be violated ... as long as the voice of a person comes through, it is a weblog' (Rosenberg, 2009, p. 63).

In this guide for best practices in blogging, we propose several dimensions for navigating the affordances and constraints of the medium, the limitations of genre, and the convergences of style. Within each dimension we pose a number of questions to illustrate ethical implications of blogging. Constructing and maintaining a blog, regardless of its genre or style, requires that consequences be considered in the following categories: transparency, attribution, responsibility, truth, and citizenship.

These categories are not mutually exclusive. Questions are repeated as they take on a different sensibility depending on the approach, and may be answered differently in different categories. There is no set of best practices that will at once cover all genres and styles of blogs and still hold enough definition to provide clear guidance. Presented here are a broad range of questions a blogger may ask her/himself and brief discussion for each. This set of best practices is meant to be applicable in a variety of blogging settings.

Many blogs encourage a level of transparency not found in other media. Authors can post items much more quickly than in other media (such as newspapers) as Andrew Sullivan (2008) notes, and a sort of conversation often develops between the blog's readers and its author(s). Blogs offer the ability to link to primary sources while offering the author's own commentary on a particular topic, thus encouraging audience members to draw their own conclusions regarding the topic under discussion. The personality you display on your blog can be personal or professional. People blog for many reasons and the distinctions of personal or professional are not mutually exclusive or tied to any one blogging genre. Personalisation and professionalism exist as a spectrum. Your blog may shift, at times being more professional, at other times being more personal. Your affiliations and your audience will help you determine the face you present in your blog. If you are blogging as a representative of an organisation, the face you present should fit with the face presented on the web by the organisation itself. You need to consider the audience you will attract to your blog; consider their expectations. Regardless of your genre, you should consider whether you want your readers to see a personal or professional face when reading your blog.

While transparency for different blogs will vary by purpose and genre, we have included a list of questions below that we believe are important for authors to consider as they create and maintain their blogs.

What constitutes a personal or professional take?

The way you present different aspects of your blog will indicate to the reader your level of professionalism. The tone of your posts, technical and design choices, and your stated and implied affiliations all add dimensions to your public face. The topics you choose to cover in your blog, and more importantly, the tone in which you write about them will influence the seriousness with which your readers read your blog. You may treat trivial topics seriously, or vice versa, but consider how that choice will impact the readers' experience of your blog. Similarly, the design elements you choose for your blog will influence how the reader reads your content. Choose design elements that do not interfere with the content of your posts if the content of your posts is the primary source of content on your blog. Additionally, where you choose to host your blog indicates a dimension of face to your readers. There is a diversity of commercial blog hosts such as WordPress.com and Blogger.com. With these free commercial hosting services, you may have less control over design, and may be required to use a host-specific domain name to point to your blog.

Will the blog be public or private?

Depending on the purpose of your blog, you may choose to make it private, or restrict access to only a few people. Some organisations (like news outlets) might want to monetise their blog(s) and require sign-in before allowing access. Of course, this will also restrict your potential audience (and may alienate those who view blogs as essentially public forums).

How much information is too much information?

Keep in mind that unless you technically limit access to your blog through password protection or blog within a closed community, everything you post is public. Any information you post is publicly available, linkable, copyable, and stored somewhere. Digital data is easily transformed, and it is easy to lose control of the information you offer once it is published electronically. Information on the web is highly accessible and pliable. Do not disclose facts, stories, rumors, opinions, or creative content on your blog that you do not want public. If it is important to disclose this type of information, you can choose to include a disclaimer to warn the reader of what is coming or to explain to the reader limits on acceptable reuse of your content.

Should you be anonymous, use a pseudonym, or your real name?

For the most part, we recommend using your real name when you blog. This provides additional credibility and accountability for the postings you create, and assures your audience of your willingness to stand behind your writing. However, there are times when using a pseudonym or remaining anonymous may be useful. This is particularly true for blogs where the material being discussed is of a sensitive nature, or where the blogger might face repercussions for the material being posted (for example, posting material about one's job that might hurt the company's reputation). It is important to remember that while blogs themselves can be written anonymously, it can be possible to trace the author if care is not taken to anonymise the blog's DNS (Domain Name System) record.

Will you allow others to comment on postings?

This depends on your blog's purpose. Again, if it is a personal journal (like many hosted on the LiveJournal website), you may not choose to allow others to comment on your posts. However, this places some artificial limits on your audience and eliminates the participatory nature of blogging, which may not allow you to reach or grow a wide readership base.

Will you moderate comments on postings?

Comments can be important ways for your audience to communicate with you and with each other. However, depending on the topics you discuss on your blog (and whether or not you are writing as an individual or representing a larger organisation or institution), you may decide to have comments sent to you for your approval before they are posted. You may want to moderate for a number of reasons. Comments can run the gamut from insightful to controversial, from inflammatory to spam, and everything in between. You may have community standards or legal obligations to control the content available on your blog, so considering how you will handle content posted by others and how you will facilitate dialogue between audience members will be an important consideration. Moderation of this content can take different forms. You may choose to simply approve or disapprove comments as they are submitted, or you may choose to approve all comments with some simple editing that preserves the integrity of two-way conversation without endorsing the particular ideas contained in a comment. For example, the author(s) can disemvowel (removing vowels in the comment) or otherwise mark comments if the blog owner considers them to be inappropriate for the discussion (Please see #4, #5 and #6 below under *Responsibility* for more on techniques and types of comments you may want to consider moderating.) Whatever technique you choose for your blog, a clear policy statement should be posted. In your policy statement, clearly outline the criteria for acceptable and unacceptable commenting behaviour, and include a list of consequences for inappropriate commenting (e.g. will the post be edited, deleted, deleted and replaced by a note indicating the reason for deletion, etc?). While moderating ensures that you have final control over what is published on your blog, it means additional time to vet comments and create a lag in the conversation among your audience members.

Should you allow advertising on your site?

This depends on a number of factors: the nature of your blog (personal, journalistic, hobby-focused, commercial, etc.); the nature of your audience; and your own comfort level with advertising. Blogs of a more personal nature may be perceived as odd or a bit unauthentic if advertisements are peppered throughout postings about one's personal life. Hobby-focused and commercial blogs are probably the easiest ones to make the case for advertising, as the former might provide ad space for specific product/services recommended by the blog's author. Certain commercial blogs might also logically include advertising; however, it is important that blog content provides more value than just promoting the company's product(s). It is also important to note that the kind of advertising that appears on your site may be out of your control. For example, while Google AdWords service may allow you to specify categories of ads you are interested in including, it is unlikely that you will be able to specify or exclude certain products or companies from advertising on your blog. This makes some bloggers uncomfortable, while others do not care. If you choose to accept advertising on your site, we recommend including this information in some sort of disclosure statement.

What about sponsorship or profit-sharing links?

Again, this is highly dependent on the kind of blog. Sponsorship can be a good compromise, as it allows a blogger more control over the kind of products and companies s/he is promoting. This is especially useful for hobby-focused blogs where readers might appreciate learning more about the products, services, or resources the blogger finds useful (for example, linking to particular books on Amazon.com where the blogger receives a small percentage of the sales if a person purchases the recommended book). Information about this sort of linking practice should be included in a disclosure statement (see #9 below).

What about including a disclosure statement for your blog?

We recommend creating an About page that includes a brief biography of the blog's author(s), contact information, and a disclosure statement that includes information about how comments are handled, what (if any) information is tracked about your readers, etc. Be clear about your intentions for blogging. For fiction bloggers, it is important to indicate that the content is fiction, or performative. For financial bloggers, it is particularly important to provide your audience with information about financial interests in any of the companies that you may blog about. If you author a professional blog, including information about the organisations for which you work/support may help your audience understand your perspective and give them a better sense of how this shapes your perspective.

Should you track visitors to your blog?

Collecting basic information about your visitors using web tracking tools (where your visitors are coming from, referring pages, etc.) is common practice online, and it is likely that your audience is used to this sort of information being collected about them elsewhere online. We recommend that you create a specific list of the ways in which you track your audience and add this to your disclosure statement so it is easily accessible if individuals have questions.

Attribution

Attribution practices in blogging help readers, sponsors, and bloggers evaluate information found on blogs. Different readers look for different things in different types of blogs to evaluate the veracity of what is posted there. Attribution is how a blogger situates his or her work in reference to other work – how he or she points to others in creating their own statements. The attribution styles reflect practices common within different genres of blog. For example, more formal attribution and citation styles are employed by journalism blogs. These blogs borrow from journalistic writing styles in other print and broadcast media. More casual styles of attribution are used in other blog genres born from personal diary or scrapbook style blogs. How you choose to notate attribution in your blog depends on the community you want your blog to fit into. No matter what kind of content you will include in your blog post a policy statement on attribution. Include a standard for how you will indicate attributions in your posts and how you expect readers to indicate attribution of cited material in comments. Also include a policy on reuse of your original content. Be aware that many blogging hosts offer widgets and tools for cross-pollinating data through your different sites in your web presence. These widgets and tools make aggregating and cross-posting creative content simple, but can easily violate copyright laws and the expectations of other people posting content to the web responsibly. Regardless of what style or technique you choose, attribution calls for reflection on how and why you may point to others' work within your own, and how you want your own work to be treated by others.

How can you protect your own work, and how can you be sure you are not violating someone else's copyrights?

Before you use someone else's creative content, always be sure to check for some copyright notification. You may be looking at a reuse or reposting of someone's work, so you may have to do some web sleuthing to find the original author's initial posting to determine whether your use of it is allowed. After you have determined that you can reuse someone else's creative work, always attribute it with a name and a link if possible. To protect and share your own work, we recommend using Creative Commons licenses. With a Creative Commons license, you can use a simple icon and link to indicate what types of reuse you deem acceptable, and how to cite your authorship. There are many media commons (such as Wikimedia) available online where you can find creative works of all formats that authors indicate as reusable with a Creative Commons license.

What are your responsibilities to your sources?

Sources can be considered two ways: as informants, or as source material. Balancing the protection of your informant with your responsibility to reveal information to your readers is difficult. Your source may want to remain anonymous, or may insist upon proper attribution for the work you are borrowing. If you are bringing information into the public for the first time (e.g. posting comments from a personal interview), we recommend that you ask permission. People perceive a difference between circulating information privately or offline and circulating information online. Your source may not be comfortable being named on your blog. Keep in mind that identity can be revealed in many ways. There are ways you may reveal the identity of your source without naming names. If your source requests anonymity, you must do your best to accommodate. We encourage linking to primary source material where possible, as this encourages a broader conversation with your audience about the topic at hand.

How should you cite source material?

You should always cite sources for any material you are quoting, paraphrasing, or otherwise borrowing from someone else. The style you choose to use should follow from what is common in your blogging genre. If you are citing a source from the web, a link and proper attribution is in order. Depending on the genre in which you blog, more links may be expected. Many blog genres are social arenas, and bloggers are expected to situate their work, using contextual links, in reference to other information on the web. Be aware that some web masters may not want to be linked to you. Links are not simply a connection; they carry meaning depending on how you frame the link from your blog. The linkee may not appreciate your frame and may request that you remove the link. When using others' images, video, or other creative content, a link may not be enough to properly cite the work. You may be violating copyrights. We recommend that you always cite your source material, and heed takedown requests you may receive. When looking for source material to include in your blog posts (e.g. images, video, audio, etc), look for hints about attribution requests by the original poster. The copyright owner may have posted a Creative Commons license agreement for you to use, or may indicate how s/he wants her or his work cited on the web. We also recommend that you use the many Creative Commons spaces online that act as open repositories for creative content for which authors allow varied use of material and give specific instructions for attribution.

Responsibilities

Like most authors, bloggers are most likely writing with some sort of audience in mind. Those readers may not agree with everything you have to say, but you have a responsibility to make what you say up-to-date, navigable, accessible and socially aware. As a blogger you are responsible to your audience, to your sponsors, to the institutions you blog for, and to the community you create with reader comments.

How often should you blog?

Whether you blog frequently or infrequently depends on the kind of blog. Frequently updated blogs can build and maintain an audience more easily. However, that audience comes to rely on frequent updates, and can be easily disappointed if the post rate drops significantly. Infrequent blogging can make it hard to build a reliable audience in the early stages, but can give you the time you need to determine the character of your blog as you get started. The frequency with which you blog depends on the genre and the topic(s) you cover, the expectations of your audience in that field, and possibly the expectations of your sponsors or employers.

Use category/tags/titles wisely to encourage readership. Blogs that cover several topics, or have many posts can be difficult to navigate. Readers may want to view only certain topic-related posts, or search for posts in an archive. Using categories and tags can help readers read more selectively or search through archives more effectively. We recommend creating a limited set of categories that make sense to you and to your readers. Depending on your genre, topic, and readership, categories may be predetermined, or may become clear to you after you have been blogging for a while.

How do you make your blog accessible?

Accessibility can mean several things ranging from browser compatibility to syndication to Section 508 compliance. It is best practice to check browser compatibility. Your blog may include special design elements that do not resolve properly in all browsers. Double check your design and indicate compatibility when necessary. Many blog readers read blogs through a central tool. Rather than navigating to a blog's URL, the reader will pull newly updated content from your blog and others to display in an aggregator or feed reader. The reader pulls updates from the blog through a Real Simple

Syndication (RSS) feed. RSS standardises blog content formats to deliver to a reader. RSS feeds can be formatted to contain all or some of the blog content, and can include ads. Since many readers of blogs use aggregators to skim many blogs in one location, it is best practice to enable them to access your content via their aggregator.

Blogs should also be accessible to people with disabilities. If you blog for a federal agency in the U.S., receive federal funding for your blog, or are under contract with a federal agency your blog must comply with Section 508 of the Rehabilitation Act – the Federal Electronic and Information Technology Accessibility and Compliance Act. Commercial blogs are encouraged to follow accessibility guidelines set by the World Wide Web Consortium's (W3C) Web Accessibility Initiative (WAI).

How do you protect the privacy rights of your readers?

Bloggers should commit to protecting the privacy rights of their readers. If you collect personal information, specify the way it will be used. Indicate whether or not the information gathered will be shared with a third party including hosts, advertisers, and traffic trackers. TRUSTe provides a Model Privacy Disclosures document to help in crafting a privacy policy. Privacy policies are particularly important on any blog that enables interaction. If you enable comments on your blog, either through your host or via a third party comment tool, you should indicate to the reader what information is required to interact with the blog, and how that information will be reused (by whom).

Do blog readers expect a level of courtesy in postings and comments?

Blog readers do expect a level of courtesy in postings and comments. Your policy statement should include a description of common courtesies you will follow in posting, and that you expect readers to follow in comments. It is common to find a list of behaviours that are encouraged and discouraged. Bloggers often list the qualities of comments that are encouraged, those that are discouraged, and those that will be processed by a moderator. Moderators may use different techniques in dealing with comments that do not comply with the comment guidelines. Some blogs request encoding of spoilers to keep content hidden from those who may stumble upon it; some blogs add editor comments to reader comments in response to comment policies; some blogs delete contents entirely, replacing the deleted post with a notice from the editor.

Whatever technique you choose to handle comments, be clear about posting it so readers have access to the guidelines. Comment moderation guidelines should include statements regarding:

1. whether comments will be moderated at all.
2. the kind of comments that are encouraged.
3. the kind of comments that are discouraged.
4. how inappropriate comments will be handled.
5. a link policy.

What responsibility does the audience have to the blogging community?

Blog readers are an active audience. They often expect to participate in comment discussions, but can often forget the leadership role they play as an active audience member. You may choose to exercise more or less control over the interactions between your audience members at your blog site. It is your responsibility to set the tone of interactivity in your blog space. You should commit to maintaining a convivial space on the web. Encourage respectful behaviour. Outline what you consider to be disrespectful behaviour in a comment policy statement. Include remedies for moderating comments, and be sure to follow the rules you outline in your own posts as well.

How should you handle damaging statements made in your blog's comments?

Unless your blog is designed as a trolling blog (this activity is not recommended), you should commit to maintaining a convivial space on the web. You should encourage those who comment to respect each other, and not make damaging statements under your title. You may enumerate to any degree the kinds of anti-social behaviour that will not be tolerated on your blog. Remedies range from altering the inflammatory text to dilute it to deletion of posts to banning readers from commenting entirely. Damaging and anti-social comments include, but are not limited to: racist, sexist, and homophobic statements; advertisements; purposefully argumentative political commentary; self-promotion; and personally identifying information about yourself or others.

Truth

For the purposes of this writing, we assume that the blogs you are writing are meant to convey the truth as you experience it. Even anonymous or parody blogs are likely to maintain some sort of true authorial voice that remains relatively unchanging. However, what happens when events, new information, or personal experiences change what a blog author thinks about a particular topic? In this case, we encourage authors to be transparent and forthright about the changes they may make to already published postings.

What do you do if new facts emerge, or there are corrections that need to be made to older posts?

We encourage making corrections to postings if the truth changes. Deleting old postings is not recommended, unless there is a compelling reason to do so. It is best to strike-through facts that are no longer accurate and provide clear updates to the posting that indicate the changes that have been made since it was first published. We assume that as additional information emerges about a topic (especially when it involves current events), a blogger may have a new opinion on the topic. In this case, it might be best to create a new posting that links together individual posts about the topic, so that readers can see how the author's perspective has been shaped over time. Again, we encourage a policy of transparency (see above), as this builds trust with both your audience and the larger communities of which you are a part.

How should you handle photo-manipulation or photoshopped images?

Before reposting an image, audio, video, or music file that you suspect has been tampered with, do some research to find evidence of the manipulation. Telling a story using manipulated images may distort the truth, and readers will call your intentions into question. If you post a creative work that has been manipulated in order to manipulate the truth or opinion of a story, you have a responsibility to inform your readers either before you post, or after you discover the manipulation. You should make a good faith effort to determine whether the file you are posting has been manipulated or not before your initial post. If your blog has a running theme of posting manipulated images as commentary, you should indicate to your readers that the content has been manipulated, and that the manipulation is part of your commentary. Manipulation in this sense indicates some sort of ill will, malice, or social engineering to tell your story. Manipulated creative content can also be a creative remix of previously existing creative work to make a new statement. If you are posting a remix, treat it as you would any other creative content, seek out permission to repost and standards for attributing authorship. When posting remixes, also include proper attribution and links to the original material used in the remix you are posting.

Citizenship

Part of what makes some blogs unique is their ability to serve as public forums (on a miniature scale) where individuals potentially engage in deliberative dialogue about social issues. This is especially true in journalistic-type blogs, although it is possible that individual posts on even the most personal of blogs will deliberate over important issues of the day. This means that bloggers have the responsibility to be good public citizens and remain conscious of their ethical responsibilities to the larger communities of which they are a part. In particular, we encourage bloggers to consider the potential impact of that which they write – especially when writing about other public or private citizens. Increasingly, the line between what is considered public and private information is blurring, making it important for bloggers to consider how their work will impact others.

How do you know what privacy individuals should be afforded?

This is a difficult question, and it is likely that each blogger will individually have to decide how they will handle disclosure of private information. In general, we encourage bloggers to be circumspect when revealing information about private citizens, who are usually afforded more privacy rights than public figures. As with many of the guidelines we offer here, the genre and purpose of the blog will largely inform the blogger's choices in revealing private information. Blogs focused on public figures may have widely different approaches to dealing with the revelation of private information about these individuals. For example, a celebrity gossip blog will likely reveal information of a personal nature that would be distasteful or potentially libellous if this sort of material were written about an ordinary private citizen. At the other end of the spectrum, there are times when even the most ethically minded journalistic blog might reveal private information about an individual if it serves a larger purpose of informing the public about important issues of the day. For more information about the differences between public and private figures, see the Citizen Media Law Project's web site.

Acknowledgements

The authors would like to thank Bastiaan Vanacker and Don Wycliff for their thoughtful review of late drafts of this text. The authors would also like to thank Don Heider (Dean, School of Communication, Loyola University Chicago). An initial meeting of the Working Group generated early ideas for the direction of the text. This chapter was adapted from a post written for the Center for Digital Ethics website at digitalethics.org.

References

Rosenberg, S., *Say Everything: How Blogging Began, What It's Becoming, and Why It Matters* (New York, NY: Crown, 2009).

Sullivan, A., 'Why I Blog', *The Atlantic* (November 2008).

Walker-Rettberg, J., *Blogging* (Malden, MA: Polity Press, 2008).

MATHY VANBUEL AND SALLY REYNOLDS

Postscript:
The Annual MEDEA Awards – Get Involved

In recent years there has been remarkable interest in the creation and use of digital video and audio in education, boosted by the increasing impact of multimedia and video based websites and applications on the internet and mobile devices. It is against this backdrop that the MEDEA Awards were set up in 2007 to recognise and reward excellence in media supported learning. They were the original brainchild of Mathy Vanbuel from ATiT and arose from his long experience of educational media production and his belief that it is only when video and audio are routine components of education and online learning that we will have an educational environment that reflects the media-rich world in which learners now live. Mathy believed that one way to foster and support excellence in the use of media to support learning was to establish a vibrant awards scheme in a sector where previously no such scheme existed.

Working with the support of partners such as University Nancy 2 in France, UNI-C in Denmark, IADT in Ireland and others, the first round of the scheme was launched by ATiT in 2007 with a dissemination campaign aimed at both professional educational media producers and those interested and involved in the production of user-generated educational media resources. The awards scheme has been in operation now for 4 years and is building up quite a track record with winners, finalists and special award recipients in 2008, 2009, 2010 and 2011. However the objectives of the MEDEA stretch beyond the organisation of an annual awards scheme and include the establishment and nourishment of a dynamic community of interested individuals and organisations who, like the organisers of the MEDEA Awards believe in the increasing importance of media to the learning process. The heart of this community is the annual awards scheme which provides an opportunity to discuss and celebrate what is meant by excellence in this field in a very practical way based on the entries and new participants they attract on an annual basis.

History of the MEDEA awards

The MEDEA Awards were a success from the start and have continued to expand and grow in the four years of their existence. On average about 150 entries are submitted each year from about thirty-five countries and they include entries from all types of educational media producer. Individual teachers from all levels of education have submitted entries from podcasting series produced by classes, animations and cartoons to linear videos and media rich websites. The following table shows the winners for the last four years with a short description of each. The reach of the awards has also grown year on year by virtue of the fact that entries can now be made in English, French, German, Spanish, Italian or Polish.

These are the MEDEA award winners and their submission areas:

Year	Category	Winner	Description
2008	Overall winner of the MEDEA Awards	*Court Introduction* by the Crime Victim Compensation and Support Authority (Sweden)	This web-based court introduction explains what happens before, during and after court proceedings to those people who are required to make an appearance in court (crime victims, witnesses, relatives and perpetrators).
	MEDEA Special Prize winner	*Anti-Anti* by Sint-Lievenscollege Gent (Belgium)	Anti-Anti is a multimedia supported pervasive game created by secondary school students to sensitise students for a national day against useless violence.

Year	Category	Winner	Description
2009	Overall winner of the MEDEA Awards	*Know IT All* for Primary Schools by Childnet International (UK)	Know IT All for Primary Schools includes 3D animation and is designed to help school staff to understand important e-safety issues and to offer strategies and information on how to support young pupils to get the most out of the Internet.
	MEDEA Award for Creativity and Innovation 2009	*Daisy and Drago* by Terakki Foundation Schools (Turkey)	Daisy and Drago is an educational animation project created by 6-year old pupils in a Turkish primary school where pupils learn to create animations at the same time as improving their English.
	European Collaboration Award	*Traditions Across Europe* by Istituto Comprensivo 'Don Bosco' (Italy), represented at the awards by Gina Mango	This eTwinning project encourages European schools to collaborate using ICT. It is based on an information exchange amongst 22 European schools about particular aspects, activities and traditions of the school's own country.
	MEDEA Special Prize winner	*Eyes on the Skies* by European Southern Observatory (ESO) (Germany)	Eyes on the Skies is a 60-minute DVD and a 132-page, full-colour book, exploring the development of the telescope over the four centuries following Galileo's breakthrough, along with all the astronomical riches this instrument has revealed.

Year	Category	Winner	Description
2010	Overall winner of the MEDEA Awards and winner of the Professional Production Award	*School Report* by the BBC News (UK)	School Report gives eleven- to fourteen-year-old students the chance to make their own news reports for a real audience. Using lesson plans and materials and with support from BBC staff, teachers help students develop their journalistic skills to become School Reporters.
	User-Generated Content Award	*Et si c'était toi?* by the Lycée Technique du Centre (Luxembourg)	The 4-minute film was produced in 2008 by 17 to 18-year old secondary school students in the framework of the project 'School without violence'. The film confronts the viewer with bullying and domestic violence and how two girls struggle to cope with isolation, depression and suicidal thoughts.
	European Collaboration Award	*Evolution of Life*, a website created by LMU Munich (Germany) and CNDP (France)	This is a website offering original teaching materials about the evolution of life. Evolutionary concepts and evolutionary biology as well as modern and relevant science are explained and shown through animation movies, documentaries and simulations.
	MEDEA Special Jury Prize	*Pocket Anatomy* by eMedia Interactive (Ireland)	*Pocket Anatomy (The Interactive Human Body)* is a range of medical education software applications to assist medical students, healthcare professionals, and the general public in visualising the complexities of the human body in a novel format.

Year	Category	Winner	Description
2011	MEDEA Professional Production Award	*Monkey Tales Games* by Die Keure Educatief and Larian Studios (Belgium)	*Monkey Tales Games* is a 3D video game series to support the learning of maths which can be used by teachers in class, but which is mainly intended for home use to help students practise the maths they learn in class.
	MEDEA User-Generated Award	*The Merchant of Venice* by the University of Education Salzburg (PH-Salzburg) (Austria)	This is an online, educational game situated in Venice in the fifteenth century aimed at accounting students, who can learn and practise double-entry bookkeeping in a fun way, learn to make decisions in a team, think about connections and networks, apply accounting, interpret results and draw conclusions.
	European Collaboration Award	*The European Chain Reaction* submitted by Qworzó Primary School (Belgium) but representing thirteen schools in thirteen different European countries	This entry is a science/art project and competition for primary schools whereby primary schools across Europe are challenged to create, film and upload a 'Rube-Goldberg/Robert Storm Petersen-like' chain reaction, for which the best chain reaction receives a trophy. In the end all submitted chain videos are merged into a big cross-border European chain reaction.
	Special Award recognising excellence in the use of media to support volunteering	*Changing Lives* by Drogheda Special Olympics Club (Ireland)	In this video the narrator explains the different aspects that are involved in organising a local sports club for Special Olympics Ireland. Viewers are guided through the different volunteer roles and learn what this means in action.

Judging process and criteria

The MEDEA Awards are supported by a highly expert judging panel responsible for the selection of the MEDEA Award winners. The MEDEA Awards Judging Panel 2011 consists of key players and experts in the educational multimedia sector as well as representatives of higher education institutions, research centres, production houses and broadcasters specialising in the use of audio and visual material in education. The annual judging of the awards begins right after the deadline for entries – usually in mid-September. The judges who evaluate entries to the MEDEA Awards recognise the primary role of effective and innovative educational design in the use of moving images with learners. This means that they will be looking first and foremost for materials and approaches that demonstrate original and successful use of media with learners to achieve clearly defined educational outcomes. The quality of the materials themselves is important as the judges will consider the following criteria, appropriate to the learning context:

1. Pedagogical quality: quality of didactics and of communication. Is there a clear learning objective? Is it likely that the material will result in good learning?
2. Use of media: the choice and selection of the type of media, the advantages of the media selected. Is the type of media chosen used appropriately and in an exemplary fashion?
3. Aesthetic quality: attractiveness of materials. Is the style and design consistent and appropriate for the target users? Is the entry appealing and pleasing to look at and to use?
4. Usability: the intuitiveness of the material. Is it easy to use the application? Is there support, a set of guidelines, the possibility of feedback or help?
5. Technical quality: are there possible flaws in the system and/or compatibility issues? Is it necessary to have unrealistic or advanced technical knowledge to be able to use the system?

The judges are particularly keen to encourage original and groundbreaking applications of moving images and sound in education. In addition to the main award, the judges may, at their discretion, present a special award to an approach or production in recognition of exceptional innovation in pedagogic or technical design.

Future plans and hopes

The MEDEA Awards have established themselves in the first three years of their existence as a unique forum whereby excellent examples of media use in education and training are recognised and celebrated. The MEDEA Awards have continued to expand through the European Commission supported project MEDEA:EU, which enabled the awards to operate in French and German as well as in English, and by specific activities aimed at putting in place a European network of support organisations as well as by harvesting best practices and making these available to the wider public.

MEDEA2020 is a dissemination and exploitation project (Lifelong Learning Programme, Key Activity 4, 2010–2012) which further extends this work by fostering the exchange of good practice amongst those actively creating and using media to enhance education and training in Europe. MEDEA2020 builds on the network created in the first three years of the MEDEA Awards and promotes educational media-supported resources created in the context of European networks, projects and initiatives. It responds to a growing pressure to provide more relevant and attractive learning opportunities to citizens through the use of ICT in general and media in particular. The MEDEA Awards are attracting more and more high-quality examples of inspirational media from those at all levels of education and training, including compulsory level education, higher education, lifelong learning and the training sector. However, this expertise often exists in 'pockets': while a great many producers and individuals demonstrate terrific skill and know-how, access to such expertise among the wider educational and training community is not evident. MEDEA2020 thus aims to heighten awareness among this community as to the value of media in learning, to raise the levels of skill by providing access to resources, expertise and inspirational examples, to enthuse and motivate practition- ers about the use of media and to raise awareness and know-how amongst policy makers about trends, development and practice in this area.

More information on MEDEA awards and how to submit an entry at <http://www.medea-awards.com/>

Notes on Contributors

YVONNE CROTTY is a Lecturer in the School of Education Studies at Dublin City University. She is particularly interested in promoting creativity and visual literacy in higher education and in the use of multimodal forms to communicate and express the nature of educational knowledge. She is the director of the research group Video linkEd and a co-director in the Centre for e-Innovation and Workplace Learning (<http://www4.dcu.ie/cwlel/index.shtml>). Yvonne was overall academic winner of the President's Award for Excellence in Teaching at DCU in 2011 (<www.dcu.ie/news/2011/may/s0511k.shtml>). Yvonne is national coordinator for the European Seventh Framework project 'Inspiring Science' (2013–2016).

MICHAEL WESCH is Associate Professor of Cultural Anthropology and Digital Ethnography at Kansas State University. He is a cultural anthropologist and media ecologist exploring the effects of new media on human interaction. His videos on culture, technology, education and information have been viewed by millions, translated in over fifteen languages and are frequently featured at international film festivals and major academic conferences worldwide. He won the 2008 CASE/Carnegie U.S. Professor of the Year for Doctoral and Research Universities and has been named an Emerging Explorer by National Geographic. His YouTube channel is at <http://www.youtube.com/user/mwesch>. His blog can be found at <http://mediatedcultures.net/ksudigg>.

ROY PEA is David Jacks Professor of Learning Sciences and Education at the Stanford University School of Education. He has published extensively in the field of the Learning Sciences and on learning technology design, and has made significant contributions since 1981 to the understanding of how people learn with technology. Roy is a Director of the H-STAR Institute at Stanford University, USA. H-STAR, the Human-Sciences and Technologies Advanced Research Institute, is a Stanford interdisciplinary research centre focusing on people and technology. His current work examines how informal and formal learning can be better understood and connected, and he is also developing the DIVER paradigm.

CARMEN ZAHN is a Professor at the School of Applied Psychology, University of Applied Sciences Northwestern Switzerland. Her main research interests are knowledge acquisition and knowledge exchange based on visual media, and cognitive processes during visual design tasks.

KARSTEN KRAUSKOPF is a research scientist at the Knowledge Media Research Center in Tuebingen, Germany. His research interests include learning and teaching with new media, Computer Supported Collaborative Learning (CSCL) and motivation in instruction.

FRIEDRICH W. HESSE is Executive Director of the Knowledge Media Research Center situated in Tuebingen, Germany. Together with his researchers he works on fundamental principles of individual and cooperative knowledge acquisition and knowledge exchange with new media and the practical implementation of concepts of virtual learning and teaching. He is also Scientific Vice-President of the German Leibniz Association, an umbrella organisation for eighty-six research institutions in Germany.

VANCE MARTIN is a post-doctoral research fellow at the University of Illinois at Urbana Champaign, studying the redesign of the teacher education programme. He has taught History for over ten years and has been deeply involved in integrating technology such as videos, online software, videogames and wikis.

THEO KUECHEL taught Art and Design in schools and colleges in the UK for fourteen years. Subsequently he worked as an ICT advisor to a Local Authority and worked in industry. Theo is now an independent consultant and researcher in educational technology. His current research covers online video, digital content and, digital archives, and how they can be integrated with social media web technologies to enhance learning.

STEPHEN J. MCNEILL is a Senior Lecturer in Media Studies at Kennesaw State University in Georgia and also serves as Director of Digital Media for the Department of Communication and Coordinator of Mobile Learning for the College of Humanities and Social Sciences. He is the author of *Digital Symbiosis: New Media in Transition.*

JOSHUA N. AZRIEL is an Associate Professor of Communication at Kennesaw State University in Georgia. His research interests include analysing how the US First Amendment applies to online social media and how reporters use mobile communication devices for journalism practices.

GLEN WILLIAMS has taught at Missouri State University, Indiana University, Texas A&M University and at Southeast University in Cape Girardeau, Missouri, where he recently was named Chair. His research interests centre upon communication education.

MARGARET FARREN is a Lecturer at Dublin City University and Co-Director of the Centre for e-Innovation and Workplace Learning. Her research interest is in the development of methodologies that contribute to personal knowledge and knowledge in the field of practice. She supports practitioner research at masters and doctoral level. Margaret is national coordinator for the European Seventh Framework project 'Pathway to Inquiry Based Science Education' (2010–2013).

JACK WHITEHEAD is currently a Professor at Liverpool Hope University in the UK, a Visiting Professor at Ningxia Teachers University in China and a Visiting Fellow at the University of Bath, where he worked in the Education Department for thirty-six years. He supports doctoral students in pursuing research inquiries of the kind, 'How do I improve what I am doing?'

SABRINA FITZSIMONS is Coordinator of Teaching Practice and lectures in the School of Education in the Mater Dei Institute of Education, Dublin. She is a member of the Centre for e-Innovation and Workplace Learning at Dublin City University. Sabrina's PhD research involved an exploration of Second Life (SL).

FAWEI GENG is a Learning Technology Support Officer at Oxford University Computing Services. Fawei currently provides support for Oxford University's Podcasting and VLE services.

CARL MARSHALL is a Technical Officer with Oxford University Computing Services and has been doing academic computing for the past five years, working on a range of products and services from Research Discovery systems to Humanities databases, creation and development of a Podcasting service and, most recently, acting as Project Manager for the JISC Steeple project.

ROWAN WILSON has been working within the University Computing Services in Oxford since 2001, supporting the work of the Oxford Text Archive. More recently, Rowan has become the licensing specialist within the JISC-funded free and open source software (FOSS) advisory service OSS Watch.

RÜDIGER ROLF started as a researcher/software developer in the newly founded Center for Virtual Teaching and Information Management (virtUOS) at the University of Osnabrück, where he currently leads the media section within the virtUOS. He has been part of the Opencast Matterhorn project since 2008.

NILS H. BIRNBAUM works at the Center for Information Management and Virtual Teaching (virtUOS) in the field of lecture recording and video conferencing. He has researched extensively the conceptual design, implementation and cost-benefit analysis for the Lernfunk content management system of lecture recordings.

MARKUS KETTERL works at Fraunhofer IAIS as a research engineer. He is also a founding member of UC Berkeley's Opencast project where he is one of the leading developers. In this capacity, he has been part of the Executive Advisory Board, a programme committee member of IEEE International Symposium on Multimedia, ACM Hypertext Conference and AACE E-Learn World Conference on E-Learning, and workshop

Co-Chair on Multimedia Technologies for E-Learning (MTEL) at IEEE International Symposium on Multimedia (ISM).

MEGHAN DOUGHERTY is an Assistant Professor of Digital Communication in Loyola University Chicago's School of Communication and Director of the School's graduate programme in Digital Media and Storytelling. She studies the preservation in and of Web culture, collaboration tools to aid knowledge production, and Web archiving as an emerging cyber infrastructure for e-research.

ADRIENNE MASSANARI is an Assistant Professor of New and Digital Media, and the Program Director for the Center for Digital Ethics and Policy, in Loyola University Chicago's School of Communication. She co-edited a book with David Silver entitled *Critical Cyberculture Studies*, published in 2006.

MATHY VANBUEL worked for the audio-visual service of the Catholic University of Leuven for more than fifteen years as director and production manager. Mathy is regularly called upon to offer consultancy services in the integration of specific ICT tools and services in the education process. Mathy is chairperson of the MEDEA Media in Education Judging Committee and Secretary of MEDEA Association for Media and Learning.

SALLY REYNOLDS has a background in remedial linguistics. She first worked in radio and television in Ireland as a presenter and producer for the national broadcaster, RTE. She is a director of ATiT, which she co-founded in 1999, where she is currently responsible for several EU projects including MEDEAnet, SAILS, Web2LLP and REC:all. She has considerable experience in all levels of European project management from concept through to validation. Sally provides consultancy and management support on dissemination and exploitation from planning through to delivery and is an experienced editor, event manager and European dissemination strategist.

Index

RETHINKING EDUCATION

Rethinking education has never been more important. While there are many examples of good, innovative practice in teaching and learning at all levels, the conventional education mindset has proved largely resistant to pedagogic or systemic change, remaining preoccupied with the delivery of standardised packages in a standardised fashion, relatively unresponsive to the diversity of learners' experiences and inclinations as well as to the personal perspectives of individual teachers. The challenge of our times in relation to education is to help transform that mindset.

This series takes up this challenge. It re-examines perennial major issues in education and opens up new ones. It includes, but is not confined to, pedagogies for transforming the learning experience, any-time-any-place learning, new collaborative technologies, fresh understandings of the roles of teachers, schools and other educational institutions, providing for different learning styles and for students with special needs, and adapting to changing needs in a changing environment.

This peer-reviewed series publishes monographs, doctoral dissertations, conference proceedings, edited books, and interdisciplinary studies. It welcomes writings from a variety of perspectives and a wide range of disciplines. Proposals should be sent to any or all of the series editors: Dr Marie Martin, martin684@duq.edu; Dr Gerry Gaden, gerry.gaden@ucd.ie; and Dr Judith Harford, judith.harford@ucd.ie.

Vol. 3 Judith Harford and Claire Rush (eds): Have Women Made a Difference? Women in Irish Universities, 1850–2010. 248 pages. 2010. ISBN 978-3-0343-0116-9

Vol. 4 Maura O'Connor: The Development of Infant Education in Ireland, 1838–1948: Epochs and Eras. 325 pages. 2010. ISBN 978-3-0343-0142-8

Vol. 5 Androula Yiakoumetti (ed.): Harnessing Linguistic Variation to Improve Education. 328 pages. 2012. ISBN 978-3-0343-0726-0

Vol. 6 Judith Harford, Brian Hudson and Hannele Niemi (eds): Quality Assurance and Teacher Education: International Challenges and Expectations. 281 pages. 2012. ISBN 978-3-0343-0250-0

Vol. 7 Mags Liddy and Marie Parker-Jenkins (eds): Education that Matters: Teachers, Critical Pedagogy and Development Education at Local and Global Level. 229 pages. 2013. ISBN 978-3-0343-0215-9

Vol. 8 Yvonne Crotty and Margaret Farren (eds): Digital Literacies in Education: Creative, Multimodal and Innovative Practices. 248 pages. 2013. ISBN 978-3-0343-0928-8

Vol. 9 Thomas G. Grenham and Patricia Kieran (eds): New Educational Horizons in Contemporary Ireland: Trends and Challenges. 399 pages. 2012. ISBN 978-3-0343-0274-6

Vol. 10 Anthony David Roberts: The Role of Metalinguistic Awareness in the Effective Teaching of Foreign Languages. 433 pages. 2011. ISBN 978-3-0343-0280-7

Vol. 11 Forthcoming.